Praise for *The Complete U*

"*The Complete U* is a must-read guide packed with heart, humor, and hard-earned wisdom that will keep you engaged until the end. With over 100 life lessons, this book feels like having a trusted professor in your corner, who, in this case, is deeply passionate about mental health and personal growth. It's insightful, empowering, and perfect for students navigating the classroom and life. I can think of no one more qualified to direct such a tour than my favorite professor, Deborah Cohan. Her expertise and *The Complete U* were built for such a time as this!"

—**Gracie Bonds Staples**, former columnist at *The Atlanta Journal-Constitution*

"Deborah Cohan offers honest, practical, and positive advice on navigating the terrain of college, urging students to savor and appreciate all the experiences—ups, downs, thrills, challenges, and rewards—that college offers them on their journey of self-discovery, knowledge, and growth. I absolutely recommend this book to any student entering or currently enrolled in college. I only wish this book had been available years ago—thank goodness it is here now!"

—**Andrea Rossi-Reder**, PhD, dean of sophomores and Ada Comstock Scholars at Smith College

"How to make the most of something as expansive as the college experience? Professor Cohan to the rescue! *The Complete U* inspires readers to plant their roots and reach for the sky, offering pragmatic and encouraging advice for prolific personal growth."

—**Lisa Wade**, PhD, professor of sociology at Tulane University and author of *American Hookup: The New Culture of Sex on Campus*

Praise for *The Complete U*

"*The Complete U* is a must-read guide packed with heart, humor, and hard-earned wisdom that will keep you engaged until the end. With over 200 life lessons, this book feels like having a trusted professor in your corner, who, in this case, is deeply passionate about mental health and personal growth. It's insightful, empowering, and perfect for students navigating the classroom and life. I can think of no one more qualified to direct such a tour than my favorite professor, Deborah Cohan. Her expertise and *The Complete U* were built for such a time as this!"

—**Gracie Bonds Staples**, former columnist at *The Atlanta Journal-Constitution*

"Deborah Cohan offers honest, practical, and positive advice on navigating the terrain of college, urging students to savor and appreciate all the experiences—ups, downs, thrills, challenges, and rewards—that college offers them on their journey of self-discovery, knowledge, and growth. I absolutely recommend this book to any student entering or currently enrolled in college. I only wish this book had been available years ago—thank goodness it is here now!"

—**Andrea Rossi-Reder**, PhD, dean of sophomores and Ada Comstock Scholars at Smith College

"How to make the most of something as expensive as the college experience? Professor Cohan to the rescue! *The Complete U* inspires readers to plant their roots and reach for the sky, offering pragmatic and encouraging advice for prolific personal growth."

—**Lisa Wade**, PhD, professor of sociology at Tulane University and author of *American Hookup: The New Culture of Sex on Campus*

THE
COMPLETE
U

Books by the Author

Welcome to Wherever We Are: A Memoir of Family, Caregiving, and Redemption (2020)

A Professor Tells You Everything You Need to Know

Over 100 Lessons for Success in and out of the College Classroom

Deborah J. Cohan, PhD

Miami

Published by Mango Publishing, a division of Mango Publishing Group, Inc.

Cover Design: Elina Diaz
Cover Photo/illustration: twentysixdepressed/stock.adobe.com, PrintingSociety/stock.adobe.com, M.Style/stock.adobe.com, ismail.stock.adobe.com, Роман Ярощук.stock.adobe.com
Author Photo: Abri Kruger
Layout & Design: Elina Diaz

For permission requests, please contact the publisher at:
Mango Publishing Group
5966 South Dixie Highway, Suite 300
Miami, FL 33143
info@mango.bz

For special orders, quantity sales, course adoptions and corporate sales, please email the publisher at sales@mango.bz. For trade and wholesale sales, please contact Ingram Publisher Services at customer.service@ingramcontent.com or +1.800.509.4887.

The Complete U: Over 100 Lessons for Success in and out of the College Classroom

Library of Congress Cataloging-in-Publication number: requested
ISBN: (print) 978-1-68481-852-5, (ebook) 978-1-68481-853-2
BISAC category code: EDU038000 EDUCATION / Student Life & Student Affairs

Author's Note: Some names in this book have been changed to protect the privacy of those quoted and/or depicted.

I dedicate this book to my mother, Naomi Marks Cohan, a badass educator who managed to get a high school kid to write poetry who didn't know how to spell his name or the name of his street. This one's for you, Mom. How I wish you were here.

TABLE OF CONTENTS

INTRODUCTION

This book is about college. It's about the difference that college can make in your life and in shaping your perspective on yourself and the world, if you're committed to channeling your energy into maximizing your experience. That's where I come in. I am here to help you do this. My goal is simple, straightforward, and gigantic—I want *you* to get the *very most* out of your college experience.

I want to share with you the wonders and joys of the college experience while also helping you survive and thrive amidst the challenging or seemingly impossible parts. I'm here to show you all the ways you can find success in and out of the classroom. And by success, I'm referring to more than achievement and productivity. I'm talking about success borne of something deeper and longer-lasting. The success about which I speak relates to how you might find meaning, purpose, connections, and profound fulfillment through the academic work you do in college and how you get involved beyond the walls of the classroom. It's a type of success you're likely to draw on for the rest of your life, and it will anchor you as you follow your life's path. The success I want to help you cultivate is both a reservoir for renewal and a buoy for survival.

Here, I share with you the real magic of college despite—and because of—recent news stories questioning the value of higher education. I demonstrate this through all sorts of things I've learned working in this field for over thirty years. This book is enriched by interviews with many current and former students and college parents. Densely packed with these rich narratives, I hope you'll find this book to be intimate and relatable.

Interwoven with this multiplicity of voices, I'll share insights gleaned from my experiences, some even dating back to when I was in my first year at college. But before you cringe and roll your eyes thinking, *oh no, not another older adult who thinks they know about college because they went years ago*, please know I offer you these personal examples because in working with young people all these years, I see all the things that have withstood the test of time. I marvel at all that has changed and all that remains the same in the college experience in terms of sources of tension and lessons learned. Because of the depth of my experience having worked at a variety of institutions, and due to my extensive research and writing about higher education, I'm uniquely positioned to help you sort through all of this. The book strikes a balance, I hope, between an authoritative, expert voice and an older friend or aunt lending support. Chock-full of tips, tricks, and guidance intended to be reassuring—and deepened by my expertise in communicating about charged and complicated emotional issues—I hope that you experience this book, and me, as open, down-to-earth, warm, and practical.

College is where the bar is supposed to be high for intellectual rigor. Along with that is something of at least equal importance: emotional intelligence. Having worked as a counselor and clinical supervisor for many years, I am unusually attuned to emotional life in and out of the classroom. The population with whom I worked was different as I counseled abusers and survivors of violence. Since I teach about issues of intimacy and violence, body image, mental health, and many other sensitive issues, I bring that expertise to you, recognizing how common these issues are for students everywhere.

While the book is designed to be something that can be read cover to cover, it needn't be read sequentially. I've organized the book into lessons so you can dip into the parts you need and find easily digestible information that meets and supports wherever you are. Designed for students in all years of the college experience, there's something here for everyone.

I've crafted this book to feel like a comprehensive, behind-the-scenes campus tour led by a guide who, in my case, is a seasoned professor who lives and breathes college life every day. You might think of this as a GPS to navigate the changing, wondrous, and rocky terrain of higher education. In this tour of sorts, I'll be pointing out all the major landmarks that define the college experience. I'll highlight for you some things to be sure to look for and consider while encouraging you to experience things for yourself. Aware of the various landmines that can interfere with student success in and out of the classroom, I try hard to help you think about how to negotiate these hot spots with more knowledge and greater confidence.

If we think of this book like a campus tour with some serious hiking involved through the aspects that can feel especially foreign and treacherous, then you'll understand why I structured the book as I have. I open the book by talking with you about the magic of college and how this time in your life is filled with promise and potential. Then, we transition to exploring all the ways that you can be successful in school. Since I see this book as a sort of extended classroom where I can reach many more students, I try to share everything I can think of that I've drawn on to help students throughout my career. We'll talk about things that come up in my office hours and advising sessions such as how to choose classes, things to ask yourself when selecting a major, how to cultivate better study habits, and rebounding from a lousy semester. We'll look at juggling hard decisions, such as transferring or taking a leave of absence, as well as how you use your time and how you can change your mindset to enhance your growth.

Together, we'll examine issues that make college feel a lot different today, including how social media is woven into the fabric of our existence, the residual impact of the COVID-19 pandemic, divisive politics, and how parents are more involved in college than ever before. These have constituted major changes felt on campuses that reverberate and send shockwaves through institutions. Importantly, these issues figure prominently in the social and emotional lives of college students, their readiness to take risks, and their feelings of happiness, health, and fulfillment.

Consequently, a large portion of the book focuses on life outside of the classroom. Issues we'll tackle include loneliness, stress, making friends, roommates, physical and mental health, family dynamics, body image, alcohol, grief, loss, sex, intimacy, and relationships. We'll consider ways you can get involved on campus and in the community through clubs, organizations, internships, and study abroad. And we'll explore ways you can find success in your senior year and far beyond, using the gifts honed in college to ignite your bright future.

Though we'll trudge through some inevitable peaks and valleys, we'll savor the most magnificent vistas from atop the summit. I'll stay with you for the parts that feel the most daunting, and I'll urge you to stretch toward all the beauty I know can be yours. I'll encourage you to look upward to see the direction you're headed, outward to notice all that exists on this path of yours to support your dreams, and inward to remind you to stay connected to your inner resources and gut feelings. So, lace up your sturdiest boots, and together, let's scale this mountain called college.

CHAPTER 1

THE MAGIC OF COLLEGE

Lesson 1: One Thing Is for Sure—College Is Full of Hope

"The very least you can do in your life is to figure out what you hope for. And the most you can do is live inside that hope. Not admire it from a distance but live right in it, under its roof."

—Barbara Kingsolver, *Animal Dreams*

" 'Hope' is the thing with feathers—
That perches in the soul—
And sings the tune without the words—
And never stops—at all—"

—Emily Dickinson, "Hope is the Thing with Feathers"

What is college all about? What is it for?

College students like you want many of the same things that students wanted decades ago and struggle with many of the same things, too. Like everyone who has preceded you, it's normal to arrive on campus with the same age-old questions of "Who am I?" and "What will become of me?" Or, in the words of poet Mary Oliver, you're likely wrestling with, "What is it you plan to do with your one wild and precious life?"

One of the most timeless and important qualities about college is that it's a structure, a dwelling, of and for and about hope—what I would call *a hope structure*. College is about educating a new citizenry. And it's also about socializing for and toward hope. I was reminded of this when scrolling on social media and noticed my friend, Dr. Kathryn Feltey, a brilliant, now retired sociologist at the University of Akron, who posted a photo of her eighteen-year-old self in which she had inscribed, "I am leaving my childhood behind as I search for my life and who I will be."

That is what college is all about—individuating from your family of origin, forging a new path, and discovering how to grow into a bigger version of yourself. Students arrive on college campuses wanting a fresh start and to expand beyond the confines of where they come from—because whether you come from a suburb, major city, or tiny rural town, almost all students seem to want something more, and something different, than from where they came.

College gives you the opportunity to reinvent yourself, develop new perspectives on how to think about issues in the world, and consider your place in it. You can reflect on your past, contemplate the future, and hopefully, vibrantly engage in the present. College becomes a place to dream big and bigger and to try out new versions of yourself alone and in relationships, in that uneasy time between late childhood and early adulthood.

Imagine for a moment the image of an accordion, how this musical instrument opens and closes and opens again, how it vibrates and produces sound. Students I've worked with resemble that accordion, going inward, expanding outward, playfully experimenting, and making new music. Or, imagine a kaleidoscope, with each turn revealing new reflections, patterns, color, and light. That's what college does—with each new course, each group of friends, involvement in new and different activities and organizations, successes *and* failures, you can try out new ways of seeing and being. The kaleidoscopic nature of college gives you the tools to develop new frameworks and outlooks, cast away older versions of yourself, and begin again. There's so much hope in that.

To become the architect of your life, to get inside and truly inhabit this structure of college, or what I'm referring to as a hope structure, you have to do it yourself. Neither your parents nor professors like me can design it for you. No doubt there will be times, based on our life experiences, when we, your parents and mentors, want to shout, "Wait, hold on, be careful, let me do that, the plans don't seem sound, the blueprint seems wrong, the roof may collapse, the ground may flood," and we desperately want to swoop in and fix things. The thing is, we're not living in that hope structure with you; we get to see your pictures of it, we get to hear about the progress or lack thereof with the building of it, and we listen to your anguish when things aren't working. But the dream home you're building—the structure to house your hopes—is made even more sturdy when you've built it yourself, even if it's harder that way.

This going-away-to-college thing is figuring out how to come home to yourself. It's about making a home and a life only you can dream of. One that works for you and only you. One that is authentic and true to your innermost needs, values, and desires. College inevitably involves turbulent transitions and difficult conversations that may rock you to your core and challenge your sense of foundation, as well as encourage you to question aspects of where you've come from and where you're going. Here, I aim to show you how, at its best, college is about inhabiting spaces more fully and creatively.

Home and place are quintessential things people struggle with; this yearning for a sense of home is central to the human condition and manifests in myriad ways. Typically, home is where we might expect to feel and behave most ourselves, and it's a primary site for where and how relationships come together and break apart, and how people come to voice and identify who they are.

Even today, when people ask me what I consider home, for example, where I went to college is high on my list. It was at the University of Wisconsin-Madison, formative for me in every possible way, that I came into myself intellectually, emotionally, academically, politically, professionally, relationally, sexually, and creatively. I've come to see that places, people, and life-changing and life-affirming experiences can all feel like home.

Going to college is a chance to begin to design your life. Like I said, you're the architect of it. Through the college experience, you get to design your interior space—your physical space *and* your psychic space. You get to choose how you dwell and about what you dwell. *This is your dream house, your hope structure.* And you can experience what gives you energy, what feeds you, and who you are at your deepest essence.

Lesson 2: Why College?

Some of you likely never gave this much thought—college was a given, an almost automatic next step after twelfth grade, with the only question being where you'd be headed. For others, college might represent a dream to fulfill as the first in your family to attend. Or, you might be going to honor a promise to a cherished loved one. Whether you're going because of a taken-for-granted assumption or because you have a grand ambition of shifting a generational story, I imagine you hope college will get you one step closer to your dreams, give you the necessary tools and knowledge base for your chosen career path, and serve as a ticket to unlock a lucrative job, and along the way, you hope the ride is fun. Sure, college can be a springboard for all of that, and I, too, want all of that for you. At the same time, college is about so much more. My many years of swimming in the waters of higher education have revealed to me things that truly distinguish the college experience and make it worthwhile. College offers you the opportunity:

- To individuate from your family of origin.
- To consider the world far beyond yourself.
- To cultivate a sense of independence and agency to make a difference.
- To live among a community of similarly aged peers with different backgrounds.
- To encounter divergent perspectives.
- To learn to more effectively communicate both orally and in writing and in ways that demonstrate critical and analytical thinking.
- To further deepen and sharpen your intellect, creativity, and emotional intelligence.
- To cultivate your identity as an active citizen and leader.

- To try new things, take risks (safely), and expect more of yourself than you ever dreamed possible.
- To learn for yourself how to recover from failure, disappointments, and other missteps. College is the best place to try, fail, and recover.
- To have the best time you can because it's over in a flash, and the memories you make will continue to make you smile decades from now.
- To grow socially and emotionally in ways that when you reflect on life just four years after entering college, even you—and most importantly, you—are struck by the remarkable transformation.

College is an opportunity to think deeply about an enormous range of topics and issues. A workplace can train a person in pertinent details and practices, but college equips a person to read more critically, write and speak more cogently, think in a more nuanced manner, and essentially live in a new way. At their best, colleges and universities aren't just about job preparation and training, but cultivating a deeper sense of humanity.

A former student compared my class to those snow globes people buy at amusement parks, where when you shake them, they become like a blizzard; he said I had shaken up his worldview. When I think back to my college experience, I think about when the most influential professors turned things on their heads and encouraged me to ask other questions and look at the underbelly, like the beauty of a sunflower turned away from you. You don't go to college to get your worldview confirmed.

College is a living laboratory where you get the opportunity to experiment and try your hand at so many things sure to emerge in adult life, including making decisions, navigating scary transitions and changes, letting go of the tyranny of perfectionism, managing projects, meeting deadlines, knowing when to rest, being in close quarters with difficult people, learning when to let go, learning when to admit you don't know something and need help, picking your battles, deciding on your most cherished values, figuring out how to resolve something after screwing up, learning to live in a diverse community that at times may be uncomfortable, cultivating healthy habits, balancing many things at the same time, deciding when to stay in and when to go out, and so much more.

When we conceptualize college as a snow globe and a living laboratory, we see the value in deep questioning, both the world and ourselves. As the poet Mary Oliver said, "Keep some room in your heart for the unimaginable."

Lesson 3: First, You Have to Get Lost

> "To be fully alive, fully human, and completely awake is to be continually thrown out of the nest. To live fully is to be always in no-man's-land, to experience each moment as completely new and fresh."
>
> —Pema Chödrön, *When Things Fall Apart: Heart Advice for Difficult Times*

Before college can feel like home, you must first get lost. Life experience reveals sometimes we need to feel lost, or even purposely get lost, to locate what we most need and want, and most importantly, to find ourselves. With answers so seemingly readily available all the time, getting lost in thought, interaction, time, and creativity ends up being a gift. Getting lost is, in and of itself, a lost art.

A dear college friend of mine shared an amazing nugget that her daughter, a first-year student at Boston University, had texted her in which she said she was "working on wandering." I'm not sure I've heard anything more astute and self-aware from a first-year student. Here's a young woman who has intuited the real purpose of college—and life. Her comment reminds me of Emily Dickinson, who wrote, "I am out with lanterns looking for myself."

Getting lost is about meandering and exploring and seeing the value in the journey over and above the destination. It's a willingness to let ourselves be surprised. Not just at what we find but what we find in ourselves. Maybe it's the ability to stop and ask a question on the way; maybe it's the ability to relish some moments of solitude, or maybe it's the newfound confidence and pride in doing it ourselves.

Robin Flicker, an attorney, recently shared this story:

"After my son was accepted to college, he gave me *Writings on Art* by Rothko. The gift was thanks for the two winter weeks we spent holed up in the apartment working on his college essays. I remember them as among the happiest of my life. We were in it together, working. His future sprawled ahead like a forest I could not see into, but knew was dense and rich. He didn't so much need help writing well as for me to say, after reading each draft, 'Good, but go in again and get closer to it.' I even had a hand signal for this. I wanted him to approach, as nearly as possible, the true note where feeling married thought and met air."

Three things strike me about what Robin said: 1) his future looked to her like a lush and mysterious forest; 2) she urged him to keep digging in and getting closer to the heart of the matter in his writing, which is to say his thinking and his feeling; and 3) when she refers to "met air," it reminds me of the freedom I tell students they'll begin to feel when they can confidently and effectively communicate in written and oral form. What I love most about what Robin said is her image of the unknown and inviting forest is akin to what I mean by a hope structure—each are filled with a promising mixture of labyrinths and light and opportunities to be lost and found.

Embarking on a journey through a forest or designing a hope structure involves surrendering to the magic of discovery. I'm reminded of a quotation from the poet Rainier Maria Rilke that hangs on my office door that I hope inspires my students as it does me:

"Be patient toward all that is unsolved in your heart and try to love the questions themselves, like locked rooms and like books that are now written in a very foreign tongue. Do not now seek the answers, which cannot be given you because you would not be able to live them. And the point is, to live everything. Live the questions now. Perhaps you will then gradually, without noticing it, live along some distant day into the answer."

CHAPTER 2

GETTING ROOTED IN THE COLLEGE EXPERIENCE

Lesson 4: Develop a Mission Statement for Your College Experience

"Dwell as near as possible to the channel in which your life flows."

—Henry David Thoreau

When people talk about college, the narrative generally revolves around issues of obtaining gainful employment after graduation. Of course, that is necessary and worthwhile as one part of the reason to go to college. However, as workforce development has become increasingly the main topic of the larger cultural conversation, I've observed another concurring phenomenon among students. Overall, they're pretty lost. Okay, that's an understatement. They're *very* lost. So, it's normal if you're feeling this right now, too. One would think that given the myopia on work and professions in which students are steeped, they would come to college with laser focus. On the one hand, many of them do, in terms of just wanting to be done, to get their diplomas, get jobs, and get on with their lives. This utilitarian way of approaching the college experience means that to them, college is at once a gatekeeper, an obstacle course, and a weighing station on the speedy highway to the next thing.

But what if, instead, we conceptualize college as a door opener? I can't begin to describe the number of students in touch with me years later, letting me know that they wish they could be back in school again and that they wished they hadn't been in such a rush to be done and get out. What if we saw college as the vigorous yet meandering mountain hike that it is, with its accompanying peaks and valleys, invisible tree roots that trip us up, occasional obstacles like boulders and a terrifying storm, breathtaking vistas, and a meditative path of reflection?

Students' *raison d'etre*, that is, their whole reason for being, often feels not only uncertain but almost unknown and inaccessible to them. But for the college experience to be meaningful and worthwhile, students benefit from having a clear purpose and a sense of intention. This doesn't contradict my earlier point about getting lost and wandering; that, too, is essential, but it's both. You'll benefit from a balanced blend of intention and free exploration. So how might you go about striking this balance?

Just as companies and organizations have mission statements, students would benefit from dreaming up theirs for the college experience. Ideally, students could and should revisit it multiple times a year, reflecting on how well their daily habits are aligning with their ultimate goals. Some questions you might ask yourself:

- What do you see as the point of college? What do you hope to get out of it?
- How have you heard others speak about college when you were growing up?
- What are you most hopeful about related to the college experience and why?

- What concerns or scares you most about the college experience?
- What do you most want to say yes to in your life?
- What would you prefer to say no to in your life?
- Who inspires you to stick to your dreams? (This person might be alive or not, someone with whom you're close, or even someone you've never met whose qualities seem worth emulating.)
- Are you hoping to finish college for reasons beyond yourself, like honoring a loved one? If not, is there someone or something to which you might dedicate the journey?
- If you're a first-generation college student, are you hoping to fulfill a dream that others have for you to finish college, or are you struggling with feeling that by going to college, you will become an outsider to those closest to you because you'll have an experience they didn't?
- What conditions are necessary to achieve your vision and mission? How might you surround yourself with a circle of people who best support these goals?
- Think about habits you've cultivated. Which serve you well? How might you let go of ones that don't?
- What are you doing, like *really* doing, to take care of your soul, interests, and heart?

We learn best when we see things with fresh eyes and with a sense of beginner's mind. Remember that tomorrow is a new day, an opportunity to start again and rediscover your dreams. Most of us benefit from taking a few quiet moments to reflect by ourselves before bouncing ideas off another person and sharing insights. From the extensive list of bulleted questions that I provided to you above, choose only one and meditate on it, and if you're doing this with a friend, talk afterward about whatever bubbled up for each of you, listening wholeheartedly to the other person's offerings. I recommend tackling a new question on another day and continuing this process. If you're doing this exercise alone, I suggest writing freehand about your reflections. You might try drawing accompanying images that come to mind, as that can be impactful and make the experience stick. Writing and drawing are great tools for soulful reflection so it might be worth spending some time on these before sharing with another person as well.

Related to mission and vision is an exercise I've done with students in which I give them a sheet of paper with the following sentence starters and have them fill in the rest. You might experiment with this at the beginning and end of a new semester.

I am ______________________________

I want ______________________________

I'm aware that ______________________________

I fear ______________________________

I hope for ______________________________

I could ______________________________

I will ______________________________

When I've taken yoga classes, one of the first things the teacher says at the start of class is to take a moment to get quiet and still and think of an intention for our practice. I've found this to be an inspiring anchor and one that works off the mat and in the classroom. When I teach, I encourage students to reflect on their intention for my course and, more than that, on their intention for the entirety of their college experience. This is an especially effective exercise for first-year students, yet it's suitable for students of any age since we all benefit from revisiting, refreshing, and rediscovering our intentions and rearticulating our visions. When students seek me out because they're floundering with looming school issues and life questions, I try to emphasize that they need not know the answer now and the point is the process of discovery. I urge them to consider intention, passion, purpose, and meaning.

I share these words from the celebrated dancer Martha Graham: "There is a vitality, a life force, an energy, a quickening, that is translated into action. And because there is only one of you in all time this expression is unique. And if you block it, it will never exist through any other medium and will be lost…"

Lesson 5: Access Your Deepest Passions at Their Root

We benefit from anchoring into the pleasures and pursuits we had when we were small children. All of us need space to listen to that still, small voice, and we need mentors and parents who are interested in listening. In that spirit, find a few favorite photos of yourself from when you were a baby, a toddler, a small child, and a few from K–12.

- Describe the personality of this child.
- Who were their best friends?
- What did this child love to do?
- What did this child not like to do?
- What was this child most afraid of?
- If fear wasn't in the way, what are some things this child would have tried?

- Did this child long to have a "louder" or "quieter" personality? Were there things this child wanted to say and held back? Did this child ever feel invisible?
- What would you like to say now to this child?
- What do you think this young person has to offer you now, especially in terms of personal transformation, self-discovery, and self-empowerment? Do the pictures give you any clues to your authentic self?
- What do you currently experience as your best traits? Alternatively, what qualities do you possess that seem to limit you, get in your way, or set you back?
- What daily/weekly/monthly habits do you engage in that seem to help you, both physically and mentally? What habits don't seem to serve you and instead sabotage your success and happiness?
- What emotional muscles do you want to develop in yourself? (Examples might include resilience, passion, curiosity, awareness and communication of feelings, etc.)
- Visualize yourself walking across the stage at graduation. What qualities and habits do you think that person (*you*) possesses? How and what do you imagine would help cultivate those aspirational, treasured qualities? How might you get involved right now in activities, alone and with others, that might pave the way toward actualizing this for yourself?

Lesson 6: Be the Tree!

Think of something in nature that inspires you. Perhaps it's the ocean or a mountain, a flower or bird, or the sliver of a bright moon in a dark sky. Take some time to meditate on what you chose. Are there qualities you associate with it? For example, the ocean may be evocative of flow, and the mountain may remind you of how far you've climbed to get to where you are. Close your eyes and conjure up this scene.

I remember a pivotal summer when I returned to Madison, Wisconsin, where I had gone to college. It was 2008, and I had just landed a new tenure-track position at a college in Boston and the trip was to celebrate that newfound stability. On that day that still feels vivid to me, I meandered downtown toward Lake Monona, where, as I was walking around the water, I came upon a tree standing high in the sky all by itself and leaning in such a way that it looked like it could fall. Yet, somewhere, deep down, I'm not sure how, but I trusted the tree. Rather than seeing it as leaning and likely to fall, I reframed it in my mind as strong yet flexible. It was grounded and sturdy, just as I had longed to be and was finally celebrating. And as it swayed, the tree showed it was agile, graceful, responsive, and adaptable—qualities I find worth emulating. All these years later, the image of that tree still inspires me to possess flexible strength.

During a trip to Madison last summer, I took a walk to visit my tree. I'm happy to report that it was still there. I think of that tree as "the little engine that could" and remind myself how strength contributes to flexibility and flexibility to strength. Sometimes in a moment when I'm nervous about something or unsure how I will perform in a situation, I close my eyes and call up that image of the tree. And then I channel something taught to me by a favorite yoga instructor; she suggested that we think of a quality we most want to cultivate through our yoga practice and dedicate our practice to that—perhaps it's compassion, equanimity, or calmness. At the end of the class, in a final seated position, she would lead us in a meditation when she told us to say to ourselves, "I am ____________," to be filled in with the quality we had thought about earlier. So, for example, "I am compassion," "I am equanimity," or "I am calmness." In those classes, I often thought about flexible strength. What used to be "I am flexible strength" at the end of yoga class has morphed into "I am the tree." Try this for yourself with whatever you've chosen in nature that speaks to you and helps you feel grounded.

CHAPTER 3

THE RHYTHM OF THE COLLEGE EXPERIENCE

Lesson 7: College Is like a Water Ride

Have you ever been on a water ride at an amusement park? If so, you know most of the fun is getting as soaked as possible. You may have even gone so far as to look at people who got off the ride to determine the best place to sit to get the wettest. Conversely, on an average rainy day, you might go out of your way to stay dry, bring an umbrella, or remain indoors. But something about that day at the park compels you to experience things differently, take risks, let go, not try to control anything (except for getting as wet as you can), and surrender to this one-of-a-kind experience.

It turns out that a water ride is an appropriate metaphor for the college experience. College is all about freeing yourself from the confines of whatever has contained you, trying out new versions of yourself, and experimenting with new ways of knowing and being in the world. And just like on a water ride, college has moments when it's momentarily dry, followed by times when it feels like everything is coming at you fast and furiously and it's overwhelming, when perhaps you wonder about the decisions you've made and how to best pace yourself and find a good balance. Try to keep the following principles in mind:

- Embrace the water; everyone gets wet
- Dive in
- Soak it all up
- Swim with the group
- Avoid just treading water
- Ride the waves
- Swim against the current
- Know when to rest
- Know the signs of when you're in over your head
- Find what anchors you
- Locate your buoys

Lesson 8: Consider the Purpose of Each Year of College

There's value in conceptualizing college not just as four years all bundled together but as discrete blocks of time that each have a purpose and characteristics. Each year marks a new transition and requires a different kind of courage and stamina. Try to begin each year with a few central, doable, and reachable goals, and review this each semester. When I talk with students about this, I describe each year in the following way. You might wind up tweaking this for your experience.

Freshman Year: Arrange Your New Life and Make Yourself at Home

A beginner's mind is often the best mindset. What is a beginner's mind? It's the ability to look with fresh eyes, to see what's common and familiar in a new way. It requires openness and curiosity, two qualities that benefit us in higher education. Beginners bring with them a blank slate, a fresh canvas, and a way of seeing that is just insider and outsider enough simultaneously. Cultivating a beginner's mind means letting the preconceived notions and judgments fall away, and it's an openness to what is. Ripe with possibility, this mindset presents us with the opportunity to recreate ourselves every day.

- Acclimate
- Adjust
- Reframe
- Explore

Look into student organizations, clubs, and intramurals on campus, and explore activities in the surrounding community where you might meet new people and find meaningful activities.

Sophomore Year: Stretch and Socialize

Sophomore year offers a prime opportunity to enjoy present-moment awareness. You're not in as much of a rush as you might think. I learned this during my sophomore year. You're not that new, yet it's still fresh. You've acclimated to some aspects and have more to discover and learn.

Half your friends aren't scattered across the globe to study abroad, as they might be next year. And you're not in the middle of graduate school applications, job interviews, and, best of all, no one yet is asking you nonstop questions about what you're going to do when you graduate. Sophomore year is the time to solidify and deepen friendships that began freshman year and to let go of the ones that didn't serve you as well, to move out beyond the ready-made social circle of roommates and dorm friends, and to chart your course. The friends you make in college will likely carry you all your life.

Use this year to have conversations with professors, coaches, and others who might become potential lifelong mentors. They may help you connect with like-minded people on and off campus. Students frequently share with me intimate details of their lives, and I'm constantly connecting them to other people who have been through something similar so they feel less alone and can benefit from peer mentoring as well. I've helped students who have lost parents or siblings, those struggling with various forms of self-injury, students who are faced with a new diagnosis, etc. It can be a beautiful thing when people can connect with a sense of mutual understanding and compassion about hard issues.

Hopefully, you're more used to your surroundings, the college routine, and the rhythm of the academic year and feel more settled and grounded. That's a great foundation from which to:

- Stretch further and take risks.
- Observe and deepen your passions.
- Cultivate a strong social network of dear friends.
- Connect with one or more mentors.

Junior Year: Focus and Fortify

Like junior year in high school, this is when things feel the most serious, but in fun ways. Things should gel more academically, as by this time, you've likely completed general education requirements if those are necessary at your institution, and you've selected a major. During this time, the following will be front and center:

- Focus your involvement.
- Solidify your major if you haven't yet done so.
- Consider and seize potentially transformative experiences such as internships, volunteering, leadership opportunities, study abroad, or research with a professor.
- Begin to think about all your options for work and future schooling, especially if you're thinking you might want to start graduate work immediately after college.

Senior Year: Get Ready to Launch

You'll be doing a new kind of individuating again, but this time, hundreds or thousands of people will be doing it with you on campus, as well as friends at other schools. Soon, everyone will scatter to different futures. Some may go after a job while others pursue graduate work, travel, or assume an internship, and to accomplish this, some may move back to their family's home or venture somewhere entirely new. Whatever it is, it's *your* launch!

Speaking of launching, I'm reminded of something. Years ago, when I was in graduate school, I discovered the figure skater Surya Bonaly. She's known for launching herself into the air. Bonaly is famed for her backflip in which she lands on one foot, an illegal move in the long skating program. Though I've never in my life attempted to even get on ice skates, Bonaly's free-spirited ways resonate deeply with me. She marched to the beat of her own drummer, defied conventional guidelines, and risked the boldest, most daring jumps to be authentic. These qualities are important to witness when you think about composing your life:

- Cultivate your network.
- Take full advantage of the community or city in which your school is situated and tackle that bucket list before you graduate.
- Keep all your options open before making decisions.
- Connect with people in your chosen field for opportunities to gather more information, shadow them, and gain experience.

Doesn't this seem similar to the rhythm of a trip? The first few days are about getting adjusted, then it's fun and relaxing and you can just revel in being; then you realize all the things you still want to see, do, and accomplish before leaving, and then you have to plan your reentry with your new lens on the world and a new sense of who you are because of the experiences you've had.

Lesson 9: College Isn't Supposed to Be Smooth Sailing

You may be wondering why things seem so hard on every level and every direction you turn. Maybe you've decided your roommate isn't so great after all; the friends you thought you made the first few weeks have turned on you; you miss your friends from high school; the workload in your classes has ramped up; you're feeling pressure from your parents; the food sucks; you didn't make the cut at the fraternity, sorority, or team you hoped for; and everyone seems to be in a relationship or hooking up but you.

These sorts of things may leave you feeling like you don't measure up, that you're inadequate, less than, or not good enough. And if you're struggling to keep up academically, you might begin to wonder how you got admitted to college in the first place and if you truly belong. That feeling is generally even more magnified among first-generation college students who, for various reasons, often question their place. But whether or not you're having a tough time with your classes, if all that other stuff gets hard and heavy to bear, it's common to question if you selected the right college, if you'd be happier elsewhere or even back at home and not attending school.

It's usually mid-October when I hear these stories, especially from first-year students, and they often share with me that one of their main concerns is how to break it to their parents that they're not doing well in school, not fitting in, or otherwise feeling unhappy. The subtext of what they tell me reveals that both they and their parents expected more smooth sailing. After all, they had gotten admitted to college, they moved in, and college is supposedly a dreamy time, so what could be the problem? And that's when I typically respond to students, "Freshman year isn't smooth sailing. It never is. In fact, it's not supposed to be."

They look at me quizzically, sense the validation, and perk up. "Really?" they ask.

"Oh yes, really. Freshman year reallllly sucks for most people." And then I try to explain. I mean, come on, how could it ever be smooth? You're in a brand-new environment with people from all over with all their different habits, preferences, and problems, living in spaces where the bathroom on an airplane doesn't look that small anymore, subsisting on the poorly replenished salad bar in the dining hall, attending (or not) classes considerably harder than high school taught by people who often don't know your name and may not care to learn it. And you're on your own for the first time, which often means managing your schedule, doing your laundry (or not), finding help when you need it, etc. Not to mention this is that formative time of life between childhood and real adulthood where you're trying out new versions of yourself, discovering your interests, and finding your way—and all of this is happening at the same time.

So, remember, it's not supposed to be smooth sailing. It will be bumpy. It will be stormy. It may make you nauseous and scared. But I can almost promise you, if you give it a fair chance, if you stay motivated and connected, if you know where the lighthouses and lifeguards are when you need help and guidance (think: offices of support, professors, and coaches), if you let your dreams carry you like the wind, pretty soon, you'll be cruising. And it will be glorious. And you'll want to keep sailing. After all, the whole point of college is to figure out how to become captain of your ship.

CHAPTER 4

ADJUSTING TO COLLEGE LIFE

Lesson 10: You're Not Alone in How Hard It Can Be to Get Settled and Find Your Way

"Hang out with people—don't binge Netflix in your room. You're in a rare situation being surrounded by other people who also want to engage (when they're not binging Netflix in their rooms), take advantage of it. Some of these relationships will become the most valuable in your adult life. Some of my closest friends (including my husband) are my college friends, even thirty-five years later... And all of these things are right there on a plate for you to engage with. It'll never be so easy again in your life."

—Alexa, mother of three college daughters

In college, so much learning and growth happens outside of the classroom, and much of it occurs in the context of the social connections and friendships you make and the intimate relationships in which you find yourselves. Some people go to college where they already have good friends or family members or acquaintances from high school, yet for so many it's a whole new world. Even if you do come in already knowing people, you have much to gain by approaching the social scene as though you know no one and with fresh eyes and an open mind. In college when so much of your life is already in flux, as it necessarily needs to be, and when everyone is trying to better understand themselves and their place on campus and in the world, it's inevitable that your impressions of people may change, and friendships will naturally shift over time. This is another great reason for being open minded rather than exclusionary in how you approach getting to know people and forming relationships. And you know what? I've never met a single college student who hasn't at one time or another felt pangs of loneliness, not fitting in, or feeling the pain of rejection, so you're not alone in trying to figure out your social life and how to find your peeps.

In doing research for this book, Ella, a rising sophomore at the University of Rochester shared great advice that applies to almost everything in college and in life: "Don't worry, no one else knows what they're doing either." What I love about this is the reminder that at times everyone feels awkward or inadequate, even people who might look like they have it all together, and so her advice feels forgiving, welcoming, and lighthearted.

Lesson 11: Sometimes Parents Just Don't Get It

Whether your parents went to college or not, most realize a lot has changed about college since they were your age. You'll benefit from having frank conversations with them about what you expect to do and experience in college as well as how often, and through what means, you want to be in touch with them. These are conversations worth having before starting college, and they're equally worth returning to at various intervals throughout college. Let your family members know how often, and via what modality, you want to check in and talk. Are you hoping for phone calls, FaceTime, Zoom, texting, or a mix? Try vocalizing your preferences while simultaneously paying attention to your parents' and siblings' wishes and reasoning without getting demanding or defensive. If you aren't in frequent or constant contact, it may be because you're building a new life on campus, and indeed, that's a great thing!

You'll likely try out a lot of things in the next few years, some of which your parents might have tried when they were your age. Try to remind them it's part of the process. Some of what you try might be just for the moment and some may be part of who you're becoming. Remind your parents that while you might rely on and value their insight and advice some of the time, it's normal to seek out perspectives from new, trustworthy mentors you come to know in college. This might be a special professor you've come to appreciate, an adviser, a coach, a counselor, or a boss at a job.

Parents often expect to be the first to know about something big, but often in college, they're not. How do I know this? Because of the amount of times that students have disclosed things to me and specifically said they haven't figured out how best to break it to their parents. Like you, they want to be heard, held, helped, and not judged. Try to explain to your parents you understand they'll likely be concerned about a variety of things in terms of your well-being and that there are some things they can do to make it more possible for you to open up. Here are some ideas:

1. Ask them for an open, nonjudgmental, and listening heart.

2. Ask them to offer you the chance to seek out professional mental health resources and medical services to get information on whatever it is you need. The two biggest things holding students back from seeking help are worrying their parents will find out and feeling anticipatory distress as to how their parents might react. This is exacerbated by the fact that students typically

already feel shame and guilt around the issues for which they need and want help.

3. Ask if they can afford to help pay for these services without judgment.

4. Convey your understanding that it might feel threatening to them to have less control, or for others' viewpoints you seek to be ones you take and act on more seriously.

5. Help them appreciate the person you're becoming, the one they might enjoy being with much more than even the you now, the one with whom they'll soon be able to clink a glass of champagne to celebrate at graduation, and the one with whom they'll relish in all sorts of interesting conversations for years to come.

Lesson 12: Navigating Homesickness

"And the day came when the risk to remain tight in a bud was more painful than the risk it took to blossom."

—Anaïs Nin

Usually within the first few weeks after the wildly hyped up drop-off, and just as your parents have almost stopped crying at the drop of a hat at the thought of their baby away at college, you're texting or calling about how homesick you are, how you haven't found your people, how you have no idea what to get involved in or how, and that you're not feeling the fit you perceived when you toured the campus last year. Your parents are getting about the same amount of sleep worrying about this as they did eighteen years ago when you were a baby and they called the pediatrician about how colicky and inconsolable you were, and that person tried to explain to them that this was normal. I'm here to tell you that what you're feeling right now is normal, you're not alone in feeling anxious or lost, and so I've assembled the following advice to help you breathe a little easier as you try to settle into your new community.

Accept the reality that this is a huge life adjustment and process. It's far too early to draw conclusions about fit and whether or not to transfer. Some people may have had more practice being away from home when growing up, while others never went to overnight camp or anything like it. Living in such tight quarters with strangers is daunting at first and especially while everything else feels so foreign—the routine, the food, the academic expectations, and the overall sense of place. Like with any life change, it can't be solved using quick fixes, and it may take some time.

Differentiate between homesickness and debilitating depression, anxiety, and panic. If you're feeling and behaving in ways that feel unsettling and alarming to you and people around you, please seek out campus counseling services. They tend to be highly responsive and resourceful and can ascertain things since they're in person with you in ways that parents far away cannot. You might benefit from seeing a counselor regularly, at least for a little while, or perhaps trying medication to take the edge off.

The grass is not always greener. In this day and age with social media saturation, we're all bound to scroll, evaluate, and compare our lives to the presentations of others. Consequently, you may get the distorted impression that everyone is having the time of their lives except you. A friend who is a therapist tells her twentysomething patients, "Don't go around comparing your insides to others' outsides."

Reframe homesickness as home-seeking. I've recently heard people referring to empty nesters—parents whose kids are all out of the house—as free birds. It's a great reframing. Perhaps we need to do the same with the word homesick. Maybe it should be home free—free of the confining ways you might have seen yourself or perceived others saw you, and you're now free to start over in a new place. Or, maybe the term is homeward bound with the understanding and intention that life is a journey to find our own sense of home. Maybe home is not one place or group of people after all. Maybe there are lots of places we'll call home over the course of our lives. And maybe college is one of those homes.

Nothing lasts forever. Soon enough, you'll graduate and move and you'll likely want to return home—but this time, not just home to see family and friends, but perhaps back to the campus where you planted your dreams, and you might beam with pride and joy at how you blossomed. Longing for home and feeling lonely are part of the process of adjusting to college. And, soon, things usually open in the most wondrous of ways. You got this! Writer Diane Hanna says this:

"You don't often know when a beginning begins. This is true of springtime and love affairs, of remodeling projects and moves to distant lands. You might notice a restlessness, a tingling around the heart. In a sweet breeze, a lingering glance, a misplaced door knob, a taste of Caribbean stew, the beginning begins. And there you are, suddenly displaced, suddenly awake, suddenly alive."

Lesson 13: Dealing with Roommates and Suitemates

Your roommates and suitemates may become your closest friends. Often, they don't. That's okay. At least in the beginning, they often function both as a launching pad and a soft place to land as you find your way on campus. Your roommate sometimes serves as a built-in person to join you at events geared for new students. Be sure to attend those events that have been planned for first-year students as everyone will be in the same boat, and it's a wonderful way to connect with new people. Roommates may provide companionship at mealtime. They can be a nice starting place for your social life. If you enjoy each other's company, that's wonderful, but even so, it's crucial to get out of your room or suite.

Not only might this person or group of people not be your best friends forever, they may even just be intolerable to live with. It's inevitable that you or people you know will experience roommate conflicts. Interestingly, the central roommate conflicts mirror that of married couples: chores, communication, money, work, and sex. Roommates struggle with differing expectations for organization, cleanliness, and clutter and how often, to what extent, and by whom these need to be attended to. They struggle with fairly sharing certain expenses for items such as a television, a mini frig, decorations, food and toiletries. Typically, roommates come with a different tolerance for noise and light, and some want music and a television on 24/7 while others need and want quiet to work, relax, and sleep. Early risers may be paired with night owls, or athletes getting up at five in the morning for practice living with people majoring in music and playing guitar until two a.m. There are the fights about visitors, especially boyfriends and girlfriends who are there night after night doing everything from having sex to hogging the bathroom. With all of these conflicts, you'll benefit from clear and honest face-to-face communication about your needs and wishes. If it doesn't work to calmly resolve things that way, then seek out the resident assistant. If after that things remain unresolved, make an appointment with the resident director or director of housing. This is something students need to advocate about for themselves.

Lesson 14: Get Out of Your Room

Over the years, schools have been catering to students' and parents' desires for beautiful residence halls with plush amenities that resemble either an upscale hotel or apartment. Students and parents (usually mothers) go to great lengths to set their kids up in a way where their living quarters feel like a home away from home, anticipating, ordering, returning, exchanging, and anguishing over every knickknack and creature comfort that will make a room feel cozy. It's big business for all the shops, websites, and artisans pushing goods and services, not to mention interior designers now specializing in dorm decor. All of this is further fueled by the excessive and conspicuous consumption evident on college-bound parent pages and dorm decorating groups on social media where people are sharing ideas and inspiration and swapping pictures that rival the covers of *House Beautiful.*

But what if I told you that you could have a winning college experience regardless of what your room likes like? If you go around and ask people what their best memories are from college, it's likely that the most indelible memories have absolutely nothing to do with one's room. Actually, this is good news for both students and parents. It takes away some of the intense financial and emotional pressure. Beauty is important and it can be pleasurable to have nice stuff, but it's useful to keep things in perspective and to remember that this is a dorm room and not a first house.

Instead of spending so much time and energy anticipating how to arrange everything in the room, students benefit from arranging their mindset for college. Anyway, you're not starring in an episode of *Extreme Makeover: Home Edition,* so rather than turn life into a massive to-do and to-buy project for what has already become Moveinapalooza, let me offer you something counterintuitive to contemplate: maybe these dorms shouldn't be so homey after all. I mean, yes, some of these dorm rooms look stunning, but there's a major thing missing when striving for these perfect room arrangements, and that's this reality: the single best thing you as students can do is to get out of your room. A lot of students love the setup of having their own bedrooms and only sharing common spaces like a kitchen, living area and bathroom.

However, this privatization and cushiness have serious unintended consequences and particularly at this juncture in history.

Students report spending far too much time holed up in their rooms, lonely, bored, anxious and depressed, scrolling on social media and worse, self-harming. It's clear that the students who've retreated to their rooms the most are less successful in school, less happy socially and emotionally, and increasingly withdrawn and isolated. They're more likely to be spending too much time in bed, sleeping, streaming, scrolling, and the like, and claiming they're depressed. Here we see a "pursuit of loneliness" to coin a term from the sociologist Philip Slater who was critical of the ways we create an alienated society for ourselves where human encounters feel abrasive or at least unpleasant. The point here is that rather than focus so much on the interior design of your room, it's vital to focus on your own interior design—that of your mind and heart.

I've come to see the positives when Pottery Barn Dorm wasn't a thing, when parents weren't hiring interior designers to create show-stopping suites, when Pinterest boards didn't exist, and the plastic crates I used for storing sweaters were enough. I'm almost wistful for that horrifyingly small room with cinderblock walls that I shared thirty-seven years ago at UW–Madison where we didn't even have space for two desks so the idea of transforming those into makeup stations was absolutely out of the question. The room was too cramped to want to spend much time in it, other than to sleep. It turns out that's the whole point—to be continually pushed out of the nest, to meet new people, to have new adventures, and to encounter new versions of yourself. For the college experience to be successful and meaningful, people have to leave their rooms. Rather than attempt to create the perfect home away from home within the room, it's crucial to remember that it's only when stepping outside of the room that you can begin to make the campus, and the college experience itself, a new space to house your dreams.

I want to address a few other practical things about time in your room. Remember that if you don't have something you realize you need, it's a great opportunity to find where and from whom to borrow or purchase it, and that gives you a chance to meet someone new—or to knock on the door of that cute person down the hall you've been afraid to say hi to. When you're in your room, especially in the first few weeks of school, leave the door open as much as possible to encourage people to drop in and chat. (When you go to sleep or leave the room, keep it locked.) If you're busy studying, you can invite someone in to study with you or suggest meeting up for dinner later on. Try to knock on others' doors and introduce yourself; people admire those who can do this. The more in-person time you have, the more meaningful, rich and deep the connections will be, and you'll be less reliant on social media for socializing.

The more you hang out in the larger common areas inside and outside campus buildings, the more you'll connect with people who have similar values and interests. For example, student unions and student centers offer great spaces to study and to hang out, listen to music, and grab coffee and snacks, and some are nestled along lakes, green spaces, and walking/biking paths with exquisite sunrise and sunset views. At my alma mater, the Memorial Union is iconic and referred to as the "living room" of the campus. Everything about it is far superior to any nicely decorated living area in a suite, that's for sure. Go out and find those amazing spaces on your campus!

The point is that the campus experience usually resembles *space*—space to enlarge one's worldview, space to think and reflect, space to create, space to explore new activities, space to try on new ways of being in the world, space to reinvent oneself—space to be and to breathe. It becomes your responsibility in these four years to fully inhabit this space. More than a responsibility, I hope you'll begin to see it as the greatest gift of campus life.

Lesson 15: Feeling Lost—The Lonely College Student

"The worst loneliness is not to be comfortable with yourself."

—Mark Twain

"Stay alive inside, don't be a stranger
Keep a line open to the outside world
Don't run and hide when everything changes"

—James McMurtry, "Walk Between the Raindrops"

Loneliness is part of the human condition, and we all experience it from time to time. College is a normal time to struggle with bouts of loneliness. You're trying to adjust to an entirely new place, and even though there are many people around all the time it's still entirely possible to feel disconnected and alone. Just as it's possible to live in the middle of Midtown Manhattan with all the hustle and bustle of activity and feel lonely, so too it's possible to feel this way at college.

Research has shown that students' reports of being lonely have continued to increase since the early 1990s. Emerging reliance on social media has made us simultaneously more connected and disconnected. For better and worse, social media has changed how we regard friendship and how we regard time alone. We may be in touch with more people than ever before and have hundreds or even thousands of "friends" on social media but the lived experience of those connections is likely more a sort of "friendship lite." Interestingly, the people we communicate with the least on those platforms are usually the ones where we share a deeper and more meaningful, reliable, and durable emotional connection. This is significant because stronger social ties are a predictor of resilience and help protect against loneliness, isolation, emotional fragility, and hopelessness.

It's important to understand that loneliness in college students doesn't only manifest at school. In fact, it's quite common for it to be acutely felt when back home on breaks in ways that can be confusing and unsettling to both students and parents. It's common to think that issues like loneliness, depression, and anxiety resolve themselves once finals are over and you're back to the comfort of your own bed and some homemade meals. But sometimes these issues and problems deepen in ways that need to be better understood.

Parents naturally want to believe these problems are external, possibly related to academic stress, pressures with being a college athlete, being over-committed with activities at school, dealing with difficult roommates, or facing a breakup. It becomes much harder to face that the locus of the problem might be internal and/or related to difficulties at home. If you're like most students, you don't want to admit to your parents the pain or loneliness you feel for fear of being criticized. It's understandable to not want to be told what to do, to not want to be criticized for a bizarre schedule or how much you want to be out with friends or how much you have no desire to attend every family gathering. But if you're hoping for your parents' empathy or support, it helps to communicate at least about some of what's troubling you. In turn, that can help them open a curious heart and suspend judgment so you can be truly heard and get the help you need.

Jasmine emailed me in the summer when, again, she found her home life difficult because of her parents' tense marriage and their drinking. She confided in me that she couldn't bear to tell her mother about her feelings. I gave her feedback and ideas for finding a therapist and recommended someone locally for when she returned to school. Interestingly, she decided to commit to therapy immediately and started making the trek, two hours in each direction. Her desperation was palpable and real yet so too was her commitment to herself to make changes. Though she felt lonely and afraid at home, Jasmine knew to reach out for help, underscoring the importance of securing trustworthy mentors.

There are numerous reasons why students may return home for the summer with newfound stresses and sadness. Simply put, as the author Thomas Wolfe said, "You can't go home again." Upon leaving for college, family dynamics often shift, the players have changed, and the game itself changes. Students return to something partially familiar and partially foreign.

The summer after freshman year can be the trickiest and potentially the loneliest; you might be eager to see friends from home and then be disillusioned when you discover those friendships have changed since high school. Furthermore, you might start missing college friends you made and then see on social media what those friends are up to, sizing up your lives against idealized pictures and updates. Some friends and acquaintances may post pictures of savoring pasta and gelato with their families in Italy while others are snorkeling in the Caribbean, all while you're home bored out of your mind from your bad restaurant job and your parents who would be better off divorced. Or, you may start to realize you're not into your friends at home and don't have the friendships you hoped for back at college either. This sense of crisis can be an opportunity for some self-reflection, for example, have you been holing up too much? If you're romantically involved with someone, consider if the relationship is fulfilling or making you lonelier. Is a long-distance relationship the best thing right now and/or when you're back living on campus?

There are things you can do to mitigate the effects of loneliness and build your emotional muscle toward greater resilience, both counting on your own strength and connecting with others. Here are some strategies for countering loneliness and its accompanying despair (and you can find many more ideas in the section related to getting involved on campus):

- **Consider the difference between loneliness and solitude.** They're qualitatively different. Solitude can be restorative and can help you recharge and renew, and it's a life skill worth cultivating now. Your future self will thank you.
- **Engage in stress-reducing activities like mindful meditation and yoga.** Deep reflection assists in any decision-making process and helps with cultivating stillness, self-reliance, presence, and peace of mind, which all enhance the joys of solitude.
- **Unplug.** Commit to turning off your phone at least an hour every day. The immediate gratification you get from a cell phone distorts your ability to find important answers from within. Experience the world outside your phone.
- **Cultivate new hobbies and passions, and try things you always wanted to do (that are legal!).**
- **Blast music and dance.** Even if you're like me and can't dance, it's hard to not feel embodied joy when listening to great music and dancing!
- **Read.** Immersing yourself in a book for pleasure is the best way to get transported, and entering someone else's world can relieve loneliness. You might even join a book club.
- **Find and make room for spontaneity.**

Speaking of spontaneity, let me share with you a story of surprising and spontaneous interconnectedness, the kind that beautifully counters feelings of loneliness as well as homesickness. One mother, Kate, told me about a remarkable thing that happened for her daughter, Sarah:

"The closer we got to school, the more anxious she got. Cincinnati is four hours away, so we'd just been talking and listening to music, and I was acutely aware of the significance of this drive… I put on James Taylor's Greatest Hits—it seemed sweet and comforting; we had gotten to see him in concert at Blossom together the summer before. When the song 'Shower the People' came on, we were just pulling into town, and Sarah started to cry. We turned into a CVS parking lot and sat for a bit. I was feeling so much love for my little girl, and showering her with it as best I could. And I know she was feeling it, too, and was anxious about leaving her family and all that she'd known. *Three years later*, Sarah was walking across campus one night after a long day of rehearsal, and a student walking toward her had headphones on but was singing along to what he was listening to: 'Shower the people you love with love, show them the way that you feel…You know things are gonna work out fine if you only will…' She called me when she got home to tell me how happy she was, after months of feeling low. She said she had this moment of connection just singing along with this random person on the path. I think—no, I *know*—we've both learned to look for the small, beautiful, serendipitous moments instead of just waiting for the big, grand experiences."

This story highlights the surprise and delight that can be ours when we're open to it, the ways that music can be connecting and healing, and how even in the moments when we think we're walking alone, in reality or metaphorically, we meet people on our path who remind us of our interconnectedness.

Lesson 16: Do Something That Scares You

It can take some practice to learn how to be alone. It takes even more practice to learn how to experience solitude joyfully rather than feeling lonely. Yet it's so worth it! The trick is to do this without being fully reliant on your phone. Many people are intimidated and overwhelmed by the idea of dining solo or going to a movie alone but these can be great experiences to try. You might find it's easier for others to strike up a conversation with you and connections might happen more naturally when you're by yourself. When you exude confidence alone, people won't feel sorry for you. Rather you may appear to others, and experience yourself to be, more self-possessed.

Hunter, a beloved former student of mine who turns thirty soon, remarked to me that she feels like she needs to take a trip all by herself to somewhere she's never been. I've encouraged her to do it now while she's able to do this relatively unencumbered. As she has faced career changes and other transitions the past few years, I can see how traveling solo feels like a litmus test to her of how well she can manage on her own, take care of herself, and serve up her own fun.

The more you practice navigating some simple activities on your own like a meal or movie, the more you'll be ready to conquer even bigger ones, and the better you're likely to feel. Doing this becomes its own form of courage training and self-care. The best part is that experiencing yourself as a worthwhile companion helps signal to others that grounded sense of contentment. This is a true gift to give yourself that will serve you well for the rest of your life and will benefit any relationships in which you find yourself in the future.

CHAPTER 5

MAPPING YOUR COURSE SCHEDULE

Lesson 17: Striking Up a Good Rapport with Your Adviser Can Make All the Difference

Advising is handled in different ways at different institutions of higher education. As a professor for three decades, I certainly love to do it when it involves talking to students about their passions, goals, graduate school, life issues, and future intentions. But admittedly, I do find it tricky to talk about classes in other departments that I can't always speak about as comprehensively. There are limitations to the model of faculty advising and it can be a good idea to seek out varying perspectives.

There are a number of things you can do to get the most out of the advising process. Perhaps the adviser you've been assigned is a professional adviser in a dedicated advising office at the college or in your field of study like an academic adviser in a business school. This person is a higher-education professional who has solid training in the ins and outs of the school and program and is in a good position to answer questions about transfer credits, resources for academic success, etc. To augment this advising experience, seek out a faculty mentor as well. Maybe this is a person with whom you took a favorite class or who compelled you to rethink your major.

You should meet with your adviser on a regular basis and before each new semester, and be sure to prepare thoroughly for your appointment. It's disconcerting how many people wait to be advised, are late to sign up for classes, and then are frustrated that they're full. It's essential to check the academic calendar for when advising and course registration starts for the next semester and to pay attention to announcements that come through via email and are printed on flyers around campus. Then, secure an advising appointment and have any registration holds lifted so you can sign up for what you most need and want. Go to your meeting prepared with questions written out in advance, and create some mock schedules you think you'd like for the next semester. It's astonishing how many students show up to appointments without even a pen and paper to take notes.

If you're attending a smaller college or university with fewer programs and faculty, as is the case where I work, we cannot offer everything that's in the academic bulletin every semester. That's just the larger menu from which we decide what to offer. So, it's a good idea when you decide to declare a major or minor, and there are specific classes that you're interested in taking, to then find out generally when they tend to be offered so that you can plan accordingly and plot out future semesters. Sometimes faculty will know what they're teaching in advance, or they'll know if they or a colleague will be on leave and not offering a class.

I've seen cases where I've been clear about the sequence of courses that a student should try to follow, explaining exactly what semesters those are offered, and how to position themselves for the most success. And all too often I later discover that they ignored my advice and signed up for a different set of classes even if the ones I suggested were actually available. Those students (and their parents) are usually the same ones to later get upset if a class is only offered in a particular semester.

It's a wise idea to check with the registrar's office about transfer credits, to be sure about certain specifications around language requirements, or any issues that seem idiosyncratic to your own record for which you need to be sure all your *i*s are dotted and your *t*s are crossed. Remember, you're the one ultimately in charge of following up on what's expected of you and making sure graduation requirements are met. While many, if not most, schools allow students to cross the stage on graduation day if they're short by a specific number of credits, try to avoid this altogether because how anticlimactic is that? Your degree isn't conferred until you've completed everything.

Advising is a great time to talk about more than just your schedule for the next semester. Your adviser may know of exciting opportunities for research collaborations, internships, and jobs. It's worth your while to get to know this person. Be honest about anything you're struggling with, and ask for resources and support. Brainstorm with this person about majors and minors and what can be done with them in the future. You can let your adviser know what sort of classes you're interested in seeing offered; we want to know what students would like to see incorporated into the curriculum as we think about designing future classes.

The rapport you create with your adviser can serve you well far beyond graduation. This person may be someone you'll want to rely on for recommendation letters, they may become a colleague should you wind up pursuing the same field they're in, and they may even remain an enduring mentor and friend later on. Do what you can to try to meet them casually over coffee to chat more deeply, or if given an opportunity to take a faculty or staff member to lunch at the dining hall with free meal passes, consider inviting this person, and show your gratitude if and when they go out of their way to help and support you.

Lesson 18: Get Out of Your Academic Comfort Zone

College is a smorgasbord. Who wants to go to an endlessly decadent buffet and only eat salad? The rich array of course offerings gives you the chance to take risks and experiment with new ways of knowing. One may not think of themselves as a good artist, yet pursuing a ceramics class or a painting class is sure to instill other worthwhile life lessons. This is an opportunity to reinvent yourself and to become surprised at what interests you.

It's a gift to take classes that you might never get to take again in your life because they're offered by experts right where you are. A prime example of this is a class that was offered when I was a student at UW–Madison, which I *still* think I was a fool to not have registered for. The class was The African Storyteller, and it was one of the most famous classes ever offered at Madison, more like an institutional rite of passage. I had friends who took it and loved it.

One day during a visit to see me, my mother, a lover of stories, sat in on one of the lectures and was mesmerized. She couldn't understand why I never took the class. At that time, I didn't see I needed it and couldn't appreciate what it would do for me. Never a fiction lover, I figured the stories wouldn't hold my attention. That outlook limited me. I'm able to see that now as someone who prioritizes lifelong learning. I didn't *need* a class to do something for me in a utilitarian way because, after all, it *would have* done something for me—it would have enriched my life. And because the professor, Dr. Harold Scheub, was celebrated for creating such magic in the classroom, I'm sure I'd have benefited from his talents in storytelling and captivating an audience.

Lesson 19: Choose Your Classes Wisely

Choosing classes wisely is one of the most important things you can do as a college student. It's an incredible thing to finally be able to do. Typically, in junior high and high school, our classes are mainly chosen for us, so it's tremendously freeing to go to college and experience a smorgasbord of what's offered. There are numerous things one can do to make this process smoother and get the most out of it. Some of my suggestions might be ones that seem like common sense while others may seem more counterintuitive. Some of these suggestions will depend on the type of institution you attend and its size. Overall, most of these recommendations are applicable anywhere, and I can say that with great confidence having taught at a variety of institutions, public and private, large and small, and highly selective and less so.

Take in the vast array of what's offered to you. Course offerings in college are a combination of an intense deepening of subjects you might have explored in high school, entirely new subjects to which you've never been exposed that may call out to you career-wise (such as what happened for me with sociology), as well as rich and eclectic offerings you might find at a community center. College becomes a place where you can take astrophysics alongside hip-hop and the history of yoga. And why not?

Having a dazzling array of experiences like this under your belt will do wonders for increasing your cultural capital—essentially the knowledge, assets, and resources that help you get ahead in the world beyond economic means. College gives you incredible access to building your cultural capital which helps you in various social and professional situations. For example, you might be on a job interview one day and notice a poster of an important painting, sculpture, or building hanging on the wall, or perhaps the person you're speaking with mentions something about literature, music, food, or theater; having the ability to comfortably converse about a variety of subjects like that reveals your versatility and depth. Another way to say this is that the college experience provides a chance to engage in an exquisite amount of world traveling, (even while remaining on campus!) that in turn makes you worldly, agile, and more fluent.

Remember that when you sign up for classes, it's an opportunity to expand your mind. It's like the expression goes, the mind stretched over a new idea, never returns to its original dimension. I was so hell-bent on taking as much sociology as I could because UW–Madison has always been one of the top sociology programs in the country, but looking back on it now, I wish I'd have taken some other classes in other departments just for that sense of being even more well-rounded. That might have involved the risk of not doing as well as I did in my sociology classes, but it would have been expansive in a different way. Along these lines, it's beneficial to take courses with a wide variety of professors. Even if you come to adore one and choose to take more classes with that person, it's advantageous to encounter new ways of thinking, knowing, being, and inhabiting the world.

Try to create a schedule where you feel some degree of balance. For example, if there are two subjects with which you know you struggle and for which you might need to devote more time or that might require you to seek tutoring, it might make sense to not take them in the same term.

Think about the sort of schedule you want and need. Whereas in high school, you couldn't choose days and times of your classes, in college, you get to have a bit more control over when you take classes and with whom. This is particularly true if various sections of the same class are offered, and perhaps one professor is teaching the class on Monday, Wednesday and Friday mornings while the other professor is teaching it in a three-hour block on Tuesday evenings. It's a good idea to think about when you're most fresh and engaged for learning.

Consider the class schedule in light of your other commitments, and be prepared to adjust things accordingly. You'll want to consider things like if you're on a sports team and when the practices and games are, or other activities you might be involved in such as musical and theatrical productions, as well as part-time jobs and other responsibilities. Over the years, I've worked with many student athletes. I'm frank with them, and if they show me their game schedule and it has them missing a dozen classes, I encourage them to drop and take the class at a different time in their college career. A young man on the baseball team became irritated with me for suggesting this, but given how important attendance and participation were for success in that class, I was advising this with his interests in mind. It turned out that he did poorly in my class, and then a number of years later took another class with me. I immediately sought him out the first week to talk about our previous experience and his attitude so that he'd know we could enjoy a fresh start. It turns out in that class he earned one of the highest grades, and it was exciting and rewarding to see how he turned things around. So, I invited him to speak to my large introductory sociology class to help first-year students avoid getting in their own way, much like he had done years prior. You could hear a pin drop in the room. He indicated that the first time around he didn't have the maturity to deal with the demands of the class and didn't understand the ways in which by being firm with him, I was, indeed, looking out for his best interest.

Determine how many classes may be too much in a given semester. If you're struggling at all academically or in other ways, avoid overwhelming yourself with too many classes. You want to aim for just the right amount to be motivating. It's like going to the gym where you don't want it to feel so impossible that you just give up, and you don't want it so light that it's not challenging enough.

Lesson 20: Consider Certain Implications and Plan Ahead

If your school offers a wide variety of modalities in which courses are offered, it's crucial to be honest with yourself about how much you want your classes to be face-to-face, hybrid, synchronous online, asynchronous online, or some other mixture. For example, there are courses I teach during the full fifteen-week semester, and there are other classes I teach in an accelerated eight-week or three-week format. These abbreviated courses can be useful for scheduling purposes if used appropriately. Unfortunately, sometimes I see weaker students or students on academic probation trying to take several of them in the same eight-week session which is usually a recipe for disaster. The same is true with students attempting to load up on shorter courses over the summer.

If you elect to enroll in classes at an accelerated pace, you can expect most of what goes into a regular semester to be condensed into the shorter time frame, and that sense of compression can be challenging. In advising sessions, I guide students to think about how to effectively spread things out for greater balance. For example, a student might be interested in taking the equivalent of five courses or more yet I might recommend that they take four classes that are each fifteen weeks long and one class in the first eight-week term and another class in the second eight-week term. This way, they come out with eighteen credits (assuming each class is three credits in this case) that are the equivalent of having taken six classes but they're only having to take five at a time. The same thing would be true if a student took three classes for the entire term and then took one class in each eight-week term, and then they would have the equivalent of five classes, but they would only have to take four in each term.

Think about course sequencing. It's important to find out if a particular order is required or strongly recommended for the courses you want to take. Knowledge building is a cumulative process so you'll benefit from knowing how these classes deepen and extend each other. Just recently, a man wanted to take three sociology requirements all in the same semester, including introductory sociology, a 400-level theory course, and a senior seminar. I told him that in no way would that be possible.

Along these lines, it's important to pay attention to when courses are offered and specifically in your designated major or minor. Schools showcase their academic bulletins featuring a dazzling array of courses that are offered. That doesn't mean that all of those courses are available at all times. It's up to students to find out the best sequence of classes for them within a major and/or minor, and when those classes are typically offered so they can graduate on time. For example, there are certain classes that I teach only in certain semesters, there are some classes I don't teach every year, and there are classes I teach in eight weeks that I don't teach in fifteen weeks and vice versa.

When choosing your courses, it's a good idea to think about if you might be interested in enrolling in summer school, or a January term if your school offers it. Some people use that as a way to catch up, and others use it as a way to get ahead. It can be a way to focus on one particular class that would otherwise be harder for you in the context of a full semester. For example, I have students who opt to take statistics in the summer for this reason. At the same time, your school might offer classes in the summer that are more experimental and innovative and not typically offered during the academic year. For example, several years ago, I created a brand-new course called The Sociology of Food that I taught during Maymester, our three-week intensive offering in May. It was incredibly well received and I loved teaching it, so I expanded it into a longer class that I've been teaching during the regular academic year. And more recently, I did this again by offering another brand-new class called Love and Intimacy. You might look into less expensive places to take a requirement in the summer, or you might find an intriguing class at another university that's not offered at your school. But whatever you do, be sure in advance that it will transfer.

Lesson 21: You Can't Always Get What You Want (But If You Try Sometimes You Might Find You Get What You Need!)

It's inevitable that at some point in the course of one's college career, most students will come upon classes they want and need that are full. This is something that students often find distressing, and then share with their parents who get even more frustrated and angry because they feel that they're paying for something that doesn't exist. And they don't want to pay for classes that might be extras. When I first imagined becoming a professor, I remember vowing that I'd never turn away any interested students from class and I would even let it be standing room only if it had to be. Now I look back on the naiveté of that in a different way. My classes fill, and I refuse to go into over-enrollment. It's not a good practice for faculty to go over their enrollment caps. Those are in place for a variety of reasons. One is that a fire marshal decided the capacity for the classroom, and the other is for sound teaching practices. The total number of students affects all sorts of things including how class time can be budgeted for worthwhile class discussions, lectures, student presentations, group work, and other activities. If presentations or group projects are required on set days and an influx of extra students are permitted to enroll, there would need to be extra days built into the syllabus for those students to participate. Faculty want the size of the class to be aligned with the purpose and goals of the course so that the learning is most meaningful. Students may not have the optimal experience if the class size is increased for a course that was designed by the professor to be more intimate.

There are some professors who are willing to have waitlists, however this can become unmanageable as it's almost a recipe for having far too many students. The professor might notice an opening and let a student know, but then in the meantime, someone else may have grabbed the spot. Instead, I instruct students to monitor the online system themselves since there's usually some fluctuation, especially around payment due dates. Sometimes a department will add additional sections as the semester approaches if other sections have filled and there appears to be enough demand. Sometimes you can't take a class the semester or year that you prefer, but eventually you're able to get into it. I had a student tell me she waited her whole college career to take my deviance class. Thankfully, she claims it was worth waiting for.

Lesson 22: Things Have a Way of Working Out, and the Best Part Is the Stuff You'd Never Have Predicted

When I was a second semester freshman, I was enrolled in a philosophy class because my father believed, perhaps rightfully so, that a college career wouldn't be complete without taking a philosophy course. For two weeks, I sat in one of the first few rows of the lecture hall and found myself nodding off in a way that was completely uncharacteristic. In the meantime, I had my name on a waiting list with the sociology adviser for a popular class called Social Problems taught by Doug Maynard. The philosophy class became increasingly unbearable to me, and I was absolutely delighted when the adviser called me on my—yes—landline, and told me that a spot had opened up if I still wanted to take it. She warned me that I'd have a lot of catching up to do as it was already the third week of school. I was so thrilled, I didn't even mind. It was in and through that class that I learned how sociology was a discipline that gave language and voice to conditions and arrangements that I had long cared about but didn't yet have the vocabulary and conceptual frameworks to understand. Before the semester ended, I knew I wanted to pursue a sociology major, and I thought I might want to be a professor. In my senior year, I enrolled in a hybrid undergraduate and graduate course just to have this professor again.

He and I have stayed in touch, and believe it or not, when I came out with my first book titled *Welcome to Wherever We Are: A Memoir of Family, Caregiving, and Redemption*, I let him know that I'd be in Madison speaking at the local bookstore. He showed up with his wife, and it's one of the most vivid and incredible memories I have from my book tour, because not only were they there, but also my former student, Annie, drove from Milwaukee to see me. She had been my student at Connecticut College thirteen years earlier. Introducing them was profoundly moving for me and still gives me the goosebumps as I write this. Together, there we were in that room as I read from my book and spoke about issues that took me back to 1989 when Doug posed questions to us in a classroom just a few miles down the road from where we were that evening, and yet here he was asking questions of me and taking me, and my writing, seriously.

When teaching and learning are powerful and transformative, they tend to move full-circle. The other thing about good teaching is that mutual mentoring is often involved. I had often counted on Annie as a wise sounding board, and I know that when she met me at age eighteen, she relied on me as a mentor as she dealt with homesickness, acutely aware of how much she struggled with change. I mentored Annie, and Annie mentored me. That's because effective teaching and learning involve reciprocity, mutuality, and collaboration.

Lesson 23: Things to Avoid When Selecting Your Course Schedule

Rather than seeking blow-off classes, search for mind-blowing experiences; rather than trying to find the easiest professors, look for the people who will challenge you. With college being staggeringly expensive, seeking out the easy A doesn't make sense. School isn't about buying grades. It's understandable to take a fun elective here or there but if this is the main approach to making a schedule every semester, then it's a problem.

Another thing to avoid is believing everything you hear or read about a class or a professor. By all means, don't rely on anonymous strangers on the internet to guide your decisions. You'd be amazed how many times I hear about smart and well-intended people checking websites like Rate My Professors as some sort of verification of whether the good things they heard about a professor are backed up by praise and whether the complaints about a professor are legitimate. The problem is that this website is methodologically flawed. Founded in 1999, I remember this site emerging in popularity in 2002 at a time when they allowed people to rank professors' hotness. I was in my early thirties when it was a badge of honor to have accumulated my fair share of their chili pepper icons. Heaven forbid had I not. I remember getting a good laugh out of the whole thing when an old boyfriend with whom I remained friends admitted to rating me with perfect scores and the chili pepper. To be sure to clarify, no, he was never my student. See, that's the thing, anyone can post ratings—and anyone does. Anyone can fake being a student on it and can post glowing or scathing reviews. Hell, I could even rate myself if I wanted. Seriously people, this is not the best way to choose classes!

Lesson 24: Always Have a Backup Plan When You Register for Classes

Keep in mind that schedules are often planned a year or more in advance and yet the reality is that life happens. Some faculty are awarded sabbaticals, others may become new parents, some require an unexpected medical leave, some leave for other jobs, sometimes someone is let go, and other times classes don't make which is to say that the enrollment is deemed insufficient to offer the class and then it's canceled. Sometimes a class remains on the books but the instructor is changed for one reason or another.

It's all too easy for students and their parents to blame the professors for these changes, but try to remember that faculty usually don't like when this happens either. We want our classes to run, we want our families and ourselves to be healthy and well, and we prefer minimal to no disruption. Many of these decisions happen without faculty input and occur because of budgetary reasons far beyond our control. If you register for classes where you see that you're the only student or one of just a few, keep a close eye on things to be sure the enrollment becomes more robust, and consider alternatives.

Lesson 25: Sign Up for a Class Because You've Heard the Professor Is Great or It's an Unusual Offering

When you sign up for classes, you're not just signing up for the content of a particular class, but you're also signing up to learn from a professor who has likely spent the better part of their life immersed in that subject area. When I'm advising students, I suggest colleagues from whom I learn a lot and would want to learn more. For example, I recommend all my advisees take classes with my colleague and sister-friend, Jayne; she and I have been guest speakers in each other's classes so I'm well aware of the kind of class dynamic she creates and how beloved an educator she is based on her decades of enduring relationships with students.

In recent decades, we've witnessed an over-reliance on adjunct faculty, meaning faculty who aren't on the tenure-track and instead on a contingent one that is part-time, without benefits, and unusually precarious. It used to be that adjuncts were relied upon to infuse a fresh kind of energy into a curriculum, and to bring something from the field to the classroom. For example, years ago, when I was teaching in Massachusetts and Connecticut not on the tenure track, I taught many family violence courses. Those weren't typically offered at those institutions but because I was there possessing that expertise I could offer that for students. When special courses like this are featured, it makes sense to take advantage of those opportunities.

CHAPTER 6

SETTING OUT ON THE PATH TO FINDING YOUR ACADEMIC NICHE

Lesson 26: Take a First-Year Experience Course If It's Offered

On campus tours and at freshman orientation, you're likely to have heard about something called University 101, First Year Seminar (FYS), or the first-year experience course. Originally conceived at the University of South Carolina Columbia in the early 70s, classes like these have emerged all across the country taking on a variety of shapes and forms at different institutions. These classes are different than those marked 101 in a particular discipline. You might take Political Science 101 or Psychology 101. But this kind of 101 is more about socialization into the entirety of the college experience. It's widely understood that the transition to college is a huge one and that it truly takes a village. That's why there are mechanisms in place to assist and support students so that the bulk of students' time and energy throughout the college experience is spent on engaging in meaningful activities, taking healthy risks for learning, and continuing to build confidence.

At a highly selective liberal arts college where I taught years ago, those of us identified by department chairs as master teachers were selected to offer highly specialized seminars with sexy names that would attract students; the intention was that the class itself would be interesting and engaging. For first-year students, it would connect them to faculty specializing in that topic and introduce students to that particular discipline. Another model for University 101 is less focused on the seminar experience as an intellectual pursuit and instead focuses more on social-emotional issues.

The institution's motivation for offering such a course, and either strongly encouraging it, or requiring it, is because after recruiting students, the most important part is then retaining them. Overwhelmingly, data indicates that students who are enrolled in a class like this tend to move on more successfully to their sophomore year. Depending on how it's framed at the institution you attend may affect how you perceive it. Sometimes when students earn less credit for it, such as one or two credits, versus other courses where they typically earn three credits, they tend to look at it as a blow off and an easy A.

At the college I worked at that I mentioned above, they offered three credits for these courses, and they were like any other stimulating elective except that they operated on a cohort model where every student enrolled was in their first year of college. Since college classes are usually comprised of students who represent all different years in school, as well as all different ages, the first-year experience is unique in terms of this cohort model. The accompanying intention of that then is that students who are enrolled in these will have a greater sense of belonging to a community of learners, feel more accountable, and grow a stronger foundation for relationships with peers and the professor.

Data shows that students who benefit from these programs include first-generation college students, low income students, students from marginalized communities, and students who may be more at risk academically if they had a tougher time in high school. In reality, everyone benefits from a class like this so that if you have an opportunity to take it, it's a good idea to do so. Some institutions will allow you to enroll in it at any point in your college career but it's the most valuable to do it right away.

You might think of a class like this as you would a trip to a country you've never been to. Indeed, college is a foreign country. There's a new language for things, and you need to know it to be able to succeed. The food is inevitably different. The sleeping accommodations may make you wish for your own bed! You'll get to find out how the locals live, and all the best hang out spots. But the trip is long and winding and you have to pace yourself, so if you start the experience with a wise tour guide and fellow passengers you might consider interesting and who could potentially become lifelong friends, you might be in for a real treat.

Many first-year experience classes will incorporate what my mother referred to as school survival skills. These are skills that help you whether or not you like a class or professor and whether or not you're acing it. First-year seminars that pay extra attention to the psychological dimensions of college and the idea of adulting might include topics and lessons that help students with: project management, time management, note taking, stress management, meditation, reading skills, writing skills, financial literacy, countering homesickness and loneliness, mental health issues, relationships, self-care strategies, work/life balance, and dealing with the adjustment and transition to college. All of these are life skills that most of us find ourselves working on far beyond college. But here you get a supportive space to brainstorm ideas that help you to live a good life in college and beyond. You might think of the first-year experience like a sort of incubator: a space with intentionality to chart your growth and ensure you're on a good path to success.

Sometimes, the same person who is teaching this is assigned to be your adviser. In a case like that, it can be a wonderful opportunity to develop a rapport with someone working at the school. Long-term mentorship is worth pursuing, and you can never start too early. These relationships will make a huge difference both in college and the rest of your life.

Lesson 27: General Education Requirements Needn't Be Drudgery

When I was a student at UW–Madison, I learned about a class designed for nonscience types like myself, affectionately nicknamed Physics for Poets. At the time, it was taught by a superstar professor, the late Dr. Bernice Durand, who was one of the first female professors in the physics department. In writing this book, remarkably, I didn't have to look up her name to remember her. Thirtyish years later and it's still indelibly imprinted in my mind. Side note: I've never understood how students don't know their professors' names, even their current ones, so it's kind of funny to be remembering someone from the early 90s. You'll do yourself a great service to get to know not just your professors' names but your professors themselves, and we'll get to that a bit later.

But getting back to my physics class, Dr. Durand knew that the hundreds of students enrolled with her every semester for that particular class had little to no interest being in it, that it wasn't their forte, but that the science requirement had to be fulfilled. And she literally almost did somersaults to make it possible for students to be excited about the material. I remember her standing on a table and doing exercises on it to illustrate a lesson about things in motion. And yes, one of my most incredibly special former students, Cody, remembers that I did a crazy dance on a table in my introductory sociology class in 2013, a class people often take only because they have to. Clearly, you see where I got the idea.

I remember going to Dr. Durand's office hours at the end of the semester, and I told her that sadly I probably wouldn't remember much of the content because it wasn't the stuff that my brain most retained but that I'd never forget the sort of professor she was. I promised her I'd take the lessons I learned into my own teaching career.

Perhaps this serves as some incentive to give your general education requirements a chance because you never know the other life lessons they might impart. And you might be surprised when such a requirement opens the door to something you choose to be your major, minor, or concentration; this happens countless times. Sometimes what starts out as a seemingly burdensome requirement you resent, turns out to be something that changes your worldview—and the rest of your life. That's part of the magic of college.

Lesson 28: Why Undecided Is a Great College Major (At Least for a Year or Two!)

College is one of the most fertile spaces we have for cultivating openness and curiosity. It's perfectly normal to be undecided when coming to college. In fact, that's what college is for. It's an opportunity for students to surprise themselves with what they can do and who they can be.

I've had countless conversations with students about declaring and changing majors. I've talked with students who feel an overwhelming amount of pressure from parents about what major to choose. Add to this the fact that it used to be assumed that students who knew their intended major even before entering college would have a greater likelihood of persisting, that is, finishing school.

Across the country, many students approach their first year seemingly set on a certain plan of study, for example: business, nursing, engineering, education, or hospitality. And there's some good reason for this. These are all relatively widely understood fields in the larger culture—people know what they are and can see a clear path to a job. There's a feeling of security—though that might be a false sense of security. Parents and students have seen nurses, business people, teachers, etc., in action. There's a bit more of a sense of what can be expected, and that seems functional and practical, and especially so in a world where so much feels out of our control. In fact, at some universities, majors like those I listed above are housed in a School of Professional Studies, wrongly giving the impression that other majors don't lead to that same cherished and hopeful destination of profession. I work with many incoming students who are dead-set on gaining entry to our nursing program thinking that their lives will be over if they aren't accepted. The reality is most won't be admitted, and they'll need to find alternative plans of study.

Sometimes students begin their freshman year hoping to accomplish whatever is necessary to secure a spot in a desired professional program while other schools offer direct admission to these programs. For some students, this immediate laser focus is motivating and helpful. For example, a friend's son who started a sports memorabilia business as an entrepreneurial young teen had his heart set on large universities with top business schools, and was admitted to several. I'm fairly certain that in his case, he'll become successful in business while being well-rounded from having attended such a vibrant public Ivy.

However, many students who think they know what they want to major in wind up with a certain tunnel vision that doesn't always serve them well in college and beyond. In their race to get their credentials to secure a job, they hurriedly and robotically move through the college experience, checking things off the list to obtain that prized piece of paper with no real attention paid to anything else about what college can be and what it can offer. These students are typically not the most successful students nor are they the most multidimensional people as they're busy overloading their schedules just to get done, getting overwhelmed, and then not having much else to show for themselves to savor and to share beyond their relentless to-do lists.

There are benefits to being undecided and undeclared. One is that some subjects are better grasped in college. That's because they're often not taught at many high schools and require a level of emotional maturity and complex, nuanced, critical thinking skills that make this coursework more fulfilling to pursue in college. This is abundantly true in disciplines like sociology and anthropology and tends to be the case with many other liberal arts majors.

Students benefit from pursuing the liberal arts as undergraduates and then pursuing a professional degree later. For example, a student might consider a major in economics, psychology, or communications and then go on for an MBA degree. In fact, with the over-abundance of undergraduate business majors across campuses, this alternate path can be desirable to employers who want an effective communicator skilled in relationship building who goes on to sharpen their business acumen in an even stronger and more reputable MBA program. Students who want to pursue law school, public policy, public administration, and nonprofit management do well with majors and minors that help to cultivate strong writing like English, history, sociology, political science, communications, and Spanish.

Instead of calling it an undecided major which sounds wishy-washy and noncommittal, it might be better referred to as "still curious" or "under construction."

CHAPTER 7

MAJOR AND MINOR DECISIONS

Lesson 29: Things to Consider When Choosing a Major

There's much to consider when choosing a major, and the point of going to college is to uncover the patterns of one's interests and passions. Some students enter with a strong sense of what they want to major in and do after college. Other students come in without a clue about either. It might be easy to assume that the students who seem to know what they want to pursue are at a significant advantage and better positioned to hit the ground running. But in all my years of working with young people, that doesn't seem to bear out in reality.

The problem with students who come thinking they know exactly what they want to do is that they sometimes take courses that reflect a narrow plan of study. For example, students who are eighteen years old, wanting to major in nursing, hospitality, or finance may realize in the middle to end of their degree programs or soon after that they're disillusioned with those fields and industries and wish they'd done something else. Therefore, the fixation on profession or vocation can constrain rather than enable as your interests and priorities might totally change by the time you graduate, not to mention how much industries themselves are constantly evolving and especially with the advent of AI. You don't want to miss out on the humanity of college and how that can further develop your sense of self. A job isn't who you are; jobs can and do change. And college teaches you to adapt.

A liberal arts degree can be particularly useful because it positions someone to think broadly and deeply for a variety of careers. There are students like my niece, Sara, who've known since they were four years old what they wanted to do. She has always wanted to be a veterinarian. I have no doubt she will be. As a junior at Washington State University, it makes sense for her to major in animal science. She's someone who can ignore my advice on this. But nine out of ten students won't be like that. In a world where people change careers many times, it makes sense to think expansively about a plan of study. In that spirit, consider these questions:

- What major feels like a natural and passionate extension of who I am and want to be?
- What major can I count on to serve me well in the present moment for the courses I most want to take?
- What major will serve me best long into the future, allowing me to grow and continually evolve into the best version of myself for the rest of my life?

Lesson 30: It's Okay to Change Your Major

College provides opportunities to reflect, reassess, reconsider, and reimagine. Not only does the experience of college serve to open your mind and to take you to unknown places in uncharted territory within yourself and in your world, it gives you an opportunity to change your mind. This might be through classes that encourage you to think in an entirely new way, to rethink what you were taught at home, and to reassess everything. It can be an opportunity to change where you thought you were headed. When I went to college, I was pretty sure I wanted to get into hotel and restaurant management. I thought I wanted this because I had a deep appreciation for travel and culture, and spent years working in hotels. But at the time I wasn't aware enough of what sorts of classes I would need for that major, and when it became clear to me that those classes weren't ones I found compelling, I had to stop and reflect on what it was I most wanted to do and what most moved me. Sometimes this is a real reckoning. It's a moment of truth, especially if you've not only told yourself what you want to do, but perhaps made it clear to family and friends around you and then have to go back and help other people understand why you needed to change your mind. Sometimes the fear of judgment can make that an agonizing experience. In the end though, college should be an opportunity to feel more liberated than constrained and to take the time to truly pause and reflect on what it is that you find most meaningful.

Some parents get overly invested in the process of their child choosing a major. I've worked with students whose parents have little regard for, or understanding of, certain fields of study and threaten to stop speaking with them or paying for school. But that sort of pressure is incredibly imposing at a time when students benefit most from spreading their wings. Students and parents fare better when there's an understanding of the need for reinvention. Your parents might be under the impression that you like or don't like certain things or want to pursue a certain career. Sometimes this is because they've seen you in action doing certain things and can't imagine you doing anything else or because of certain interests and activities you were involved in as children. Perhaps your parents want you to follow in their footsteps with a similar career trajectory or to take over a family business. Or it might be that your parents are adamant that you select something entirely different and don't want you to fall into the same trap that they fell into in their own career. The thing is students need to figure this out on their own. Do your best to help your parents understand that making demands and threats only makes everything worse and jeopardizes your relationship.

A few years ago, I had a student, Bailey, who came to the university to study nursing. Her parents were incredibly jazzed up about this, and to her it seemed like the logical next step because that's what had always been assumed. Introductory Sociology is a course that pre-nursing students need to fulfill as part of their requirement and Bailey got entirely immersed in it, so much so that she realized how little nursing was sustaining her interest. She was admitted into the nursing program, but soon was miserable, having an identity crisis of sorts, realizing this wasn't what she wanted after all, and felt desperately lost. She regretted how hyper-focused she was forced to be with a rigid curriculum and wished for greater flexibility and creativity. What compounded the distress was dealing with her father who threatened to disown her if she left the nursing program, and her mother colluded with him. Bailey was dependent on them for her car and health insurance and felt trapped. I kept thinking to myself, well, if they want nursing so badly, maybe they should return to school and major in it themselves but why project their dreams onto her? She took more sociology classes and got more swept away in it. Initially, she wasn't forthcoming with her parents because of all the judgment and threats. Eventually, she wound up telling them she dropped out of the nursing program. I'll never forget when Bailey came to tell me; she looked visibly relieved, as though the heaviest weight was lifted off of her, and she could finally actualize her own dreams.

I've worked with students over the years who've changed their major multiple times, as well as changed it and then gone back to the original decision. Similarly, I've had students who have transferred out of the college and some have even transferred back. There's something worthwhile to be learned in these stories, and that is you'll benefit from discovering that most decisions you make can be revisited and reworked, and that few things need to be permanently set in stone, especially in regards to school, work, or relationships that aren't serving you well. Students who courageously make these sorts of changes show an adventurous ability to take risks and try again which are worthwhile qualities to have. The problem is when this causes delays that increase financial distress or put students into debt. But when it's done with minimal disruption, it can be part of the process of learning and growing.

Lesson 31: Are Double Majors and Minors Necessary?

I'm often asked both about double majors and minors. The reality is that neither are necessary. That said, it can be helpful to have a double major and/or to have a minor. But few people will care or ask one day if you earned a double major or minor. In speaking with a brilliant friend recently, she had actually forgotten that years ago she had double majored. We're in a current moment of thinking more, more, more must equal better, better, better. If a double major or minor doesn't significantly extend time in school, then it can make sense. The trouble that students get into is when it extends the time to graduation and/or deepens their debt. Sadly, these are the same reasons why many schools push for students to do these.

Students do well by combining seemingly disparate fields of study in ways that creatively synthesize their interests and talents and highlight their multidimensionality. For example, research shows that a great many physicians, especially surgeons, play musical instruments. It's reasonable to imagine a student who is undecided pursuing a double major in biology and music and later going on to medical school. Furthermore, minoring in a language can put a student at a fantastic advantage in terms of gaining cultural capital and future employment.

When asked if a minor is worth it, I usually explain to students that if they find themselves repeatedly choosing classes in the same discipline, and creating a cluster of courses that they've enjoyed and succeeded in, it's a natural thing to do. In fact, that's what I did with earning a certificate in gender studies when I was in college. It happened organically; I didn't set out to do it, but I was already accumulating classes in that area. Some students benefit by choosing a major that feels dreamy and intriguing to them, while choosing another major or minor that feels more practical and applied. Or vice versa, students might choose a practical, vocationally driven major and augment it with one that might feel more ethereal.

Overall, a minor or a double major can serve the following functions:

1. An added bonus

2. A good contrast from the other major field of study

3. A meaningful augmentation to the other major field of study

CHAPTER 8

CULTIVATING THE MINDSET FOR ACADEMIC SUCCESS

Lesson 32: Learn the Secrets of Highly Successful, Happy, and Well-Adjusted Students

There are observable patterns in the attitudes and behaviors of the most successful, happy, and well-adjusted students and ways that you, too, can learn from them. Successful students are multidimensional, possessing an interest in the intellectual enterprise of college and attuned to socio-emotional issues in ways that demonstrate emotional intelligence. I've found that students like this are interesting people whom I and others want to get to know. Some of my former students who were the most thrilling to teach and get to know as people didn't necessarily earn the highest grades, but the way they inhabited their lives and still do has a richness and aliveness that served them well in college and beyond.

Over the past six years or so, I've noticed a shift in students, and in talking with many colleagues across the country, they've confirmed observing something similar. I've found myself admitting in almost hushed tones to faculty friends and former students who are now friends that many students seem increasingly one-dimensional. I know, it sounds terrible and mean of me to say. I'm not blaming students for this. Recently, a colleague remarked to me, "The students are like zombies." The sociologist in me senses that something much bigger is going on. No one is born to be this way, and no one needs to remain so. Life isn't meant to be lived so narrowly and flatly. I see how larger social forces are at work here.

Sociologist George Ritzer coined the term the McDonaldization of society to describe how qualities of the fast food industry like efficiency, predictability, control, calculability, and standardization have come to dominate more and more aspects of our lives, even in intimate and personal arenas of life where we might least expect or desire it such as the wedding industry or childbirth practices in the United States. McDonaldization flattens our lives and risks rendering them more boring. The boredom we feel in our daily rounds can translate to our personalities seeming more boring as well. It's as though the bureaucratic practices that go hand in hand with McDonaldization contribute to more bureaucratic and boring personalities.

This flattening of society has infiltrated the academy in insidious ways. A variety of things have conspired to produce some of the boring, zombie-like qualities of which I'm speaking, and these include but aren't limited to: the seduction of technology and the pressures to conform both in physical appearance and in thinking; the pandemic squashing possibilities; parents caving to the demands of their kids and doing things for them; holing up alone in one's room with a phone or video games; being disconnected from the natural world and all that the wilderness offers; not reading for pleasure; not being connected to the cultural arts, etc.

The good news is that the qualities that make for successful students are ones that resist the flattening. Those of us who crave more organic, authentic, spontaneous, passionate, vibrant, and creative experiences in our daily live have to go to greater lengths to cultivate these. The most successful students either intuitively know how to do this or they seek out peer mentors and other adult mentors to help them achieve this. When students share with me careers that interest them, I often put them in touch with people I know. Students are surprised by how extensively I'm willing to share my contacts and many have seized the opportunities presented. What's proven baffling and disappointing is when I learn that a student didn't follow up, and that typically seems due to a fear of initiating that first move. Often though, people in the field are welcoming and well-situated to make solid recommendations and it behooves students to follow up.

Qualities and behaviors of successful students:

- Curious
- Possesses the desire to grasp ideas over and above just knowing their grades
- Self-aware and aware of others
- Self-motivated
- Interested in constructive feedback and improvement
- Possesses an understanding that the world is much larger than themselves
- Shows comfort in solitude without it turning to loneliness
- Seeks help before things spin into a much larger and unwieldy problem; this is true for class performance and emotional and social issues
- Possesses the courage to try, regardless of the outcome
- Tries to find answers on their own first
- Has other passions, causes, and things they care about
- Willing to accept responsibility

- Expresses gratitude
- Strives to become a more effective communicator, both orally and in written communication including formal papers, informal writing assignments, emails, video calls, phone calls, and class presentations
- Has excellent follow-through; doing what one says they will do and communicating if and when things change, especially when others depend on them
- Able to talk with others face-to-face and over the telephone
- Reads, not just for classes but to grow as a human being
- Coachable and mentorable, actively seeking out people to be mentors for them
- Experience seeker who takes advantage of pursuing internships, invitations to build networks, opportunities to shadow people in an industry, and informational interviewing
- Senses that learning is, and will continue to be, a lifelong process

Lesson 33: The Struggle Is Real and Necessary, and Nothing Needs to Be as Perfect as You Imagine

Over the years, struggle has become a new buzzword. What seemed to capture something about arduous work in a most authentic way has now come to be about anything, even something requiring a modicum of time and effort. Coupled with this is the overuse of the word confused. On emails and in person, students reach out to faculty like me reporting that they're struggling because they're so confused. But when I ask questions and dig deeper into the source of the struggle and confusion so as to best help and support them, a pattern has emerged in recent years. What I am seeing is that students are declaring a struggle and confusion before even giving something a try. For example, students will tell me they're confused by the reading or by the instructions for an assignment and after a few questions and some chatting, I come to find out they in fact never read what was asked of them. It's almost like pre-struggling with something or being pre-confused, right? I can relate.

During the pandemic lockdown, I, like others, indulged in some things for my house since I was spending an awful lot of time there. As someone who routinely spent hours working at Starbucks, I wanted Americanos and lattes at my fingertips at home so I purchased my first ever espresso machine. It arrived one day when I was out for a walk, and my husband unpacked it and started putting it all together. When I returned home to this scene, I was so excited for us to make drinks but had zero desire to learn how to use it. Suddenly, it looked too hard and too irritating to deal with and I wondered if it was even worth it or if we should return it. Mike laughed and rightly jabbed back at me, "There's a syllabus that came with it. You should read it." Okay, very funny, now the joke was on me! He knows I find instruction manuals for any technology like that to be aggravating to read and so I overly rely on him for translating only the most essential information. But he was right, this was a fun gift to myself that I owed it to myself to learn how to use well and enjoy rather than getting in my own way. I regard it as one of the best investments I've ever made, and I save a lot of money on coffee!

Lots of things account for the impatience around quickly understanding and mastering something. We live in a push-button, microwave culture craving instantaneous and satisfying results, and we live in a time-distorted culture as a result of that, constantly feeling sped up yet yearning to slow down.

The thing about college is you're supposed to struggle. It is okay. Just like how I talked with you about how college is not supposed to be smooth sailing, it's not supposed to be easy. Struggle and confusion are—and should be—part of the process. When we normalize that rather than normalize instant clarity and perfection, we'll do everyone a service. Here, I'm referring to struggle and confusion borne of hard work at a developmentally challenging time between childhood and adulthood.

A mother on a college parent Facebook page claimed that she was confused because the college stopped using a grade of A+ and she wanted that as a possibility for her high-achieving child and was concerned she'd be less competitive than her peers for jobs and internships. The mother seemed to be creating a struggle where none needs to be. I'll bet that no employer has ever asked at an interview why someone earned only As and not A+'s. In fact, most won't ask your grades. They'll want to know you'll shake their hand, look them in the eye, hold a conversation without a struggle, take initiative, show good follow-through, collaborate well, and be a delight to mentor. Being coachable involves not claiming constant struggle and confusion and instead asking good questions, making connections, and accepting feedback to improve.

Lesson 34: Learn to Pivot and Let Go

Dream, plan, and remember that the impermanence of life's circumstances means anything can happen, and you can *still* realize your dreams. For example, I had always wanted to write a book and I was so excited when my first book came out on February 14, 2020. I had an extensive national book tour planned which of course got stunningly abbreviated in mid-March due to the pandemic. I was disappointed and frustrated for a few weeks and tried to let myself grieve, and then I tried to seize and create any opportunities I could over Zoom. I had to work with what I had. It wasn't at all what I expected or dreamed of. But I had to tell myself I could either keep being sad and angry about it or surrender to what was happening in a global moment so much larger than my own little world. I had to make beauty out of chaos. I had to find light that would vanquish the darkness. Or as my mother would sing to me when I was a little girl and stumbled and fell, "You've got to pick yourself up and start all over again." As long as we're human, we'll always stumble and fall. It's up to us to pick ourselves up and start over, again and again.

When we get overly attached to something, anything—a plan, an object, a way of being in the world, a person, a goal, or an idea, we tend to cling. Our grip tightens. We're likely to feel constrained and pressured and with fewer options because the over-attachment creates myopic vision. As a result, we wind up getting in our own way.

On the other hand, when we loosen our hold on something or someone, we create breathing room and spaciousness, both of which are necessary and helpful for creating flow and growth in all aspects of our lives. When we begin to let go, we see what else is possible. Suddenly more options and ideas seem available to us which in turn builds our confidence for whatever next thing we're trying and hoping to do.

CHAPTER 9

PREPARING FOR ACADEMIC SUCCESS

Lesson 35: Always Consult the Academic Calendar

Plan ahead, and plan appropriately. Before you make plans, review the academic calendar that is posted on every institution's website. I've had students email to tell me they missed an exam so they could have a long weekend with a boyfriend or that their parents booked a big trip and they'll be missing a week of a three-week summer class to travel to the Bahamas. Faculty understand that you have lives and plans outside of class—we do too—but scheduling these sorts of things with no regard for the academic calendar in tandem with what's on the syllabi for your classes is not a good idea. By all means, if you must go away, be sure to take your laptop and necessary books with you so you can work remotely and not fall behind.

Most institutions post the current calendar as well as calendars for the next few years so you and your family can plan accordingly. You'll find out when semesters (or quarters) begin and end, when breaks are, when certain holidays are honored, when final exams will take place, the deadlines for dropping and adding courses, and dates for commencement. It's worth paying attention to the fact that some universities change days around, and that is typically noted on the calendar. This is so that the same class days aren't repeatedly impacted by cancelations.

Lesson 36: Read the F*cking Syllabus!

Quite literally, most everything you need to know to succeed in a course is indeed on the syllabus. At one point, I wanted to title this book "Read the F*cking Syllabus and Other Advice for College Success" because it is *that* important!

Sure, some syllabi aren't written in a friendly way and sound overly punitive, warning students of all the ways they can lose points in a course. I see the syllabus as a letter to students conveying my intentions and hope. Much to my delight, a student referred to mine as a "course welcoming document." She was onto something. Indeed, the syllabus is an invitation to a new way of thinking, and it can be your friend.

Several years ago, a post circulated on social media about a professor who had stashed fifty dollars in a locker, and in his syllabus, had provided the locker combination; at the end of the semester, he returned to the locker expecting to find it empty of the money yet the bill was exactly where he left it. Most of us bemoan that students don't appear to read our syllabi despite our best efforts. At the beginning of every semester, I explain that the syllabus is like a GPS for success and that students who read it thoroughly do much better.

I adapted that professor's idea. Rather than offer money, I inserted a line in my syllabus indicating that if students emailed me in the first few days of the semester with a response to a question I provided, I would give extra credit points toward their first assignment. Out of seventy students enrolled in the course in which I offered this incentive, do you want to guess how many did this? Four. But many more than four students emailed me at the end of the semester begging for extra credit opportunities. They weren't even aware it had already been offered.

Some students think I'm snarky for insisting they refer back to the syllabus. But it's not even all about the syllabus. What I'm trying to do is cultivate the conditions possible for students to trust that, often, they can find the answers on their own. On a thank-you email after the semester ended, a student wrote to me, "I remember the second day I asked you a question, and you just took a big sip of coffee and then turned your mug around that said, 'It's in the syllabus.' But when I needed help or had big life questions, you were always open to hear every student out. That's what mattered. And from now on, I'll always be more careful reading the syllabus."

As soon as you see the syllabi for your courses, go ahead and note all due dates, exam dates, holidays, classes that might be canceled in advance, special evening events that might be expected of you, etc. It's not up to the professors to remind you, and many won't. By logging due dates into your calendars, including stages of project management, you can get your work done at a good pace.

Lesson 37: Read and Be Prepared for Class

Ben, a recent graduate of the University of Redlands told me, "The majority of students I know, in some classes, don't complete a single reading (start to finish) throughout the semester. From what I've seen, well over 50 percent of assigned readings never even get opened! It's okay to miss one occasionally, but to fail to even crack open the book—classes are designed to reward those who actually read and provide evidence from the text."

Ben is right. Reading is a big part of college, and like writing, it's an important life skill. And he's correct that students who show mastery of the reading and connections to the ideas and concepts in it generally do much better. It's pretty easy to tell, both in class and on papers, who has done the reading and who is faking it.

Buy the books that are required for the course and consider purchasing any supplemental, recommended texts if you can afford them. Be sure to pay attention to the edition of the book you're assigned so that what you purchase matches the one your professor is using. And don't wait until the last minute to order books. Claiming "Amazon delays" is never a good excuse.

Lesson 38: Read for Pleasure

To succeed in school, it's important to read what's assigned. It's also important to read for pleasure. Why? Because it makes you more interesting. People who read have a greater sense of fluency of ideas and perspectives that they can bring to bear on conversations and they possess stronger vocabularies. All of this gives people an edge both socially and professionally. Referencing something you read and learned that resonates with you or naturally relates to a conversation at a job interview, for example, helps position you as someone with insight and depth.

The other thing to remember is that the habit of reading often translates to greater agility with writing. This is because you have more exposure to a variety of ways that ideas are expressed, and you're able to gather more information to craft what you want to say.

College is a great time to discover what exactly it is you like to read. This is especially true if you're coming to college with little interest in reading. The lack of interest is often due to not having much say in what you got to read in high school. So, now's the time to think about what you gravitate to most. What do you find most moving and compelling? Maybe it's fiction, nonfiction, creative nonfiction, or poetry. Whatever it is, reading is like a passport for the experience of world traveling which is a gift you can give yourself.

If your parents read to you when you were a child, they may have shown you the value and joy of reading. I've started directly asking my students if a parent or guardian read to or with them and what their favorite book was as a child and what their favorite is now. What's most sad is when students aren't able to name a single book and instead tell me they "never read," "never had a parent read to me," "hate reading" or "never finished a book." But even if the value of reading was not instilled in you growing up, it's not too late to develop a habit of reading for pleasure. Find something that potentially interests you, put your phone away where it's not even visible, grab a fun drink or snack, and curl up in a cozy space and read. Try just fifteen minutes at first. If you like it, keep going. If you find yourself restless or sleepy, try to push through a bit longer and if that doesn't work then go do something else and make a commitment to yourself to return to this the next day. Typically, those in the regular practice of reading and enjoying it generally find it easier to be alone and enjoy solitude.

Lesson 39: Discernment Is a Crucial Quality to Develop

Students with a greater capacity for discernment are able to think more critically and creatively, think things through to their logical conclusions, consider unintended consequences, make healthier and more constructive decisions, and know what to let go of and how to resist catastrophizing.

One primary way students reveal they lack the ability to discern well is in how they come to talk about the main ideas of a reading assignment. I find myself telling students to think about the three main ideas of their reading as a way to prepare for writing a paper or taking a test. When asked to state those main ideas and discuss them in class, too many students are at a loss and, instead, bring up things that hardly qualify for even the minor points an author is making.

It's clear to me that this correlates with an overall lack of reading in the first place. We have to read more to read better, to think better, and to write better. Too many students shamelessly state they don't read and haven't finished a book in years or a lifetime.

I get it; I didn't like reading as a junior high and high school student because I wasn't assigned reading that held my interest. But when I got to college and was assigned reading in my major that finally spoke to me, in a genre to which I gravitated most (nonfiction), I was off, and my imagination soared. This is why I tell students that it helps to find something, anything, that they enjoy reading and by doing so, other aspects of their lives will be enriched.

I'm sympathetic to a generation coming of age with oversaturation of information. I didn't grow up this way and still feel inundated by the overwhelming amount of content, not just in terms of reading but also in terms of podcasts to listen to, series to binge, and movies to watch. It's a lot coming at us. It means discerning the good stuff from the junk. This is important in terms of how we spend our days, which is to say, our lives. And it means discerning accurate information from misinformation. This is crucial for a responsible, ethical, and learned society.

Liberal arts disciplines offer ample opportunities for students to see how most things in life aren't black and white and how ambiguity is a powerful space from which to think, learn, and make decisions. When I teach, I ask my students to formulate questions about the materials as a way to see what they're discerning. If people can ask insightful and thoughtful questions, they usually show a better grasp of class concepts.

Adding to the challenges and complexity of strengthening one's ability to discern is the advent of AI and students who rely on it. Without previously achieving strong skills in reading, writing, clear thinking, and asking good questions, the use of AI is shockingly bad. Using it well demands discernment.

Knowing how to be more discerning isn't just reserved for academic and professional life; it's also essential for our personal lives. It helps us distinguish between what's important and what's urgent. It helps us think about how we choose to spend our time and with whom.

In order to have meaningful intimate relationships and friendships, we have to be able to discern what constitutes healthy, happy, loving, and respectful ones from those that aren't. In talking with students about intimacy and violence, it is abundantly clear how this is anything but obvious. For example, young women are likely to mistake someone's jealous behaviors for interest in them rather than as the possessiveness it actually is. Those errors in discernment can set in motion patterns of vulnerability in controlling relationships.

CHAPTER 10

HOW TO SHINE IN CLASS

Lesson 40: Get Your Ass to Class!

As my friend, Marian, tells her son, "Get your ass to class." She's right. And anyway, so much of life is about showing up. It should go without saying that good attendance and class participation are key elements to your success in college courses. Being present means more than simply occupying a seat in the room regardless of if that classroom is face-to-face or online; it means that you become active agents in your own learning and that you engage in the group dynamics of the classroom in order to build a learning community. Each person is a valuable member of the group process, and in this way, class discussions will be most vital and meaningful when everyone is there.

Being actively engaged in a course doesn't mean talking the entire time or attempting to dominate class discussion. Sometimes, in fact, I have seen relatively quiet students make only a few comments in each class meeting or in a given week, but if these are made selectively, they can be just as thoughtful and significant as comments from someone who speaks often in class. And remember that instructors don't call on students to be mean but because they want to increase the diversity of perspectives in class discussion.

Class time is more engaging and thought-provoking when people have thought in advance about questions, reactions, and ideas about the material. Developing thoughtful questions is a crucial part of writing well and thinking clearly.

Just because attendance is likely not mandatory for your classes doesn't mean you shouldn't show up. When teaching my introductory course face-to-face on Mondays, Wednesdays, and Fridays with mainly first-year students, I've seen a marked drop in attendance on Fridays. It has made me more likely to assign in-class writings that cannot be made up, to present important concepts and terms, etc. On the face of it, it sounds mean. But if you sign up for a class that meets three days a week, Friday doesn't become optional. Even when Thirsty Thursdays precede it!

Understandably, there may be times when you need to miss class for good reason such as illness or an important family obligation. When that happens, be sure to ask multiple classmates their perceptions of what they learned that day and ask to see their notes. Getting the perspective of more than one person is most useful. You can offer to reciprocate the favor if and when they're absent, and it might lead to becoming study buddies which is always helpful. Whatever you do, please don't ask your professors if you missed anything. Of course, you did. Don't you hope you did? I hope so for you! It means that time is precious and well-used. And if your professors are like I am, they might send you this fabulous poem by Tom Wayman titled, "Did I Miss Anything?"

Nothing. When we realized you weren't here we sat with our hands
folded on our desks in silence, for the full two hours

Everything. I gave an exam worth 40 percent of the grade for this
term and assigned some reading due today on which I'm about to
hand out a quiz worth 50 percent

Nothing. None of the content of this course has value or meaning

Take as many days off as you like: any activities we undertake as a class I assure you will not matter either to you or me and are without purpose

Everything. A few minutes after we began last time a shaft of light suddenly descended and an angel or other heavenly being appeared and revealed to us what each woman or man must do to attain divine wisdom in this life and the hereafter. This is the last time the class will meet before we disperse to bring the good news to all people on earth.

Nothing. When you are not present how could something significant occur?

Everything. Contained in this classroom is a microcosm of human experience assembled for you to query and examine and ponder.

This is not the only place such an opportunity has been gathered but it was one place

And you weren't here.

Lesson 41: Be a Good Classroom Citizen

"Know that learning is not something professors provide. Learning is what we do together, what happens between us. We—you, me, and others in class—construct our learning together. My job is to skillfully facilitate your learning and your job is to own it...to make it your own."

—Jayne L. Violette, Professor of Communication Studies at the University of South Carolina Beaufort

Being a good classroom citizen is a little like being a good passenger and seat mate on an airplane. Here are some tips to remember:

- Come to class on time. If for some reason you expect to be late on occasion, consult with your professor as to their policy and if it's okay to show up a little late.
- Come prepared having done the required reading so you're able to engage in discussion and group work that is assigned during class time. Being prepared creates the possibility of deeper conversations and more intriguing classes that in turn help connect the dots and make the entire course come together more logically.
- Bring your own school supplies. Assume that your professors aren't carrying around extra writing utensils, paper, or a stapler just for you.
- If your professor permits food in class, don't be the person who brings something to eat with a pungent odor or intense crunch that will bother others.
- Save internet shopping and watching games for when class is over; it's distracting to people around and behind you and a waste of your own education.
- Don't be the person who's constantly coming and going during class. Yes, of course, it's reasonable to occasionally need to leave class to use the restroom, and I cannot fathom professors who try to police this as some do, but try to do it in as limited a way as possible.
- Silence your phone, and stash it in your bag during class. It's never good to be the person whose phone starts ringing in class, especially if your professor has asked that all cell phones be put away. Your neighbors don't want to be the ones mistakenly glared at because of you. Of course, if you're anticipating a call related to someone you love who's in surgery, for example, your professor is likely to be compassionate and grateful if you

notify them in advance about the possibility you might need to leave the room.

- Determine what's best to bring up in class and what should be dealt with privately. For example, when a professor starts class by asking if you have any questions, check yourself first. Are the questions that you need to ask ones that apply more broadly to others and from which others will likely benefit, or are they related specifically to your own individual circumstances? Remember again, college is about community. For questions that are for your own benefit, make an appointment to discuss things privately.

- Avoid having side conversations during lectures and class discussions. It's distracting and disruptive to everyone involved, including you.

- Observe yourself and your interactional patterns and consider how talkative or quiet you are, and borrow a bit from the opposite way of being. If you consider yourself talkative, think about what helps you to listen with more presence and/or share the forum with others. And if you tend to be quiet, think about what helps you open up. Being actively engaged in a course doesn't mean talking the entire time or attempting to monopolize class discussion. Contributing in a thoughtful and balanced way is key.

- You may enroll in classes that demand a great deal of emotional intelligence and social grace. This is particularly true with some of the classes I teach related to the body, violence, race, etc. For matters that are deeply personal, it's best to recognize the limitations of the classroom and/or online discussion boards for what they are. If you wish to disclose something personal, think about how you're sharing this information since the classroom cannot be a place for therapy; however, the learning process can be, and often is, therapeutic. If you find that fellow classmates disclose information that you understand to be personal, do everything possible to recognize the challenges that people face in sharing difficult information.

- Try to listen and pay attention closely with a sense of presence, and respect issues of confidentiality and privacy—meaning that it's okay to discuss the themes, process, and content of what emerges in a class but that it's not okay to reveal other people's identity in relation to what is being discussed. It's useful to be able to sit with some of the discomfort and silences that occur when navigating the natural turbulence of discussing central social issues of our time.

- Wait until class has ended to pack up to leave. Otherwise, you risk being the person who creates a domino effect where other students follow suit and the room gets noisy at exactly the same moment the professor is speaking about material that will appear on the test.

Lesson 42: Take Note of This

It takes practice to learn how to take good notes. This is because notetaking is about capturing and discerning what is memorable in a lecture, class discussion, or text. I can remember how in high school and early college whatever I was reading turned neon—yellow, hot pink, and orange—because I was overusing my hi-liter pens and not knowing what to mark up. Come exam time, this wasn't a useful strategy because I had lost sight of the forest from the trees and had to go over it all again. Then, I began the habit of taking a ballpoint pen and underlining on top of only the most crucial highlighted material while making notes in the margins, often using one word to summarize the section or writing "key point" so I would be sure to zero in on it later. Little by little over the years, I developed new systems that worked for me that I still rely on to this day. It's a process and a practice, and it's totally worth it.

Ideas about notetaking have taken on an interesting evolution in college over the past few decades. When I was in college in the late 80s and early 90s, it was understood and expected that students would take notes during class lectures, discussions, videos, guest speakers, and when reading. For the bulk of my career teaching college students, these same expectations held. In the past ten years, there has been a notable difference in ideas about notetaking, and whose responsibility it is.

Students ask me, "Where are the notes?" or on evaluations they might say, "I wish she gave us notes." The first time I heard that I was confused because I didn't even understand what that meant. How could an instructor provide notes on what a student finds interesting and memorable? While I don't use any PowerPoint in my teaching, of course many of my colleagues do, and even they remark that students ask for notes in addition to a PowerPoint lecture. So interestingly, even with the advent of PowerPoint, which some might think would assist in more structured notetaking, that, too, has rendered too many students helpless for thinking about notetaking. In fact, my own position on it is that notetaking can get strengthened more effectively in the absence of PowerPoint, which is largely why I don't use it. Plus, I've never attended a lecture where I've seen anyone make their point in a powerful way through that methodology. In fact, it's usually uninspiring, and I find my eyes glaze over.

Notetaking extends beyond the classroom and is an important professional life skill. For example, when I go to a doctor's office, I want to know that the practitioner is listening to what I'm sharing, and that they have the ability to summarize it in their own words in my records and in ways that will help treat me best. When I've been on interviews for jobs, I've taken a legal pad on which I've come prepared with questions to ask and notes about the employers' needs and interests. If I'm interviewing with more than one person or group during the day, I'm able to look back on those notes to see what it is I still need to ask or need to elaborate on in terms of how I might be able to contribute to that workplace. In meetings, I take notes on initiatives that are being announced, deadlines of things I need to remember, and aspects of substantive discussion. The point of these examples is to show that the notetaking I might do as a participant in a given situation is different than the notetaking that you or your friend might do. This is because each one of us will remember different things that feel meaningful. We may encounter things we don't need to write down so we can just sit, listen, and pay attention while maybe those are the things someone else needs to write down. Often when I'm meeting students, I ask to see their notebooks so I can get a sense of the types of things they're writing down, how they're deciphering what's important, and how they're organizing their notes. Usually, the students who struggle the most are the ones who either end up showing me a blank notebook or notes with information that is less vital. I offer them an idea for practicing notetaking while doing something they already enjoy like watching a movie or TV series, and to try taking notes on it, capturing details of key scenes and important quotes and then comparing notes with a friend.

While it might be tempting to use recording devices in class, you'll need to be sure to ask for permission from your instructor, and it behooves you to consider what you're asking, especially if the material is highly controversial, emotionally fraught, and invites your peers to be vulnerable with sharing information and experiences that they likely don't want recorded or shared.

I hope the following tips will assist you in a new and fresh way when taking notes on reading. You can adapt these to use during class and after class when reviewing lectures and discussions:

- Why do you think this reading was chosen, and how does it fit into the rest of the course?
- Distill the reading down to three to five central points.

- Copy down three pithy passages from the reading that capture the essence of the piece and that are intriguing and provocative or made you question your own taken-for-granted assumptions.
- What possibilities have opened up for you by reading this? What questions do you have?

Lesson 43: Finding Your Way in a Big Class

Ideas vary as to what constitutes large classes. Some may say it's the 200-person chemistry class or the 400-person nutrition class at a major research university. At a smaller liberal arts college, a thirty-five-person psychology class may seem big whereas at many schools this is just an average size. When a college is filling classes in rooms the size of large movie theaters with amphitheater seating, we can probably all agree these are enormous classes. It's crucial that you find your way in them. If you attend a large university, big classes can serve as a living laboratory for how to devise strategies to gain confidence in public speaking, finding your people, and generally making a big school feel a whole lot smaller.

Some of your professors may do something similar to what I do which is to ask students to fill out a questionnaire on the first day to help reduce anonymity and to get to know students as learners and human beings with their own interests, quirks, hopes, fears, dreams, and passions. On my forms, questions range from their course schedule that semester to if they hold a job outside of school or have caregiving responsibilities for elderly or ill relatives. I ask about their favorite books, music, and movies as well as social problems they're concerned about or that they believe they could be passionate about to participate in activism. I always ask what I can do to be the best teacher for them, their learning style and personality, and if there are things I should be aware of that might make learning about the material more challenging or painful. It's here that I often find out about mental health issues, body image issues, a history of sexual and domestic violence, parents who are divorcing, are addicted, have died or are in prison, stories of extreme poverty, LGBTQ+ identity, etc. Some of the responses break my heart, but they're all informative and have become a springboard from which I can connect with students. So, remember that many of us are indeed interested in you as more than just learners, but also as people worth getting to know; do your best to get to know your professors and let them get to know you. Often, they can share resources and help you get on a path that leads to greater success, wellness, and happiness.

Take the opportunity to think about how you can make yourself stand out in large classes in a positive way. You may be reticent to do this, but trust me, it makes all the difference.

Lesson 44: Academic Freedom Is Essential for Transformative Teaching and Learning

One of the things that distinguishes college from anything else is what's referred to as academic freedom. In fact, it's the bedrock of college. An intellectual atmosphere that promotes as wide an aperture to a free and open exchange of ideas is necessary for life in a civilized democracy.

This means that professors may assign readings or other visual materials that bother you or go against something in your faith or upbringing. For example, my dear friend, Kim, teaches anthropology in which issues of evolution are explored and some students dismiss it outright saying they only believe what they learned in the Bible.

But Kim makes it clear she isn't out to convert anyone; rather, she's explicit that she's providing scientific evidence and research with which students can engage and develop new ways of seeing things. On a related note, I assign a book in my Sociology of the Body class related to father-daughter incest, and a student told me she wouldn't read the book. I figured that perhaps she had endured something similar and I was then of course prepared to give her resources to best support her learning. Instead, she told me that the issue was the writing of the book and some of the language, and she deemed it "immoral." I responded by asking her to rethink immorality for the thing that was immoral was the sexual abuse, not the writing to heal from it. The situations in both Kim's class and mine are good reminders of how crucial it is to be exposed to a wide range of ideas and how college isn't about keeping you comfortable in your preconceived notions. I can say for sure that Kim and I each carefully run classes that are regarded as open, safe, and comfortable yet with content that can push people to the edge of their thinking and feeling.

In a day and age where so much is preceded by trigger warning hashtags, it's good to remember that it's unrealistic to expect that faculty can provide trigger warnings for everything that could possibly warrant it as perception of social phenomena varies greatly. I've never met a professor seeking to do harm to students through chosen materials. It behooves you to remember that context is everything, and that content and materials were likely chosen for legitimate pedagogical reasons. In my own example, I don't teach about domestic and sexual violence to showcase gratuitous violence but rather to help students understand sociological causes and consequences of violence.

Lesson 45: Turn Off Your Damn Phone

The spiritual teacher, Ram Dass, was known for saying, "Be here now." This seemingly simple advice is amazingly challenging in the era we live in, and yet the qualities of presence and mindfulness needed to do this are vital to our performance, our well-being, and any depth we might hope to access and enjoy.

You'll want to get acquainted with your professors' policies on technology. If they don't permit laptops and phones, don't test them. To quote a flight attendant, "Keep your electronic devices turned off and stowed." Resist the temptation to check your phone during class. There's no good reason to have a phone out during class unless it's part of a required class activity. This isn't the time for online shopping and checking sports scores. You have no idea how often I have asked a student why they're texting in class and the response is "Well, my mom wanted to ask me something." To that, I respond, "Tell your mom you're in class!" or "Put her on speaker and we can all say hi." Like I tell my students, if you're smiling down at your crotch when I'm talking about violent crime for example, I'll assume you're playing with yourself. And then I tell them to keep the vibrating devices in their bag. That usually results in laughter—that is, unless they're still too busy texting to know what's going on.

Lesson 46: Turn On Your Damn Laptop—How to Succeed in Online Classes

Over the years, we've witnessed a surge of online and hybrid course offerings and degree programs across colleges and universities. It can take some time to adjust to this way of learning and there are things you can do to improve your experience.

First of all, it's a bad idea to use technology as an excuse. Many of the technological excuses sound like the modern version of "My dog ate my homework." Certainly, there are outages and technical details, but here I'm referring to the various ways that students lie with the assumption that faculty won't know any better. A student tried to tell me near the end of the semester that her online discussion postings had somehow vanished and she claimed that this happened in another class, too. Another student insisted that she'd been locked out of her account the day a paper was due. Numerous students feign "confusion" and "stress," which could possibly be reasonable claims until one learns that they'd never accessed the syllabus or read the assignment to have anything to be confused about. Remember that professors can and will call their colleagues in the IT department to get more information. Years ago, I befriended a lovely man in that office who showed me how we're able to see every single keystroke a student makes in our courses as well as the number of hours, minutes, and seconds they've spent on every item in the course. Yes, there most definitely is a creepy Big Brother quality to all of this and yet dishonesty is not the answer.

Be sure to build in time for technology problems that inevitably arise at the worst possible times.

One thing that people find appealing and that they tend to appreciate about asynchronous online classes is that they can be done at one's own pace. The flip side of this is that asynchronous classes demand good time management and self-motivation. Students have to rely on themselves to make the class a priority. No one is making students report to a designated classroom, and no one is standing in front of them aiming to both educate and entertain. Don't let an online class become "out of sight, out of mind." It's imperative to transfer some of the online information into your own systems, so for example, put all due dates in your calendar as well as dates by which to start projects in order to stay on track. Regularly review the entire syllabus for what's expected of you. Just because you've had the same professor for other online or face-to-face classes, don't assume everything is laid out the same way.

Always remember the importance of online discussion boards if they're part of the course. These are a place for class participation, and the typical expectations are that you create original posts and give peer feedback. What's so great about these is that even quiet students who are hesitant to speak in a face-to-face class have this opportunity to contribute, and as a result, it's your chance to hear from classmates you otherwise might not have. So much of your learning is through peer interaction. If you skip out on these, it's the equivalent of not attending face-to-face classes for days or weeks at a time. If posts are due by 11:59 p.m., for example, it's best to not race onto the learning management system to try to write something up at 11:57 p.m. Would you rush into an eleven a.m. class at 11:47 a.m. that is scheduled to end at noon, blurt something out, and dash out the door? Hopefully not. Your learning and performance are enriched by the sort of citizen you are in this learning community. Students tend to do better on papers and exams who are steady participants in discussions, and that's true regardless of class modality.

If you're taking synchronous classes and you're not required to have your camera on, try having it on. You'll likely find it changes the way you show up to the whole experience and how the experience reflects back to you in a more meaningful way. When students admit that in synchronous classes, they log on and then go nap, take a shower, or leave for a run, these choices probably won't support success.

Remember that it's people who make up online classes. This sounds like a given but it isn't. Before online classes became popular at my school, I had a student from an in-person class ask seriously if her online class was taught by a robot, Sadly, because of the nature of so much of social media culture and its accompanying alienation, objectification, and hostility, some students project some of that onto faculty and peers, forgetting these are human beings worthy of respect.

It's vital to pay attention to the way you talk about online classes. For example, try to rethink this dominant and counterproductive narrative: "I'm taking online classes and it's like I'm teaching myself." There exists the assumption and mythology that when students are taking online classes, they're just teaching themselves. Actually, professors are still facilitating learning. They cull and curate materials for class, dream up discussion prompts and activities, post original video lectures they deliver or the written equivalent of these, create assignments, grade them, post articles and book chapters, find powerful visual material to share, meet with students, etc. The assumption that the student is doing everything and the professor is doing nothing is faulty as it devalues and insults educators and is rooted in the notion that students can simply show up however they want for a class and professors should accept that as enough. Education is supposed to be about becoming active learners, getting students to think for themselves, and to be creative and resourceful. If the online format, or any format for that matter, demands more of students than they might be used to, it's a great thing.

When you take online classes, you have to be even more intentional about building non-screen time into your day to get outside, exercise, read, or daydream. None of us can stay sane and happy if we're exclusively tethered to screens. If you find yourself taking online classes, you'll benefit from some extra technology detox from time to time.

If a class is offered in multiple modalities, be realistic in deciding which one suits your preferences and needs. Some students have grown to love online courses, learn a lot, and feel successful in them while other students don't care for them, know they struggle, and flounder. For example, if you fall in the latter group but the in-person section is offered at a time you don't like such as nine a.m. or six p.m., that still might be the better alternative to online. Furthermore, students sometimes make the mistake of thinking an online class will be much easier when that's certainly not the case.

Lesson 47: How to Succeed in College with a Disability

So many things can present potential challenges to a student's ability to thrive in school, and certainly one is disability. When we talk about this, we're referring to a range of physical, intellectual, cognitive, developmental, and emotional disabilities.

Quite frankly, most faculty, while experts in their subject matter, don't have prior training or certification in special education. That said, we work with many students who present with a range of issues. When encountering students with disabilities, most of us are concerned with making sure these students, and everyone for that matter, have the tools to be successful in our classrooms. Most of us want to follow the law, ensuring that our classrooms are as barrier-free as possible. Generally speaking, the things that make education more doable for students with disabilities make education a more positive, equitable, and ethical experience for everyone anyway.

Consider what is meant by "reasonable accommodations" and how that relates to your own strengths and limitations. Years ago, I was a visiting professor at a selective liberal arts college in Connecticut, and I remember striking up a great rapport with a woman who served as the director of the Office for Students with Disabilities at that time. I had contacted her because I had a student who was doing poorly, and I wanted to be sure I was doing everything right by the student and in compliance with the law. I'll never forget what she said to me: "Students registered with this office still have the opportunity to fail." And then she described to me a situation she had dealt with in which a student who suffered from extreme agoraphobia signed up for an elective art class that had required field trips to museums and other crowded places. Of course, it would be amazing if an experience like that could help a student overcome such debilitating fears, but my colleague explained to me that at a certain point, she and the professor had to explain to the student that perhaps this class choice was neither realistic nor practical. This is because there would have been no reasonable accommodation that could be used in place of the field trips and the written reflections about them. The point is that these offices can work hard to set up students for success, and most faculty will do whatever is possible to make it a successful experience, but students must think about what they're expecting of themselves and others.

If you're a student with a disability here are some things to consider to have the best chance at success:

- Be sure to have all of the necessary documentation from your physician when you go to meet with someone in the Office for Students with Disabilities.
- Within the first week of class, make an appointment to let your professors know your situation. This is best done by bringing the letter of accommodations to your meetings and then talking it through with your professors as to what each of you can expect.

- Don't just toss a letter at a professor on your way in or out of a classroom; it's disrespectful and it misses the point of good communication that is necessary in these situations.
- Be sure to carefully review the syllabus as to what is expected. Sometimes, students approach me about accommodations for which they wouldn't be needed for that particular class; for example, I have seen letters that indicate the need for priority registration, special calculators, and a particular testing environment but when a student gives that to me for an upper level sociology course in which there are no tests and no mathematical equations, it appears that they haven't thought through their needs with each class.

While some students present with disabilities that are permanent or with illnesses that are chronic, there are students who find themselves temporarily disabled, for example due to a broken arm or leg, or acutely ill for a long stretch of time, or in the throes of undergoing extensive medical testing to determine a diagnosis. The Office for Students with Disabilities on your campus is the best resource if you find yourself in these situations as they can support you in making transportation arrangements, securing a notetaker, communicating with faculty, etc. Because of the high number of students with co-occurring diagnoses such as ADHD and bipolar disorder, or visual impairments and anxiety, it's often beneficial to connect with mental health counseling on or off campus to supplement whatever accommodations are provided.

Mary shares an alternative perspective on working with her disability throughout college:

"I had accommodations due to an intellectual disability I've struggled with since I was very young. College was especially hard for me and I struggled immensely with focus and testing. I lacked confidence without my accommodations and it stood as a safety net for me during much of high school and college. One professor not only advocated for me but also pushed me to reach my full potential. I remember many occasions where we'd have a quiz or test and she'd always ask privately, 'Would you like to try and take your exam with the group?' She never forced or pushed me, but encouraged me to try. Eventually, I was easily taking quizzes and (some) exams *in* her class without my accommodations. In other classes, tests and quizzes became easier to take without accommodations because of her pushing me to reach my full potential. My advice to other college students with accommodations: 'Push yourself—You have no idea the doors that will open for you if you'd just be willing to push yourself just a little past your comfort zone.' It definitely wasn't as easy at the time to see how she was molding and shaping me to be the professional I am today but now looking back I can see the bigger picture, and I'm so incredibly grateful for what she has done for me. I'm now a twenty-eight-year old social worker who is completely unmedicated. This is something I never thought that I could do or accomplish."

CHAPTER 11

PAPERS AND PROJECTS AND EXAMS, OH MY!

Lesson 48: Writing Is a Crucial Life Skill

"Wrestling with words gave me my moments of greatest meaning."

—Richard Wright

Typically, when students enroll in classes outside of the English department, they don't expect their professors to hold them as accountable for the quality of their writing. But the thing is that you're better served thinking of all your classes as writing classes. During the semester, students insist, "This is like writing boot camp" and complain, "But, this isn't an English class so why does grammar or sentence structure matter, why did you count off for this?" And then, like clockwork, months and years later, students routinely get in touch to tell me what has become one of the best things I could ever hear: "Your class made me become a better writer." That's what one of my dearest former students named Michael said who had me at the University of Connecticut, Storrs in 2003 as he claims my rigorous standards for writing helped him gain admission into a doctoral program from which he has launched a successful career as a therapist and new business owner. Eighteen years after having me in class, he sent a gorgeous bouquet of flowers to my home in South Carolina. But things surely didn't start out so easy. We *still* joke about the first paper he ever submitted to me. He earned (not "got," but we'll get to that later in Lesson #55) a C+. He approached me after class, flabbergasted, begging for extra credit and incredulous that he "never got C's." I tried to gently explain that I wasn't offering extra credit, there wouldn't be a redo and that I hoped he would improve for the next one. Every piece of work he submitted after that, in both classes he took with me, earned A's, but it's what he revealed to me later on that's had such staying power. He acknowledged to me that he was used to turning in "crap" as he put it and still seeing A's; in this case, I can't say earning A's because even he would admit he didn't. Many students don't react as well to grades they don't like and simply blame the professor. What's amazing about Michael's reaction is how he recognized the average quality of his initial paper and the fact that I wasn't playing the game he'd been used to. He saw my tough love for what it was: holding the bar high for students with the hope that they, in turn, would hold the bar higher for themselves.

The ability to write well—and comfortably and confidently—is one of the greatest gifts you'll ever give yourself. Through writing, we come to learn what we know, and through it, we think and grow. Writing is a life skill, a means of survival. The process of writing and revising can be incredibly frustrating, but at its best, writing can be sustaining and nourishing. The problem is that in high school and college, writing is generally regarded as drudgery and generates dread and stress. What's missing from that framing is the fact that knowing how to write well opens up possibilities for stronger communication in other arenas of life where there's a lot on the line and you want to feel understood. This might include writing such as: cover letters, love letters, personal statements for applications of all sorts, wedding vows, condolence cards, and almost anything else you need or want to write.

I often find myself telling students that the form of their writing will either clarify or obscure the content. I convey to students that the goal has to be to move from muddied, unresolved writer-based prose—what is in the mind of the writer—to clean, smooth reader-based prose which means that the writing lands in the lap of the reader the way the author intended it. Furthermore, writing is the key to cultivating our own authentic voice and identity. The reality is that knowing how to communicate effectively on paper can bring success, freedom, and joy.

Here are some tips to enhance your writing practice and process—and believe me, writing is indeed a practice and process:

- Read over the assignment multiple times and, if it helps you, have someone else read it to you aloud. You wouldn't believe the amount of times I'm grading papers and dumbfounded as to why some students just make up their own assignment with no regard for what was asked of them, or admit to me they never bothered to even read the assignment.
- Find a classmate with whom you can partner, discuss the assignment, brainstorm together, read each other's work, and provide feedback. Of course, your paper should be entirely your own unless you've been told you can write a collaborative paper.
- Pay attention to things such as: thesis statements, structure, main arguments, introductions, conclusions, demonstrating the ability to make connections between seemingly disparate class materials, substantiating your points with vivid examples, transitions, grammar, etc.
- Build in the necessary time for revision.
- Your campus likely has a dedicated Writing Center staffed by professionals and/or peer tutors. Make an appointment with them, and find out about workshops they offer.
- Go to your professor and/or teaching assistant's office hours. Bring with you a copy of the assignment, the ideas you've

already sketched out, a rough draft, paper to write on, and a writing utensil. In this way, your instructor can get a sense of the direction you're taking, and the time spent can be more productive. The more you do to prepare for the appointment, the more help you'll receive.

- Unless your professor is able to offer the opportunity to the whole class, there are typically no rewrites for better grades, but it's always useful to seek help for the purpose of improvement. Energy and emphasis should be placed on forward progress rather than on prior grade readjusting.
- Think about your workspace. When might it be better to work in your room, the library, or perhaps at a favorite café?
- Make paper writing easier to return to so you're not struggling to find your way back into it. Write notes to yourself as to where you're leaving off on a project and what you plan to attend to next—create an intention. As a result, you'll probably look forward to returning to your project and getting it done.
- Consider keeping a journal. You need not have to feel obligated to do this daily but it can help with expressing feelings and thoughts, clearing mental cobwebs, and strengthening your writing muscle.
- One of the worst things is when students submit papers with little to no analytical connections to class materials. It's as though they could have written it for any other class in college or even back in high school, and it lacks the specificity of how being in our class, exploring what we did and learning the concepts, vocabulary, and theories, informed and shaped their thinking. So, ask yourself before turning in any paper: have I clearly demonstrated how the materials in *this* class contributed to my thinking on *this* paper at *this* current moment in time?
- "Defiantly don't take it for granite" that your paper is all ready to submit! Every time I grade student papers, I see mistakes like these. And remember, I teach sociology, not geology! Carefully

proofread your papers, and then read your paper aloud to yourself to hear its rhythm and how well it flows. You might consider doing this with a study partner and swapping papers to read each other's work and give feedback. It can be beneficial to have someone read your work aloud back to you in order to hear how it sounds.

Lesson 49: Take Deadlines Seriously and Don't Blow Off Assignments

Submit your work on time. Don't show up in the middle of class or when it's over to submit the paper you were busy finishing during class time, and don't try sliding it under your professor's office door when you think they've left and then emailing an excuse. These are the oldest tricks in the book. Lateness and absences on the day something is due are telltale signs of problems. A problematic trend that has increased in frequency over the past few years is when students attempt to submit late work via email and either do so without a note or they say something like what this student emailed me: "Here's my paper. I couldn't turn it in yesterday because I've been depressed. Thanks for understanding." Inappropriate for multiple reasons, it presumptuously claims that acceptance of it is a fait accompli when that's not the case, and it reflects a distortion of roles.

Another thing that's never made sense to me is when students who've been neglecting to do assigned work all along suddenly emerge asking about extra credit and/or wanting many more assignments thinking that will help bring up their grades more than existing chunkier assignments worth a good deal more. It's foolishly misguided to complain about not being able to stay up to date with the required workload yet asking for more. Furthermore, a few additional extra credit points won't save someone who neglected major assignments. The workload in college is likely to be more rigorous than high school—as it should be—so you can't rely on doing a minimal amount and still doing fine.

Lesson 50: Be Sure Your Work Has Integrity

It seems to me that if you're enrolled in school because you want to learn, then you should go about this honestly. While the majority of professors want to be open, flexible, approachable, and responsive to students' needs and interests, plagiarism is something we won't stand for. In this current societal moment, there are so many outlets pushing people to pursue their work with no integrity; there are businesses, websites, and all sorts of technology that will enable you to cheat and turn in work that isn't yours. Recently, I had a student who submitted written work using ChatGPT which on its own was bad enough but the offense was made more egregious because she had been assigned to respond to questions about something I had published! I'm not sure how she imagined she would not be caught. What is clear in these situations is that students resort to making bad choices when they feel desperate, when they neither acquired nor read the required text, or when they didn't give themselves the necessary time to complete their work. Misguided decisions like this show a level of disrespect on many levels: toward the professor, the class, the material, other students (if the work is copied from a current or previous classmate), and most of all to the student who does this as it reveals a lack of self-respect for one's present and future.

Most of the time, professors can detect plagiarism and AI even without electronic detectors. If you're suspected of cheating, your professor will likely want to speak with you directly to gain more information and to give you a chance to fess up. Even though it's embarrassing, it's much better to tell the truth. In these situations, I ask students these two key questions: 1) how would you handle you if you were me? and 2) how do you want to be remembered? These questions are meant to compassionately confront students on problematic behavior and on actions and decisions that lack integrity and honesty. By asking these questions, I push for accountability, empathy, pause and reflection, and emotional rigor. Like I tell them, I hope that the responsibility you feel for your own educational experience and future will help you to resist any inclinations to participate in dishonest work.

Lesson 51: Learn to Manage and Maybe Even Like Dreaded Group Projects

Group projects and presentations are an opportunity to collaboratively explore and master a topic in a course. There are certainly a variety of pros and cons to being assigned group work and especially when grading is involved, and I've experienced and witnessed this both as a student myself and as a professor. Overwhelmingly, the pros have always outweighed the cons so up until the pandemic it was something I incorporated often.

Great contributions in groups can surprise the professor and lead to unusual opportunities. For example, a recent alumnus, Cole, was part of a group investigating sociological aspects of fatherhood and for his part spoke about helping his mother escape a lethal domestic violence situation. Since then, I've invited him to speak at evening events I've hosted on campus and at classes on the effects of domestic violence on children. Speaking passionately and convincingly, Cole has served as a mentor to so many, especially reinforcing the importance of bystander intervention and an alternative to toxic masculinity.

In the best of circumstances, students hold themselves and their group members accountable, there's a feeling that more brains together are better than one, and sometimes friendship or romance even emerges. I have had a number of students over the years who met doing a group presentation or a project in pairs who went on to become dating partners or close friends, and some remained tight even after graduation. I, too, have four special friends I met through working together on projects during both my undergraduate and graduate education. This is another one of those moments in college pushing you to be open to what is possible.

Even if you're not assigned to work in groups, it's beneficial to connect with classmates outside of class as study buddies where you can deepen discussions and share resources. If you're taking online classes, you can usually access class rosters and reach out to peers via email and then ask for contact information for texting, Snapchat, etc.

Lesson 52: Advice for the Very End of the Semester

As each semester draws to a close, students are stressed, cramming for finals, and finishing major projects. Many will claim to being up straight for two days to do this, strung out on coffee and Red Bull. As everyone is clamoring to finally be done, here are suggestions for finishing strong.

- **Make a list** of what you need to do for each class in the order in which due dates occur.
- **Review the syllabus for each class.** This may seem an odd time to do this, but it can make a difference. A good class is like an intricate puzzle, and while each piece contributes to the whole, it's not typically obvious at first what the purpose was of a

particular unit, assignment, text, film, etc. When you reread this document, the rationale for how the course was constructed can become clearer and, in turn, you can begin to see the class you took as more than the sum of its parts. Doing this might even help you with your final exam in terms of how materials come together. Class policies and your professor's teaching philosophy typically make more sense after participating in the course. In reviewing the syllabus, you give yourself an opportunity to see if you've fulfilled everything.

- **Make a commitment to care for yourself even during stressful times.** Stress won't be lessened on no sleep, bad food choices, no exercise, and too much coffee. Performance anxiety, junk food, and caffeine overload can do a number on your stomach. Take it from me—I guzzled diet Mountain Dew at one a.m. in college and it left me feeling gross, a bad mix of wired and tired. When you get good rest and eat real food, you're likely to feel better in your gut. Occasionally staying up late to finish a project can be okay, but too many nights of that in a row and you wind up feeling depleted, depressed, out of sorts, and almost broken in your body. As we've all become increasingly mindful of illnesses post-pandemic, it's also true that a lot of poor choices can leave our bodies even more vulnerable to illness.

- **Find study buddies.** These may be people enrolled in class with you, and you can share notes, discuss materials, and quiz each other. You might seek out study buddies who aren't in your classes but are friends with whom you can quietly and respectfully share a space and study together to keep each other accountable and motivated.

- **Mix it up.** Consider studying in a new place like a coffee shop. Another idea is to see if the classroom in which you take the class is open in the evenings, and you might consider studying there. Research shows we perform better in the same space in which we learned the material. You can visualize more of how you were taught things.

- **Try to avoid catastrophizing.** When people are stressed, they tend to worry about the worst possible thing that could happen. Perhaps you're earning a B- or a C+ in a class and then submit a paper and worry you'll now fail the class. Think about how to keep this situation in perspective.
- **It's normal to feel nervous.** When you're especially nervous about a final exam or an important presentation, it can be most helpful to take a few moments, close your eyes, and try to visualize an image that will encourage you. Years ago, before I defended my dissertation, I was extremely nervous and a therapist suggested I do this and it continues to sustain me in nerve-racking moments when I feel like I have to be "on." The image I routinely call up is of a tiny clown car filled with people I adore (including some former students I talk about in this book!) and then spilling out of the car and lovingly cheering me on. What's great for me about this image is it also makes me laugh; it's hard to imagine dozens of people with pompoms and signs emerging from a car the size of my old Mini Cooper without giggling, and that playfulness and lightness calms my worried mind and heart.
- **Visualize the finish line.** Think about how good you'll feel when you finish the semester. Envision what your body and mind will feel like when the term ends. How do you want to celebrate? Perhaps you want to plan an evening with friends, a day trip with someone special, or a hike in a beautiful place. It's always good to have something to look forward to, to take stock of what we've accomplished, and to create rituals that mark the end of one experience before transitioning to the next.

Lesson 53: Believe It or Not, Finals Can Be Beneficial

Finals week is when emotions are running high and stress is all consuming. Of course, you'll find that some professors have done away with final exams while others still rely on them, and some faculty choose instead to assign final papers, projects, and presentations. But whatever it is, there's always the sense that everyone's frantically, maniacally trying to finish and anxiously awaiting the break. Here, I identify reasons they may not be so bad after all.

Preparing for finals is an opportunity for mastering time management and project management. It becomes an awakening moment and you have to figure out how best to get it all done. This might serve as a reminder to seek out resources and support upon entering the next semester so that crunch time at the end is less frenzied. Examples of such resources include tutoring, counseling, time management workshops, meditation classes, meeting your professors in office hours, etc.

Finals is an opportunity to get better at stress management. This is a lifelong project, and every step helps. Most industries have super high impact time where the stakes are high, and this is preparation for that. Most careers that students will go on to engage in will have their own cycles of when things are the most busy, intense, and stressful, and the opportunity is presented again and again for how to gear up for that, sustain the momentum, and find ways to stay relatively calm in the midst of it all.

Finals can help students make choices and become more discerning. As more information comes at us all the time, and as we're faced with increasing responsibilities as we get older, we have to learn to know how and where we can best cut corners and skim material and still do so in a way in which little is compromised.

Finals don't go on forever. My stepfather always said, "This, too, shall pass" as a sort of mantra whenever I shared with him that I was stressed about something. At the time I dismissed it as cliché but now I see how it's actually quite helpful and comforting and makes a lot of sense. It's a reminder of how everything is impermanent and how preparation for finals, however arduous and tiring, is something that doesn't last forever.

Sometimes, we just have to get through it, whatever it is. Finals, both the act of preparing for them, and the act of taking and doing them, is good practice for that. It's a reminder of how something not fun can still usually be tolerated for a limited duration of time. That way of thinking still serves me now when I have to push through a final professional hurdle in writing or editing, or even something in my personal life I prefer to avoid like a medical procedure I don't want to endure.

Perhaps the best part of finals is the sweet reward and pleasure afterwards. This can take many forms like getting to sleep late, indulging in hedonistic activities, looking forward to play, having more time with friends, catching up on movies and shows, etc. When I was in college, I remember how we'd ask each other when we'd be done to find out who we could get to hang out with or party with as soon as we finished our last exam and before heading back home. I remember not wanting to immediately jump on a plane to fly home because the down time with college friends with whom we had just weathered so much seemed worth savoring.

The ritual of finals reminds us we're not alone. There's something about the communal experience of gearing up for finals, procrastinating and anguishing and somehow pushing through coupled with the communal experience of the anticipation of pleasure-seeking, that is a beautiful thing. It's not that the stress itself is so fun, but there are aspects of those stressful days that can bring fun and funny moments built into them. In my own case, it was wandering from the Helen C. White Library to the Memorial Union at UW–Madison to get coffee and popcorn at eleven p.m. to keep me going and then talking with friends in the library lounge before getting back to work. We'd study there until the place closed at 2:45 a.m. and stumble home together knowing we'd be right back at it together the next evening. Right below the surface of that hard work and exhaustion existed a durability of relationships undergirding it all. I don't see that happening so much anymore as there's more holing up alone in rooms these days. Yet when the ritual of finals is a shared, collective, communal experience, and the relief and pleasure-seeking is as well, this does mitigate the stress of it all.

CHAPTER 12

COMMUNICATING AND CONNECTING WITH YOUR PROFESSORS

Lesson 54: Practice Good Email Etiquette

If there's one simple thing you can do to bolster your chance of success, it's this: understand the necessity of email for school and work and how to craft appropriate messages. Also, online learning systems have features through which professors post information about assignments and grades that generate emails to students. Students need to check email to stay abreast of updates in their classes to enhance their chances for success. I can tell a lot about my students by how they handle email. I've even found myself complimenting students who send highly professional emails: it's rare, and it distinguishes them.

Be sure to use only your school email account for contacting personnel there and for seeking opportunities outside of the college. It's hard to take students seriously when they have email addresses like chocolatebunny, biggolfballs, or hardasarock at gmail.com. Yes, indeed, I have received messages from emails with those names! Even if the email makes it through the Spam filter, you won't be taken seriously. Think of emailing professors the way you would a boss; after all, that's what they are. School's the job for the next four years. Be professional and courteous. Include a salutation and not "Hey." You'd be amazed by the different ways that students email their male and female professors and how often I've been addressed as Mrs. Cohan, yet I don't think they meant to contact my mother! Female faculty earned doctorates too; students should use Dr. or Professor in the email salutation unless the professor encourages students to address them by their first name as I do. And it's best to avoid asking about grades, or posing challenges about grades, over email. **When students send emails to professors, they should remember that this is a short letter and not a text.** So be sure to include subject headings stating the name of the class since the professor has many students across numerous classes, and check salutations, grammar, spelling, signing off, etc.

Email can indeed feel overwhelming. We get messages about educational and career opportunities amidst party invitations and department store coupons. Yet life is a process of discerning what's urgent, what's important, and what can wait and email provides constant opportunity to practice this life lesson.

Recognize when to send an email and when not to. So many questions that students email professors about are already answered in the syllabus. For example, it never fails—every semester, at least one student will email to ask if the required book is "necessary"; that's a foolish way to make a first impression. I tell my students that email is to be used primarily to make appointments and for emergencies and not to email me about matters pertaining to grades or assignments that are better clarified during in person meetings or conversations over the phone. Like many other faculty members across the country, I have nearly 120 students every semester, and if every student asked questions via email about things that are already addressed and answered on the syllabus and assignments, it would get to be too much.

More recently, when students email me asking questions that I have addressed multiple times in person and online, I direct students back to those documents to find the answer themselves and I ask them to email me again when they have found the answer so I can be sure they've figured things out. Below is an email exchange with a student that proved fruitful; I did my best to convey to her, "You got this!"

"I wasn't trying to be snarky by having you find this on your own but more because I want students to know that they usually can find the answers and resources themselves. So much of what you need to succeed is already there for you but it's just that people are often not paying close enough attention despite all my best efforts. I want students to succeed and students must do their part to make it possible."

Her response shows that she was open and receptive to the lesson I was trying to teach her:

"I completely understand, it was a very helpful learning experience to have someone who doesn't just hand things to me. I guess I thought I was on the right track, but I'm still not quite used to having a hybrid class. I think I'm still trying to get used to it but it's helped me realize I need to stay more on top of things and look through the syllabus more thoroughly."

Students need to be in the practice of regularly going through emails, responding to necessary ones in a timely fashion, filing them appropriately in ways that allow them to later find and track them with ease, and deleting others. When a student emails me a question, and I write back with a response of what they need to do and ask a question of them, I expect a reply. You cannot imagine the number of times I've immediately replied to an email offering times to talk, gone to class days later or the following week, and that same student approaches me asking if I got their email. When I explain that I responded days before, they look at me dumbfounded and admit they hadn't checked their email! When professors extend an invitation to students to come to office hours, it's vital for students to reply and arrange an appointment.

Lesson 55: Let's Talk About Grades

I have to confess. I was the sort of student who was obsessed with getting A's. My mother tried to tell me over and over that I'd get much more out of my classes if I focused less on the outcome and more on the processes of how to think, how to learn, and how to write than on the grades.

The joke's on me as I find myself telling students the same thing and that ten years from now, they'll likely forget the grade they got in my class, but my hope is that what will stay with them is a new way of thinking about the world and their place in it. The writer and teacher bell hooks said that teaching and learning is not a paper/grade exchange but an exchange of ideas and humanity, a relationship of mentoring and mutual growth—a meeting place if you will. Hooks and my mom had it right. The students who get this do better. Every single time. It's the essence of an education well lived. It's where and how joy emerges, both for the student as well as for the educator.

I often wish we could do away with grades as they render education—a potentially transformative experience—overly transactional, with students and parents reviewing them like an itemized receipt from Walmart or a bank slip at the ATM. However, given various constraints under which we're operating, grades are here for the foreseeable future. Yes, there's some movement afoot where some faculty are employing alternative grading practices in class such as "ungrading," "specifications grading," "contract grading," and peer evaluation, but in the end, we still have to submit actual grades to the registrar.

And because of that, it's important for students to develop a greater understanding of grades.

When students want to talk about why they "got" what they did on an assignment, I always say that students don't "get" grades because professors don't "give" grades. Based on their professional expertise, faculty assign numerical value or letter grades to what they determine the student has earned. So, resist the urge to engage in grade grubbing. It's a bad look. It's one thing to gently and respectfully question a grade if there's a true mathematical error or to ask how you might improve going forward, but otherwise, you need to understand that a grade is not given; rather, it's earned. Grades aren't malleable. So, if you've earned grades in the 60s and 70s yet you want a B, don't go declaring to your professor that is what you want, expect, or need. It's crazy how often faculty hear this request. Your professors aren't magicians and cannot pull higher grades out of a hat that you've never even earned simply because you want or need it to apply to a special program, keep your financial aid, stay on a sports team, or because you believe you tried hard.

The truth is most faculty hate grading for multiple reasons including the sheer number of hours it takes, the shenanigans we often encounter in the process, and some students' reactivity that follows. Students complain from every point on the grading spectrum; some just want to pass, some want a C or better, and some are distressed with an A- or B+.

A recent alumna, Ashley, told me:

"We had talked multiple times about how those in online classes tend to just go through the motions of read a chapter, answer a question and respond in an agreeable manner with two classmates for discussion. I became that guilty person that we talked about with one of the papers. I just ran through the motions. You told me my grade was lower because you knew I needed to push myself. Some students would have thrown their hands in the air, but that comment was exactly what I needed to kick my ass into gear…That's such an important lesson to learn as a student…I don't complete a single thing now in my professional career simply by going through the motions. I always push myself to make whatever I'm doing the best I can possibly do. Being hard yet fair is such a difficult thing, and honestly, not all college students will understand. I try to walk that fine line with my team at work, and you instilled that in me."

Your parents, too, might need a primer on grading in college, and it might likely behoove you to initiate a conversation with them about expectations. Up until this point, they may have been used to the electronic systems to monitor your grades. But in college, you as a student have a choice. Parents no longer have the same ready access to monitor your progress or lack thereof. For many, this is a hard pill to swallow since if they're paying for a significant portion of the experience they often believe that should give them some right to have a clearer picture of what's going on. Other parents may prefer to have you take the lead on telling them how you're doing. You can give your parents access to both your grades and to talking with officials at school and you can choose not to. Generally speaking, that sort of surveillance diminishes trust for all involved, and if you've earned a great grade worth celebrating, you should be the one to get to share the news. Likewise, if you didn't do as well as you'd hoped and anticipated, I believe you should get to tell your parents. One thing is for sure—try to help your parents see that threatening you about grades creates undue agony and an adversarial relationship between you and how you come to regard school. I have students who tell me their parents will only pay for college if they earn straight A's or A's and B's. This isn't always realistic at the college level. A wonderfully sweet guy I had in class in 2012 was so worked up about needing all A's due to his father's threats and pressure that he dropped out of school and died by suicide soon after. Grades need never be that defining and heartbreaking.

Lesson 56: Things to Consider If and When You Complain or Challenge a Grade

In highlighting the myriad ways to cultivate academic success, it's also important to acknowledge some things that get in students' way (including themselves!) so you can do your best to avoid the same pitfalls. You'll see that some things that may have worked in high school simply don't work anymore.

Showing up is great and so is effort, but they're not enough. I hear students say, "But I came to class" or "But I tried." You should do all that, but the work you do must stand on its own to be meritorious. Occasionally, students earn zeroes on papers in my class and then share with me how stunned they are since they were used to getting half credit for at least turning in something.

Recently, I had a student who earned forty-six on her first exam. Unfortunately, the test wasn't out of a possible fifty but rather a hundred. When she came to my office in late February, I asked to see her notebook, and only a third of one page was filled with notes from the first week of school in mid-January. This means that in six weeks of school, she had only taken a third of a page of notes in class. She told me she didn't have any other notes and shamelessly admitted she'd never read the syllabus or even obtained the books. Smiling, I pointed out, "Wow, you got a forty-six doing *that*? Imagine what would happen if you did *everything*!" I told her I couldn't and wouldn't help her until she started to help herself. Students have to come at least part of the way.

After the second exam on which she earned a grade in the 70s, I emailed her to say I was happy to see the improvement and invited her to meet again. I asked her what she had done differently and what her advice would be to future students and to me in similar situations. She admitted that I'd done all I could and she just needed to do the work—and that once she did that, the material was actually interesting and made her want to learn more. Imagine that!

Every semester, I, and every other professor I've ever spoken with, have students who email wanting to make up missed assignments due weeks and even months before. In desperate emails, they ask what they can do. I'd love to tell them they need access to a time machine. It's like the old saying, "too little, too late." These are students who've never shown up to a single class or submitted any work whatsoever and email me the last few weeks of the semester to try to salvage things, conveying the message that education is something they believe they can squeeze in during momentary bursts of time, even at three a.m. after a shift at a restaurant and hanging with friends at a bar. Every semester has to end. Or, as I tell my students, the ride must come to a complete stop. Students usually want the semester to be over but they don't want it to end until they get what they want grade-wise.

Think about what you're asking. Refrain from asking professors for special individual favors like extra credit, endless chances for redoes, or grade bumps. When you do this, you're asking a professor to be unethical. No student would want to discover that their professor offered extra opportunities for improvement to only a select few and not the rest of the class. When students ask me to make an exception just for them, I remind them of this and the larger lesson of my sociology classes, which is that the world is larger than ourselves.

Larger social forces are at work here that have shaped students' attitudes and behaviors. You've grown up seeing many older adults doing terrible things in the public sphere, facing no consequences, and instead often being rewarded. You've come of age in schools that mandate educators to assign passing grades even when the work wasn't up to par, and maybe you've even participated on teams where everyone is rewarded, even if only for effort. College becomes an opportunity to interrupt this line of thinking, accept more responsibility, and increase your sense of humility.

Lesson 57: Respect Boundaries

"Between stimulus and response there is a space. In that space is our power to choose our response. In our response lies our growth and our freedom."

—Viktor E. Frankl

Faculty can tell a *lot* about a student by how they handle email. A mature, respectful email from a student shows me that they learned good manners. It shows that they understand boundaries when an answer has to be "no," and they close the loop on any actionable item. I worry about the students who don't seem to know how to do any of this.

For example, a student was unhappy with the final grade she earned in my class and was worried it would prevent her chance of admission to the nursing program. Distraught, she called me six times on my personal cell phone, left three voicemails, and sent two text messages and three emails, all within two and a half hours. I gave the students my cell phone number because I was teaching asynchronously online, and I wanted them to still find me available and accessible. When I finally spoke to her, I identified that her behavior constituted harassment. Her actions demonstrated that she had poor judgment, no boundaries, and lacked the ability to carefully and thoughtfully ascertain and respond to a real emergency—all essential things to grasp if one wants to succeed in nursing. Unfortunately, many students believe we'll cave if they wear us down enough. This student earned a D in the same course the previous year with a different professor. Yet, she still didn't seek help from me earlier in the semester. She had missed the biggest lesson of all from my sociology class which is that the world is so much larger than ourselves.

I'm still floored by the young man in my class who texted me over Thanksgiving weekend to ask questions about how to study for the final exam and to see if we would have more discussion boards online. Evidently, he had saved my number from a phone appointment we had several weeks earlier. Numerous students do text me—once they've finished my classes and graduated. In fact, I have former students, now friends, who text me regularly. I welcome that. In fact, I love that. But in no way can I manage well over 100 students texting me random questions at all hours of the day or night on my personal cell phone as they're freaking out about grades. I told the student I wouldn't reply and he'd need to email me. My concern is that students need to respect their professors' need for personal time on evenings, weekends, and holidays.

Think about what you're asking of your professors. My colleagues and I deal with overflowing inboxes where we're flooded with students' questions and pleas for second chances to redo their papers and retake tests or who want extra credit or who simply want "just a few points" added to boost their grades to whatever they need and want them to be. Somewhere along the line, they've been told, "Well, it can't hurt to ask." I'm here to tell you that to the contrary, it *most definitely can* hurt to ask. When students do this, they signal that they believe they should be treated in a special way. My reply is always the same: "If I offer this to you, I'd need to offer it to everyone." So, think about what you're asking of your professors, what position this puts them in, and how you want to be remembered. And rather than email professors only about grades, talk with them about how you can improve for the future with other classes and as you move further along on your path.

Lesson 58: Determining If and When a Grade of Incomplete Is Warranted

Schools will have policies about taking a grade of I for "incomplete" for a class. In addition, faculty members will likely have their own policies. I do everything possible to help students avoid incompletes. Sometimes they're implemented in ways that are appropriate, but all too often they're not a good solution. If, for example, a student regularly engages with a class and has performed well all semester and then a few weeks before school ends is in a scary car accident requiring surgery or has a parent diagnosed with cancer and needs and wants to be home, then an incomplete would make sense. This is largely because the student had a good track record and handled everything well that was within their control; they established a solid foundation so that they can sustain a crisis. Consequently, when an accident, illness, or death occurs for which no one has any control, it's appropriate to arrange for accommodations for a successful finish.

However, incompletes aren't appropriate as a cure for having checked out all semester, being noncommunicative, and then desperately trying to find an alternative to failing or dropping a class. For this reason, the vast majority of schools and individual professors will rightfully insist that determining eligibility for an incomplete requires that a certain percentage of work had already been completed in a manner that was at least satisfactory or better.

Lesson 59: Go to Office Hours

Office hours are a unique part of the college experience. This is dedicated time when you can sit down to talk one-on-one with your professors about questions you have related to classes, to life, and your future. You want your professors to know your name and who you are. Anonymity poses a great risk for students already in jeopardy academically and psycho-socially.

Typically, faculty are expected to hold a certain amount of office hours per week and usually post their scheduled office hours on their doors and in the syllabus. Be sure to seek out your professors during the times they say they'll be available. If they're open to scheduling appointments outside of those office hours, then you might send an email asking for an appointment, indicating what the meeting is about and how much time you anticipate you'll need so they can plan accordingly. This reduces the back and forth and lets the professor know you're prepared. And if you need to cancel, be sure to let them know. Find out if your professor offers alternative ways of meeting such as virtually or over the phone. Go to your meeting prepared for your time together and with some questions written down in advance demonstrating a sense of purpose, focus, and a willingness to interact. Be sure to turn your phone to silent in advance of your meeting.

Access to professors in college is quite different than in high school, and this is related to a number of factors. One main reason is that along with our teaching responsibilities, we're expected to do research, to present our work at conferences and other venues, to write, and to publish. By being part of the construction of knowledge and engaging in the larger conversation in their disciplines, your professors are able to bolster the classroom experience. Faculty are also expected to engage in service on campus, to our respective disciplines, to the local community, and to the region and nation. Service takes the form of things such as: serving on committees and boards, being officers in professional organizations, editing scholarly journals, partnering with nonprofit organizations, conducting peer reviews for publication, and being interviewed by media outlets about our expertise. As you can see, this means that faculty aren't always in their offices. Try to respect and trust that all these other professorial activities deeply enrich the college experience you receive because the more active and involved your professors are, the more they have to offer in the classroom.

Some students choose to never make use of individual time with faculty and unfortunately and predictably, they're typically the same ones who struggle, wind up on academic probation, and feel lonely and distressed. The large majority of students who come to office hours admit they were initially a little intimidated, are glad they came, and grateful for the additional resources and recommendations I give in that setting that are unique for each person. It's one more opportunity for me to learn their names and what's capturing their interest or what's of concern to them, in the course and in their overall experience.

Regardless of whether you have a scheduled appointment, it's good to remember that your professor is one person trying to assist and support students who come forth with a range of issues related to class as well as to other personal, life issues and emergencies, so try to be patient if they're running late. It can become quite challenging to teach multiple classes on a given day in various buildings across campus, attend meetings, and then hold office hours with students; no wonder, most of us joke about when we'll have time to eat or use the bathroom. So it's good to remember that professors are people, too.

We're living in a day and age in which it seems rare to have someone's undivided attention and for someone to sit across from us, listening closely, and offering feedback. My own life experience tells me that's worth waiting for. In fact, like I tell my students, when they're in, they're in, meaning that even if they had to wait a bit, I'm committed to answering all their questions and helping them as much as I can. I borrow this approach of true presence from a gynecologist I saw for the eighteen years I lived in Boston—probably the best doctor I've ever had—and fun fact, Mindy Kaling's late mother. Yes, *that* Mindy Kaling!

Lesson 60: Invite Your Favorite Professor to Coffee

In the fall of 1996, I was in graduate school at Brandeis and simultaneously hired to replace someone on a semester sabbatical at Wheaton College in Massachusetts. There, I had a remarkable student named Amy; she was twenty at the time, she's now approaching fifty, and remains one of my dearest friends. Wheaton offered to all students the opportunity to invite their favorite professors to lunch for free in the dining hall, and Amy asked me to be her guest. I was thrilled and touched that she chose me, I was impressed that Wheaton created this possibility, and I've been delighted to see that tradition occurring at other schools across the country.

There's something to breaking bread with another person. Sharing food and leisurely, unfolding conversation is a way to enjoy the immediacy and intimacy that can emerge between teachers and students. It's hard for teaching and learning to get reduced to a crude grade exchange when a meal has been shared and both the teacher and student can embrace the multidimensionality of the other person.

Let me share with you an influential memory that relates to how breaking bread helped me come to see this whole business of teaching and learning. Starting in nursery school and then continuing in elementary school in the 70s, my mother, who taught at another school in Cleveland, invited my teachers to lunch at our house every year. It was a warm, sweet gesture, and the teachers welcomed a homemade lunch with my mom's winning presentation of food. She prepared a bountiful spread of homemade chicken salad sandwiches, crudité, homemade soup, usually lima bean, homemade bread, and decadent chocolate desserts. And every year at holiday time, I made handmade gifts for my teachers. One year, my mom took me to buy clay flowerpots, and we painted them and put plants inside. In fourth grade, I had the same teacher as I had in second grade, and we went to her house to bring gifts for her new baby, hand-me-downs for her older daughter, and cupcakes for the whole family.

Nowadays, this would strike people as bad boundaries or trying to get on the teacher's good side for my grades. The truth is, I did well anyway, and I'm able to look back on this and see what my mother was trying to instill. It was never about the lunches and the gifts, or about them only insofar as those are used to express love. I think my mother was trying to convey to me a sense of teachers as human beings for whom we express empathy, gratitude, and respect, people with whom we can break bread. So, at a young age, I learned to value the role of teachers in my life.

Simultaneously, my mother showed me the value of students in a teacher's life. When I was growing up, we enjoyed many visits with a woman named Ellen; she had been a student of my mother's when she was just twelve years old when my mother was in her mid-twenties. Amazingly, Ellen is now in her seventies and they enjoyed a deep, lifelong friendship until my mother died in 2020. Now, I have my own Ellens in the dozens of former students, now treasured friends, who've made an incredible impact on my life. Just look what happened with Amy!

If your school doesn't offer meal passes to be able to invite your favorite professor to lunch, suggest the idea. If it still doesn't happen, then ask your professor to join you for coffee. They're likely to be delighted and honored. Most faculty crave these conversations because we got into this wanting to connect with students over spirited conversations about subjects that drive our passion. We want to hear your perspectives, interpretations, insights, hopes, and fears about the world. When students contact me or my colleagues to only inquire about their grades, it's empty. While it's normal to be concerned about grades, it shouldn't be the only reason you seek a professor out. There's more to you and to us, and to the work happening between us, than the grade could ever possibly represent. When you get to know a professor as a human being and you allow that person to get to know you, you help transform what would otherwise be transactional into something relational and potentially profound. You never know what might unfold from these conversations and connections. So, break bread with this person or enjoy coffee together, and allow yourself to be surprised.

Lesson 61: Seek Out Mentors

In 1997, journalist Mitch Albom published *Tuesdays with Morrie*, a book—well actually more of a tribute and a love story—in which Mitch, upon hearing that his cherished professor, Morrie Schwartz, was dying of ALS, returns to Boston on a series of Tuesdays to visit with him and gather his nuggets of wisdom and hope. Appealing to a wide range of readers and tapping into something universal, the book became an instant bestseller. It hit a nerve. Most of us need and want that great teacher or coach who single-handedly changes our life. In fact, as a culture we're obsessed with these stories. There've been many movies chronicling the same sort of storyline. It's particularly ironic in a society that so deeply devalues and under-values educators. But despite that perverse paradox, books and movies abound revealing to us this deep longing.

One of the single most important things you can do in college is to find yourself at least one mentor. An implicit and explicit mission of the college experience is to assist and support students as they individuate from their families of origin. Students generally do better in school both academically and socially, and experience greater satisfaction in college, when they've identified and nurtured relationships with faculty and staff who become mentors to them. When they get ready to graduate and launch into the world, these are connections that have the potential to lead to job opportunities and other sources of enrichment.

I hear parents talk about how they want their children to have relationships with professors so that they can obtain letters of reference for graduate programs or recommendations for jobs. Some parents suggest that the connection will help boost the student's grade. I don't know about that, but what I do know is that those are utilitarian reasons for trying to get to know your professors. The deeper and more sustaining reason is because lifelong mentoring will, in fact, change your life.

The marine biologist and conservationist Rachel Carson said, "If a child is to keep alive his inborn sense of wonder, he needs the companionship of at least one adult who can share it, rediscovering with him the joy, excitement, and mystery of the world we live in." For our purposes, we can take the word "child" and replace it with "young adult" and her observation holds just as steady and true. And this is why mentors are so vital.

Amazing relationships can be cultivated with faculty. They might become mentors from whom you'll eventually seek reference letters. They might become your thesis advisers, research collaborators, and even your friends for years to come. I've been known to introduce people and facilitate friendships among current and past students suggesting that people meet because of certain shared interests, struggles, quirks, goals, etc. Professors may be aware of people in the community searching to hire good workers or organizations looking for possible interns or volunteers. Or they might be able to suggest places or people they know connected to a specific passion or dream of yours in order to help you with networking. In the best of circumstances then, professors play a facilitative and generative role in students' lives.

Hundreds of students have stayed in touch with me over the years. I've attended numerous former students' weddings and was invited to speak at one, I've gone to baby showers and even a funeral for the three-year old daughter of a favorite former student. These are priceless connections. I treasure them. And I know and trust these students do as well. For example, recently, I was in touch with a former student, Jamie, whom I consider to be more of a friend than anything else. She took classes with me twenty years ago and is working as a senior staff member at a college in another state. We laugh and rant about issues in higher education, and we reminisce. Recently, she found herself in a particularly fraught personal situation that she shared with only her best friend and me. She was beginning an affair, trying to leave her husband, and concerned about her children. I'm honored she chose to confide in me like that. Here it was, twenty years earlier we were in a class titled Families in Society of all things, and fast forward to the present moment and we're living out and talking deeply about what once were theoretical issues. Those hours spent over coffee on campus talking about her assignments, her college boyfriend, her family, and her hopes and dreams laid a sturdy foundation from which she could reach out to me, whenever and about whatever, knowing she had someone safe to tell who would understand and wouldn't judge her. Jamie intuited I'd be there for her as I was. This is what I call long-haul mentoring.

You may wonder, how would you find a mentor? Think of someone you feel you can open up and talk to and to whom you can ask hard questions and take risks. That person exists somewhere on a Venn diagram of great life coach; cool aunt or uncle; fiercely, protective, big sister or brother; and tough love parent. And don't underestimate the power of gratitude. My friend's son reminded me that when he left for college, I suggested to him that if he felt connected to a professor or loved a class, he should let that person know by writing a handwritten thank-you note or an email at the end of the semester. I was so glad to hear that he did this and saw that it made a difference, especially in a small program where he had the same professor multiple times. That can be the seed to growing a mentoring relationship. I'm reminded of a Buddhist saying, "When the student is ready, the teacher will appear."

Whether you reach out to an impactful professor soon after the end of the term or find them years later to let them know the meaning they had on your life, this expression of gratitude will be appreciated. Hearing from students years later is one of the most exhilarating things about this job. Planting seeds and finding out how they've taken root, bloomed, and flourished is a beautiful thing.

Soon after graduation a few years back, another student, Matt, made it a point of posting on social media photographs and messages of gratitude to those of us who mentored and stood by him for years—I was in good company with a few other colleagues, his mother, and his grandmother. What's beautiful to me about what Matt did on Facebook is that he made visible that which needs to be made more visible all the time—gratitude for educators and the sheer joy in deep mentoring.

Another student, Brianna, whom I had in three classes, always made a habit of leaving every single class session thanking me in the most earnest way. It was unusual and amazing to hear this from a twenty-year old multiple times a week for several semesters, and it made an indelible imprint on me. Even more interesting is that she failed my class the first time she took it and struggled to earn better grades after that. For her, the experience transcended the grades. Besides expressing gratitude, it seems that Brianna learned another lesson, and that is to consider how you want to be remembered. I've come to see that the way students communicate and behave, *especially* during the last week or so of a semester, is revealing. This is because the way we exit any type of relationship tells a lot about our emotional intelligence, who we are, what we're capable of or not, and how we'll be remembered.

I'll never forget receiving an email from a first-year student, Nina, soon after my last introductory sociology session of the semester who thanked me for all that she believed she learned in the class and about herself in the world, and then asked me to serve as her mentor. I hadn't had a student ask it like that to me in a formal email, and it was unusually refreshing. I wondered how early in her freshman year she knew to do that. I was struck by the fact that she'd given thought to what such a rapport could do for her academically, professionally and personally. I responded immediately with a resounding, "Yes, absolutely, of course!" As it turns out, she didn't major in sociology, and instead chose a related major. Nevertheless, she felt a connection to me and sensed I had something special to offer to her. And though Nina graduated several years ago, she has remained in touch with me, surprising me with delightful messages and curious about how I am. She checked on me during the pandemic and after my mother died. The care that she experienced from me in college is care that she has returned tenfold.

Regardless of how old we are, we all benefit from having mentors. I see this with my many nontraditional age students as well. Personally, I'm grateful to be able to count numerous mentors who've left indelible imprints on my life. Transformative mentoring tends to be a multidimensional, mutual, reciprocal thing. It's professional and it's personal; it's academic and it's social. I think back to the summer of 2007 when Mary Gilfus, one of my favorite professors from UW–Madison who over the years became a dear friend, invited me to join her at her second home so I could enjoy a place to retreat and write. This gave us time and space to each do our work and ample opportunities to share at the end of the day what we had done. Together, we made dinner, ate, took walks, read our work to each other, and gave each other feedback. Mary is a woman who single-handedly changed how I saw the world and myself. I've come to see that there's no comparison to the feeling of a former teacher taking you and your perspectives seriously *and* having fun with you years after classes are over. I'm lucky to have that feeling both as a former student and as a teacher. This leads to sharing with you one of the most significant mentoring experiences I've enjoyed in the course of my career.

In the spring of 2013, Cody was enrolled in my introductory sociology class and emailed me late in the evening after a class session on body image and eating disorders. In that message, he disclosed his experiences struggling with self-harm, specifically anorexia and cutting. That email led to hundreds of other email exchanges and to him enrolling in five more courses with me, becoming actively involved in the Sociology Club I advised, and a continued conversation and friendship that we've sustained since he graduated in 2016. His voice for change around issues of violence against women was powerfully felt, and his wisdom, far beyond his years, was hard-won as the result of witnessing a rapid succession of deaths of those close to him. I invited him to speak at classes and events I hosted about body image, self-harm, masculinity, loss, trauma, recovery and what it means to be an ally. He quickly became an exquisite model for his peers. Now, he's married to a fantastic woman, they have a darling daughter, and he works as a family support specialist at a mental health center for at-risk youth. We communicate with each other often for feedback and reality checks and ask deep life questions related to topics such as education, mental health, social media, and violence. I always value his opinion, and he never fails to make me laugh. Embedded in those texts are traces of our classes together, conversations that started long ago that I trust both of us expect to be lifelong. And if I teach long enough, who knows, maybe I'll get lucky again and his adorable daughter will wind up in a class of mine. It's this mutual, long-haul, full-circle mentoring that can change lives—both that of the student and the teacher.

CHAPTER 13

WHEN THE ACADEMIC ROAD GETS ROCKY

Lesson 62: Know the Warning Signs of Students Who Struggle So You're Equipped to Help Yourself or a Friend

- Demonstrates little to no curiosity, and this extends beyond class material and relates to others, oneself, relationships, nature, and the larger world around them
- Unsure of the purpose of college and why they're there
- Self-sabotaging
- Lack of follow-through
- Waiting too long to seek help and wanting a quick fix
- Unwilling to seek help or follow up on resources provided
- Claims "I don't have time to get a tutor" even when getting that support would likely save time in the long run
- Poor communication skills, orally and/or in writing
- Poor choices in peer groups
- Shows signs of substance abuse and other forms of self-harm

- Doesn't engage in project management to be able to successfully complete assignments on time
- Blames circumstances and other people, especially professors, for the grades they earned
- Does the bare minimum
- Has problems showing up, both in terms of actual attendance and in terms of a sense of presence
- Doesn't pay attention to the parameters and demands of assignments and submits whatever they want
- Ignores course requirements as spelled out in the syllabus

Lesson 63: Locate Academic Support at the Earliest Sign of Trouble

Seek help right away when you find yourself slipping. This is true with academics and seeing your professor and a tutor, and it's true with your emotional life and seeing a counselor if you need a professional sounding board and resources. Take time to honestly reflect on where and how you need to take more responsibility. Rather than saying, "I didn't do well because the professor didn't post the notes," it would serve students better to ask themselves the following:

- Did I seek help from the professor and/or teaching assistant in office hours to learn how to better take notes?
- Did I seek support from a tutor at the student success center?
- Did I find a study buddy or study group?
- Did I do all this as soon as I saw things going awry, or did I wait too long when it was too late?

- Did I neglect to submit any assignments?
- Did I make excuses?
- Should I consider seeking help at the counseling center for dealing with anxiety and depression or other issues that have caused distress?

To further illustrate, below is an actual email exchange with a student that reveals the numerous ways she dropped the ball: not reading the syllabus, otherwise she would know how to craft an email, writing to me twelve days before the semester ended having never reached out to me before that, showing concern with nothing but the grade, and confusing what it means to pass with what it means to do well. After I replied and offered an appointment, she never followed through in a substantive way.

> **Sent:** Sunday, April 9, 2023 2:54 p.m.
> **To:** Cohan, Deborah <DCOHAN@uscb.edu>
> **Subject:** Class
>
> Hello, Ms. Cohan I just wanted to know whether you believe I would be able to pass your class and get a good grade. I'm just curious since I feel like I'm not doing all that well in your class, and the course is almost over.
>
> **From:** Cohan, Deborah <DCOHAN@uscb.edu>
> **Sent:** Sunday, April 9, 2023 4:46:35 p.m.
> **Subject:** Re: Class
>
> Hi,
>
> Good to hear from you. I'm not able to adequately predict grades weeks in advance like this. If you earn another good grade on the next test and continue to participate, I would think you could earn a C or hopefully even a C+ in the class but this is a guess at

this point. I hope you do well on the next test. If you were having trouble in the class, I wish you had reached out to me before now so I could best help you. If you need an appointment, let me know. I hope you have enjoyed the class material and are doing okay in your other classes.

Best,

Deb

Sent: Sunday, April 9, 2023 5:10 p.m.
To: Cohan, Deborah <DCOHAN@uscb.edu>
Subject: Re: Class

Yes, ma'am, thank you.

The key is to be honest about where you're having trouble, meeting with the necessary people to strategize steps toward improvement, and following up so you can best position yourself to reshape your habits for the new semester and beyond.

Lesson 64: How to Recover from a Lousy Semester

It's typical for students to struggle (academically and/or socially) during at least one semester and sometimes in ways that can be hard to recover from. The good news is that there's hope, and students can, indeed, find success after a rough semester. Here are some tips to ensure a smoother subsequent semester.

- **Before heading back for a new semester, consider where and how you floundered.** What was hard and why? Were the struggles academic? Social? Roommate related? A bit of all of these? Assess the patterns. Think about your role in these struggles.

- **Consider time. How much were you manifesting your own life?** You have new freedom, and you get to make your own schedule. How can you make that best work for you, honoring your own rhythms and finding balance? Did night turn into day and day into night? Did that work? Sometimes it does, but often it doesn't. "Social life in general got in the way in my first year, learning to balance social life and academic life was a much bigger challenge than I expected going into college," admitted Cody.

- **Invest in a paper planner or find an app that will help you make your schedule and remind you of upcoming important dates.** I can't begin to tell you how many students reveal to me that they don't use a calendar. It's the first thing I ask about when students show that they're having trouble with deadlines and project management. This is a great time in your life to try out different systems for staying organized and on top of things to see what works best for you. Again, you're creating lifelong habits.

- **You'll want to record due dates in your calendar including stages of project management so you can get your work done**

at a good pace. Over the years, I too have gotten into the helpful habit of printing out all my syllabi and sitting down with them and my planner and entering in important dates for all the classes I teach, including things like exams, paper due dates, dates I should set aside for grading, dates by which I should post review sheets for exams, etc. In addition, I keep a master list of all the work and writing projects I need to complete and include these items as well. This helps me pace myself for the next fifteen weeks and I know in advance which weeks might be busier and which ones have more flexibility. As a result, it helps me think about weekend commitments and travel plans. Doing these things actually creates the structure and scaffolding to make time for more spontaneity and a sense of spaciousness.

- **When you think about time, consider your online habits.** Did an hour just pass when you were scrolling? When you think about what you did when you were supposedly out with friends, do you recall the conversation or just the fact that everyone was on their phones? Consider turning your phone off and putting it in a drawer while you're studying to minimize distractions; the best thing is this will actually shorten the amount of time the work will take. Echoing this is Ben who told me he blames phones for what he calls his peers' "horrendous ability to focus." He acknowledged that "While I cannot go a day without my phone like everyone else, I at least have the ability (and discipline) to turn it off for thirty to sixty minutes at a time (usually, I set a timer and throw it in a different room—then lock my door—until it goes off). However, I'm not convinced I have a single friend who could do this. I notice hardly any of my friends can even wait twenty seconds in line without reaching for phones. It's *amazing* what can get done in two hours of 100 percent focus—and the damage this may be doing to us when we do otherwise."

- **Think about the habits you've cultivated since you've been at college.** Which ones are serving you well and which ones are no longer serving you? How might you let go of what is not serving you?

- **Evaluate your life outside of classes.** This is the time to think about how to make college your home. Maybe you can join clubs and organizations on campus that resonate with your interests and that have the potential to help you develop your leadership abilities.

- **Think of a new semester as an opportunity for a fresh start and a chance to reinvent yourself and rediscover your dreams.** Take some time to sit down by yourself in silence with a paper and pen and close your eyes for even just a few minutes and anchor into the place within you that intuits your own hopes and dreams, To get motivated, you might take a short walk to your favorite café, treat yourself to your favorite nonalcoholic beverage and then bring it back to your room or find a relaxing, quiet space outside or in a campus building. It's fun to find your own nooks and crannies on a campus that you can escape to and call yours. Then think about a word or phrase that comes to mind that best captures your intention for moving forward? What are you wanting to cultivate in your life? What do you need less of going forward? How might you shed that stuff and clear space? What do you need more of going forward? How might you hold space for that good stuff? Try writing about this. Make a list of how you might get there. Then, meditate on all of this, reconnecting with the word or phrase that motivates you. When you open your eyes, take out a sheet of paper and write this down anew, perhaps drawing an accompanying image that brings this mantra to life. You might benefit from keeping this in your calendar, on your nightstand, or in a journal to refer back to for inspiration.

- **Get to know a professor.** This can make all the difference in how connected you feel to your intellectual work and the campus more generally, and this person might become someone with whom you stay in touch for years to come.

- **Evaluate your friendships and intimate relationships.** Are the people with whom you're interacting fulfilling for you and giving your life meaning, or are they sabotaging you in any way?

Consider how to strengthen the relationships that feed you, and let go of the ones that don't enhance your well-being.

- **Consider ways you might meet new people.** This might be through classes, clubs, Greek life, student organizations, intramurals, teams, etc. Approach and talk with someone you've never met.

- **Consider volunteering in the community.** This can be meaningful and fun, and it provides a way to meet new people. When I was in graduate school, I volunteered at a domestic violence agency and, after just a few months, that led to a part-time paid position that lasted for years and led to multiple other professional opportunities that continue for me to this day.

- **If you did poorly in a course and are retaking it, make an appointment with your professor to discuss how you can create a fresh start and improve.** Just last semester, a student took my class again and earned an A when the first time she had failed. I was thrilled for her, and she was rightfully proud of herself for the strategies she implemented that made such a huge difference.

- **Think about how you might first rely on yourself and your own inner resources before contacting your parents.** It's always apparent who has first tried to find answers on their own and who's emailing me because of a knee-jerk response asking questions about things that are clearly spelled out in multiple places. It can feel good, and can build your confidence, to first try to locate answers on your own and to remember that often, the answers are inside you.

- **Commit to self-care.** Is there a healthy habit you're curious about and imagine you'd benefit from doing regularly? All you need to do is start with just one new habit, even if it's for fifteen minutes, do that regularly for three weeks and then consider adding a second one. Perhaps it's meditation, yoga, reading, writing, painting, walking or running, getting better sleep, learning to cook, etc. Maybe you'll remember something you loved to do as a child and since abandoned. You might consider ways to return to that activity you enjoyed.

Lesson 65: If You Wind Up Having to Retake a Class, Remember This Advice

Sometimes you'll get another chance to make a different impression, so use it wisely. If a student does poorly in a class and has to retake it, the student should make an appointment early on with the professor to create an improvement plan. I've had students earn failing grades twice and have to retake the class a third time, and even when I've made overtures to help those students, they most often neglect to follow through. When a professor contacts a student, there's usually a good reason. I make contact to try to be helpful and provide resources and support for improvement. It makes sense for students to respond and make an appointment. When students struggle during the semester, it's important to reach out to the professor for guidance immediately. It's misguided when students contest a final course grade having neither appropriately responded to a professor's initial concerns nor sought help.

CHAPTER 14

DECISIONS, DECISIONS

Lesson 66: Should I Stay or Should I Go Now?—Thoughts on Transferring

Talk of transferring is common, and it's a real gamble. You're weighing two things against each other—one being the place you are that you likely haven't fully experienced and the other being a place in the abstract that somehow sounds dreamier. Often, it's just part of the process of anxiety and adjustment the first year and nothing to be alarmed about. Some students decide that college isn't right for them or for their goals and dreams, and while this can produce real anguish, this too, may be a healthy decision so that students put in effort, passion, and energy that approximates or matches the high cost. I've seen students transfer more than once during college, and I've seen students return back to the original place a year later. It's not just the grass that's always greener; sometimes the cinder block is too.

By the holiday break, students have a semester of college under their belts and are taking stock of where they've spent their time and what lies ahead. They go home for break, usually eager to see old friends but not sure how their experience compares to and measures up to their peers. Did they choose the right college after all? Might someplace else be a better fit? Conversations about transferring, as well as about taking time off or dropping out, emerge more frequently in this time of transition between semesters.

Perhaps a student dreamed of attending a particular school and wasn't admitted the first time and wants to try again. Or maybe a student came to X school with the intention of using it as a steppingstone to transfer to the flagship in a public system or to another sort of college entirely. Students sometimes overestimate the issue of size, thinking a school of more than 5,000 will be entirely too large and they'll feel lost, only to find themselves at a much smaller school feeling claustrophobic and wanting more opportunities. There are students who choose a school because of it being in a more densely populated urban area and then yearn for sprawling green space between buildings on a hill, that sort of idyllic campus setting we see in movies. Conversely, there are the students at campuses in more rural and remote locations craving the pulse and vibrancy of a city.

There are many reasons to want to transfer, some better than others. There are usually good reasons for staying and compelling reasons for going. It's helpful to remember that for most students, freshman year is hard; well, okay, it usually sucks, at least in the beginning. That may not be the best time to make such a big decision and forge a transition. Let's take a look at what to consider when the desire to transfer comes up:

- **Recognize that these thoughts are normal.**
- **Consider if you've given the experience a fair shake.** Have you truly given the school—and yourself—a fair chance and explored new things?
- **Consider intended majors and minors.** Are the areas of study you most want to pursue available at your current school as well as at the institution to which you might transfer? Is the program strong and robust? If you're a student who prefers face-to-face classes and avoids online classes, will you be able to enroll in the face-to-face classes you need and want?

- **Find out about research opportunities.** Many professors would love to involve students in research and collaboration that might lead to students becoming exposed to professional conferences and publishing.
- **Assess the underlying reasons for wanting to transfer.** Avoid transferring for boyfriends and girlfriends.
- **Consider your friendship circles.**
- **Consider the level of vibrancy of campus life.** This includes what exists in terms of extracurricular activities, including Greek life, intramural sports, clubs, etc. that might be meaningful and rewarding. Have you taken advantage of what is being offered? Try to explore if there are opportunities to assume leadership roles in clubs and activities to experience a sense of real contribution. How likely is it you can secure a good internship? Unless the only things you get to do are water plants and stuff envelopes, it's likely that the time spent in an internship will serve you well for making real-life, practical applications with theories in class, and it can help nurture connections for effective job seeking. Is there a great study abroad or study away experience available to you as a way to broaden your horizons?
- **Meditate.** Deep reflection assists in any decision-making process and keeps you calmer.
- **Consider counseling.** Reflect on how much of this struggle about transferring relates to the ways you think about making decisions and trusting the decisions you do make. If you don't work out the underlying reasons for wanting to transfer, you're likely to simply relocate your troubles.
- **Network.** Talk to alumni as well as older students at the school. Learn from them what shifted and made their experience better as time went on. Ask them for their guidance and tips and what they'd do over if they had the chance.

When I was in my first year at UW–Madison, despite my excitement about sociology, I still had it in my mind that I wanted to transfer to the School of Hotel Administration at Cornell University. I applied and was admitted. My parents put down a large deposit so I'd be able to secure a space and a room. At that age, I said what so many young people say—"I just want to work with people. I want to help people." It's well-intended but totally vague and meaningless. Everything will involve working with people in some capacity. At nineteen, I already knew how much I loved to travel and had the privilege, as an only child, to do that often with my parents. We stayed at historic and boutique hotels around the world. Throughout high school, I worked in hotels in Cleveland. I did my senior project in high school at the famous Broadmoor Resort in Colorado since my mother and I were joining my father on an extended business trip there. My parents pointed out to me that managing a luxurious resort someday would likely not carry with it the same allure and magic as traveling. But I didn't care. And after all, what did they know anyway, right?

In the early summer after my freshman year, I was set to go to Cornell. I had said goodbye to dear friends I already made in Madison and figured, even pre-social media (I know, I know, horror of horrors!), that we'd find a way to stay in touch and see each other. I wasn't yet overly connected and wedded to the university or to Madison itself. It held some appeal but I was clearly in limbo. I hadn't truly found my place yet so a move at that point felt doable. Plus, I figured I'd get to experience the prestige of saying I went to an Ivy and the best program for hospitality management. I'd surely be able to land a plum job at an amazing place. It all made sense. Sort of.

That summer, my mom and I regularly met up in the late afternoons to take long walks when she was done with work. We talked a lot about this idea of transferring and what it would mean for the present and for the future. In the meantime, one weekend, my dad took me to visit Cornell so we could see the campus and the dorm I was assigned and get a lay of the land. I met with an adviser and saw the schedule I'd have to take to be on track, and when I was truthful with myself, the classes barely interested me. Then, we stopped at the student center that was nothing like the Memorial Union at Madison, and I sat down on the steps and cried. My dad couldn't figure out what was happening and what went so terribly wrong. But I was too unhappy during that visit and couldn't shake it.

I came back from that visit, walked more with my mom, and she pointed out to me that it seemed like I was going to transfer for what appeared to be an endurance contest, for classes that in no way excited me, and with eyes set solely on post-college and not the experience of actually being there. She expressed concern that I was solely interested in the end result and not the process. I worried about telling my friends I was coming back, like I had gone back on my word or prematurely quit something. I knew Cornell had a thriving Greek life and though I had less than zero interest in joining, I figured I'd have to in order to make new friends as a transfer student. I was worried my parents wouldn't be able to get back the over $6,000 they had deposited. I think I wanted the sense of the present of what UW–Madison offered to me and the sense of the future that looked so promising if graduating from Cornell. But, of course, I couldn't have both.

On one of those walks with my mom, the craziest thing happened. I was wearing a red Wisconsin tank top, one I still wear thirty-six years later though threadbare, for all the good luck it seems to still provide. We were at a traffic light waiting to cross the street, and a woman we'd never seen before was in her car stopped at the light, and she rolled down the window and asked if I went to Wisconsin. I said I had gone there but not for long and was just about to transfer. The light turned green, and as she started to drive away, she yelled out: "Don't go! Wisconsin's the best!"

Neither my mom nor I had time to respond as the woman drove off. We always wished we had known her so we could properly thank her for that moment of perfect serendipity. She affirmed and validated what I felt down deep. Ultimately, I returned to Madison, and my sophomore year was my favorite part of college. I got heavily involved in arts programming for the university, World AIDS Day, and rallies for reproductive rights. I gave tours for prospective students, helped with orientation, exercised a lot, met my college boyfriend, developed closer bonds with friends, and became active in sociology, the very discipline that became my life's work. And though I had been consumed with the idea of being at the number one program for hotel and restaurant management, I instead found myself in the number one rated program for sociology. It all worked out. I probably would have made it work just fine had I gone to Cornell, but I'm glad I stayed and let myself enjoy the benefits of a true liberal arts education.

When it comes to deciding whether or not to transfer, there's usually not a right or a wrong answer. The tough thing is that you can't live out both choices, get to the end, and compare the outcomes; you have to pick one and trust it. Most people I know are happy with where they went to college and can look back on it fondly. There are probably multiple schools that could be a good match for each person. The reality is that it's a little like dating and wanting to be in a good relationship or eventual marriage. Is there just one right person for everyone, one true soulmate? Probably not. In a world this vast, there are likely a variety of people with whom we could partner, love and be loved, and enjoy a good life. Are some people better matched for us than others? Definitely. But we're not going to date and become involved in long-term relationships with millions of people across the globe to try everyone out.

At some point, all the fretting about transferring takes away from your ability to be in the present moment and awake to the experiences right in front of you, just as they are. Throughout life, we have to make the best decisions we can with the information we have at the time, and we cannot always know something for sure far into the future. There are no guarantees. The sooner you can stop the rattling noises in your head about the agony of if you should stay or transfer and trust your gut to decide what you want and can live with, the sooner you can "start where you are" (Pema Chödrön) and make the most of it.

Lesson 67: Determining If You Need to Request a Leave from School

In addition to considering transferring to another college, sometimes there are other reasons for leaving school, some of which are voluntary and others mandatory. These may include the necessity to consider a medical leave related to your physical and/or mental health, addiction and self-harm, a family-related leave because of a terminally ill parent or sibling or a significant death of someone like that, academic suspension, or other violation. While these situations can feel painful, shameful, and disorienting to students and parents alike, the opportunity to leave and get the support and resources one needs can wind up being a gift in the long run.

Often, when students take a break to access the help and support they desperately need, they can then heal and return with greater focus and drive. If the most basic pillars of a student's health, well-being, and success are structurally compromised and cause anxiety and despair, they're too preoccupied and overwhelmed with all of that to achieve the self-actualization that college affords.

Here's a useful analogy. For many years I worked as a counselor and clinical supervisor for abusers in domestic violence intervention programs, and sometimes we had clients who were active substance abusers as well. Before we could effectively work with them on their attitudes and behaviors in their relationships, we always urged them to first get clean and sober and return after that. Otherwise, they lacked a sturdy foundation from which to do the hard and necessary work of honestly and clearly reflecting on their violence and the effects that had on their partners and any children.

The same is true for students where there's cause for pause; when students are frequently absent, neglect to submit work, feel too depressed to get out of bed, or are otherwise not functioning well on a daily basis, they owe it to themselves (and older adults in supporting roles owe it to them, too) to first take care of their most basic and pressing needs and return to college when they can gain more from it and have more to contribute.

CHAPTER 15

FRIENDSHIPS AND RELATIONSHIPS

Lesson 68: Meeting New People Can Be Scary...Until They Become Your Friends for Life

"I get by with a little help from my friends."

—The Beatles

Friendship is incredibly important in college and as we age. For many, friends can feel like family, and if family dynamics are fraught with tension and competing demands, relationships with friends can provide an alternative source of support and comfort. Just like following a good diet, getting plenty of exercise, sleeping restfully, and reducing stress are significant for our short- and long-term health, so is friendship. Engagement in social life, being active and connected with others, and enjoying intimacy are equally important markers of good health. Friendships serve as a buffer from work and tensions in the larger world, etc. Friendships can help counter some of the loneliness and fear we feel and remind us that someone else in the world is looking out for us, is concerned, and will be there in a time of need.

Maintaining friendships from growing up, as well as maintaining friendships you make in college, will support your life and serve as an anchor. Our friends are like our memory banks, providing us with information about our past selves, dreams, and desires, and this can serve to keep us on track to pursue our passions, to chart our growth, and to develop future possibilities. Research on friendship tends to categorize and make a typology of different friendship groups. Broadly speaking, there are lifelong friends, best friends, good/close friends, and acquaintance-type friends. Of course, there might be overlap with these categories. These categories needn't imply a hierarchy of friendships where one is deemed more important than the other, where for example lifelong friends are somehow better than friends from activities we do in our daily lives. Rather, it's helpful to remember that each category of friendship—and the personalities of our various friends—can serve different purposes and functions and fulfill different emotional needs, all of which can nourish and sustain us.

We benefit from friends on all levels—friends with whom we share a history, akin to sibling relationships who anchor us to our early years; friends who have known the major players in our lives and have been with us through life's major ups and downs; and friends we can enjoy doing certain activities with, where perhaps the conversation is less intimate but where there's fun and laughter in doing something that counters isolation, for example, exercising, eating, or watching a movie together. Friendships can provide us with a person to help us think things through, for doing activities with us that can be more fun in the company of another person, and for challenging us to become the best versions of ourselves. Through intimate relationships, including friendships, we learn a great deal about ourselves and our wants and needs. This helps serve us in other relationships as well. We might benefit from learning something new from a friend—perhaps something to do with the other person's culture, religion, or political viewpoints. With a friend, hopefully, we can be more open and ask and answer questions more honestly, even about touchy subjects. This can lead to vulnerability, openness, and growth. Enjoying a diverse group of friends at the various levels of friendship alluded to above is healthy. The problem comes when a person becomes overly reliant on one person to fulfill what a variety of friends could and should provide.

Some of us may know people who have tons of friends but even in a case like that, that person likely feels super close to only some of them and maybe even just a few of them. In addition, friendships can emerge and be sustained online. For some people, those friendships spring from social groups or acquaintances or even online support groups. Indeed, some of us have had the experience of becoming close to someone through email and social media with the hope and intention to eventually meet in person.

Consider carefully who you become friends with and who you can trust. One way to decrease your overall isolation in school is to forge community with people who help you to hold yourself to the highest standard possible and where you feel like you're learning, growing, and liking who you are more than ever. In working with Cody for all four years he was in college and enjoying a friendship with him since his graduation in 2016, I've had the unique pleasure of knowing his friendship circle, and much to my delight, all of them were my students as well. Cody had a best guy friend in college and their three dearest friends were women with whom they remained platonic and are close to this day. Their tight circle always reminds me of something out of a movie or the romantic vision of enduring college friendship that so many of us hold. Their loyalty to each other and their great love for each other is the real deal, and it's refreshing the way that Cody looks back on their time together in college, recognizing the positive influence it had on him. Particularly special is the way that Cody regards these friends as family he got to choose, as I've always loved hearing that sentiment from students over the years:

"My friends and I made it somewhat of a tradition to either go out to, or cook, dinner together once a week or just have movie nights in the dorm to spend time together. The sense of family that came with that helped ease the stress of academic life. It was those simple things that always made it easier to refocus and get through the week. Alcohol got in the way at times, being able to obtain it at any time, especially when stressed, led to bad decisions a few times. I'm thankful though that my closer friends didn't drink much which helped keep me away from it."

When it comes to friendship, my best advice for you is to prepare to be surprised. Start up a conversation with strangers because they may become your friends. It might even start by asking for help. In fact, this is how I met one of my dearest college friends. We were sitting next to each other in carrels in a study room in the basement of our residence hall. I asked the woman next to me if she took French because I had a question about my homework. I had tested into third semester French, and as it happened and lucky for me, she had tested into fourth semester French. She was able to answer my question, and then we proceeded to ask each other's names and where we were from. Laura had come to Wisconsin from Toledo, Ohio and I was born and raised in Cleveland, just a couple hours apart. She asked where in Cleveland, and when I told her I had attended Shaker Heights High School, she laughed because her mother had graduated from there. That was the first night of hundreds that we spent talking, laughing, and hanging out together. Quickly, we became inseparable. We got to know each other's parents who became like extended families for us. And it turned out that our parents knew some of the same people. Twenty years later, long after my parents were divorced and my mother was re-partnered with my stepdad in Massachusetts, we learned that Laura's mother was friends with my stepdad's sister in Florida. I'm sharing all this to say that the world is small, and when you get to know people you often encounter connectivity that will surprise and delight you. But it requires a certain amount of openness, risk, and sharing. In reality though, this is how the sweetest connections can begin.

Sometimes college friendships, like any friendships, emerge from an unusual interaction or a bizarre set of circumstances. And perhaps we find ourselves leaving a less than desirable impression on another person, or they on us. Take for example how I met one of my favorite people on the planet, a man named Tom I met in my first semester of college. Let's just say he initially left me with a most unsavory impression of himself. We didn't know each other at all but found ourselves getting hot drinks in the dining hall one night after dinner. Rather than use a serving utensil, he dug his bare hand in the bowl of miniature marshmallows and scooped out a handful to plunk on top of his hot cocoa. Standing at barely 5'3" and he at 6'3" and built like the football player he was, I looked up at him, glaring nastily, and all I could muster was, "Oh my god, that's so disgusting," and I walked away. I assumed that anyone doing that was not just gross but also not that smart. You can imagine what Tom was muttering about me!

Fast forward a few months later and we found ourselves at the same large table for dinner; as it turned out, we shared mutual friends who were eating together and had us each join them. I came to learn that this big, tall, strong guy had an even bigger heart and was more like a teddy bear underneath it all and was enrolled in one of the university's most challenging majors: chemical engineering. He came to learn that while simultaneously a neurotic germaphobe who knew how to speak my mind, I indeed had a capacity for kindness and was pretty nonjudgmental with my friends. Thirty-seven years later, and Tom remains one of my most brilliant and treasured friends. And funny enough, he wound up with a hugely successful career in, of all things, food safety, specializing in sanitary design of processing and packaging equipment for the top food corporations in the country and slathers on Purell just like I do! I learned from this that we can't judge someone that quickly, and that when we're open enough and take a chance to get to know someone, they can surprise us.

Lesson 69: Surround Yourself with People Who Believe in You and Your Potential

When we feel supported, we tend to thrive. And we're more likely to take risks for our own growth and well-being when we trust that people who care for us are rooting for us. You'll benefit from having a posse of people including but not limited to family members, friends, professors, coaches, etc. These are people you can rely on to listen, cheer you on, challenge you with questions that help keep you on track, call bullshit when necessary, and hold you to the highest possible standards. They believe in you and want the best for you and will say the hard things to help you get out of your own way.

Lesson 70: The Best Relationships Are Drama-Free

Students share a lot with me about their relationships, and I'm often hearing about how they're filled with drama, drama, drama that to them feels natural and almost inescapable. They report constant arguing, feeling jealous, not feeling trusted by the other person, and feeling anxious overall. They've normalized all this, assuming this level of angst might just be the natural course of things in a long-term relationship. They think that by sticking it out they will be more heroic. Women students, in particular, are often determined to think they can help a boyfriend or change him.

I try to counter these sentiments by saying things like, "If a relationship is this hard now, imagine later on when things are hard in life with jobs, kids, bills, homes, extended families, etc. What do you think of being in a relationship that so often leaves you feeling this unsteady and uneasy?" I try to get students thinking about and questioning these things and their overall assumptions about relationships, and one of the main ones is something we've all heard which is the idea that relationships take work. I'll try to show you what I show them which is that dating and intimate relationships need not be work, and that the best ones are more play than anything else.

When I hear that relationships require so much work, I feel weighed down and tired, don't you? It sounds like drudgery. Work implies something we *have* to do, especially in order to achieve some sort of desired outcome for the short and long term. We work for money, for the hope of success, and for getting ahead. If we're lucky, we may find meaning through our work and feel valued for doing it. Work typically contains aspects of control and hierarchy and often power struggles and resentment. At work, we're often inundated with, and constrained by, rules, procedures, and guidelines; we're motivated by outcomes and deliverables. Relationships that feel like work drain our energy. This is because we're spending a great deal of time trying to get through to the other person in order to feel understood.

On the other hand, play implies freedom, experimentation, adventure, spontaneity, and creativity. The play I'm talking about is not to be confused with all easiness and just fun and games, but rather the quality of ease. It's the ease of trust, comfort, calm, and a sense of knowing and being known. It's the knowledge that you're assuming the best in the other person and the confidence that they assume the best in you. When that happens, there's less to struggle over and less to prove.

One thing I observe in women students that has been true for decades is the number of them who impose a lot of pressure on themselves and their dating partners about the future. Often, women have decided in advance, even if they're single, the age at which they want to be married and have children. At age twenty-one or twenty-two, they start to feel rushed and frenzied wondering how it will be possible to do all they want and find the right person before their mid to late twenties. I try to remind them to not rush their lives away and to keep in mind how their thoughts on marriage and children might shift over time.

Relationships that resemble play have the advantage of feeling lighter, freeing, and more spacious. We get to reconnect with our authentic selves, even our sense of our inner child. A huge benefit to a playful relationship is that it tends to be built on affection and admiration, rather than contempt, jealousy, and control so our time and energy can be directed to other things that matter to us in our lives, and we can return to rest in the trustworthiness of the relationship. My hope is that you'll get to experience these qualities in your relationships both in college and far beyond.

Lesson 71: Long-Distance Relationships

Some students enter college with their heart somewhere else, perhaps because the other person has remained in their hometown or chosen to attend another college, and some students may meet someone special online, through friends, or in the course of traveling. A long-distance relationship isn't inherently "more work" but it certainly demands something different of the people in it, especially in terms of trust and a higher tolerance for time alone, for example.

The main thing to honestly reflect on is how much you want to be both here and there, mentally and physically. Leaving on weekends for visits, or having someone visit for short bursts of intense time, may be satisfying to some people but not necessarily at all stages of their lives. It's worth weighing if college is a sustainable time for this or if it pulls you too far afield from the present moment experience of your campus.

Lesson 72: How to Deal with Parental Reactions to Your Dating Life

Maybe you're not swept up in hookup culture and instead find yourself in a dating relationship. Often, students anticipate their parents won't approve of whom they're dating, often leaving them feeling increasingly isolated and torn between family and peers. This is a perennial issue. Before introducing your favorite person to your family, you might want to remind your parents of this:

- Years ago, you, too, were young and crazy in love, often unable and unwilling to listen to your parents about love, sex, and relationships.
- Being in a relationship is proving to be a great way to get to know myself much better, and to grow and stretch. I need the opportunity to do this and to clarify my own needs, interests, values and priorities in intimate relationships.
- Like other adult children, I yearn for some amount of parental approval and acceptance.
- Like many adult children, I may come to recognize that you were right about these issues but please refrain from saying, "See, I told you so."

I want to share a story with you that brings this home. A young woman came to my office to let me know her absences were due to being diagnosed with genital herpes. She went on to say that she'd only had this one boyfriend, lost her virginity to him, and her mother never wanted her to date him. Consequently, she was hesitant to tell her mother anything and worried about needing health care and medication. I sat and listened, held space for her, and then gave her many resources and contacts so she could get help; but all the while I knew her shame was a direct result of her perceptions of maternal judgment which would remain a big obstacle for her.

- Please check at the door any prejudice, bias, racism, religious beliefs, homophobia, biphobia, and transphobia.
- Get curious about why I find this person I'm involved with as special as I do.
- Please don't make threats toward me about my dating choices or attempt to withhold things from me to force me to break up with this person. This will likely alienate me, and if we continue dating, I'm less likely to share with you if and when I encounter any problems and truly need your help and support.
- I might wind up in a study abroad program and fall in love and want to remain there for the summer or move back there after graduation. You may have hoped I'd live nearby or at least an easy drive or plane trip away and not across the world. But I might crave an unusual life in a faraway place. I might need to live out these questions now and at least try this journey. I might come back—or you might get a fabulous new place to visit if you stay open to this.
- Please keep an open mind. You might see me in a new way and can witness a newfound happiness and sense of peace wash over me.
- If you notice things that confirm your suspicions and worries be sure to distinguish how much of that is simply a self-fulfilling prophecy and how much is accurate, and then approach me without criticism. If you think I'm being abused in any way, then it's definitely time to let me know and to be proactive, but be gentle with me.
- I may share with you a problem in my relationship or I might want feedback about something, but please don't use that as an excuse to judge me and my boyfriend or girlfriend or to hold a grudge against them forever.
- Please resist the urge and tendency to fantasize and worry far into the future.

CHAPTER 16

THE TETHERED STUDENT

Lesson 73: Honestly Evaluate Your Social Media Presence

Think about creating a responsible social media presence that has integrity, and aim for what closely mirrors who you are and aspire to be in real life. The implications of this are vast, both for your personal and professional lives.

Young women tend to hypersexualize themselves on social media thinking it will make them more dateable and desirable, yet doing this comes with many risks they're not always thinking about or prepared for when engaging in these sorts of curated, filtered, and sexualized performances. I've had numerous students who participate in this hypersexualization, with some working in local strip clubs to make extra spending money, getting jobs at Hooters, and developing liaisons with much older men known as sugar daddies where they serve as escorts or engage in sexual activity as a way to defray the costs of college. Of course, the trouble is that these risky behaviors and the emotional toll they ultimately take on young women wind up being even more costly on so many levels.

In a globalized economy heavily reliant on the internet and where it's so easy for people to obtain so much data about us, it's crucial to think about what we're projecting to the outside world. While there's much information that surfaces over which we have no control, it's worth evaluating that which we can choose and be sure it's what reflects our authentic self and our core values.

Lesson 74: Got a Complaint?— Pause Before You Text Your Parents

Societal crises in which students like you have come of age certainly have not helped make the process of growing up and letting go any easier. Emerging as young children soon after 9/11, you're defined as a generation of students who have been largely "overparented" (Lythcott-Haims, 2016) in a "culture of fear" (Glassner, 2018) where the worries range from post 9/11 culture to school shootings. Conversations about safety and protection have dominated how you've come of age. It's understandable if and when you've internalized some of this fear, distress, worry, and panic. We know that students like you are far more tethered to technology and less comfortable with solitude yet by virtually all accounts are lonelier and feeling more awkward in their own skin. Psychologist Jean Twenge's term for your generation is iGen (2018). Growing up hyper-scheduled with so much already engineered for you, it's no wonder if and when you demonstrate less ease and fluency with creative risk-taking and semi-structured or unstructured assignments that demand curiosity and original, critical thinking.

Yours is a generation of students in college understandably aching to let go and generally not knowing how to do this. Every student I meet wants to embody and live out the ethos articulated by Kathryn Feltey earlier in the book in which she said, "I am leaving my childhood behind as I search for my life and who I will be" and yet they're often feeling rigidly confined and stuck. Your generation might have the most to gain from breaking away from families of origin to begin anew yet you're being subjected to greater surveillance because of the myriad ways that parents have more ready access to what's happening on campus in real time.

I witness firsthand as students struggle to individuate from families of origin, eager to make their own choices, follow their own passions, discover their own values; most wish for parents who will be present and supportive along the journey but not judgmental, neglectful, intrusive or smothering. I will tell you what I tell them: you play a crucial role in how your parents respond and the extent of their involvement by more carefully thinking through what you share, how you articulate your grievances, and what you expect and hope for from them.

One way in which the current landscape of higher education looks different than it did years ago is what I have come to see as a symbiotic relationship between students and parents; that is, we can see the extent to which students are going to college both together and apart from their parents in significant ways. We've seen rapid transformation in technology and in the ways that shapes identity and interaction both on campus and between young people and their parents.

Parents are indeed taking to social media in record numbers to seek support as they navigate with you through this confusing maze between high school and college. Many universities offer parent listservs while Facebook showcases parent-run discussion pages reaching hundreds of thousands of members addressing a wide variety of issues. How might you respond if you found out that your parents reposted to your school's parent group on Facebook a screenshot that you had sent to them when you were complaining about something at school? Would you be surprised, embarrassed, angry, happy, or upset with them that they took your rant and made it their own, asking for advice from other newbie and seasoned parents? Let's unpack this, shall we?

On these Facebook pages, some parents have even taken to orchestrating their students' social lives. Let's say it's your parent who posted this and you share the same last name; what might be your reaction to being set up for a playdate?

"SEEKING FRIENDS FOR FRESHMAN DAUGHTER: I figured if my daughter can't seem to find girls to hang out with, maybe I could help. If your daughter needs someone to watch Netflix, go to the gym, shop or just hang out and talk, PLEASE, PLEASE PM ME…maybe we can get them together."

In another group, a father posted a photo that his daughter had texted him; all one could see were her short shorts, her bare thighs, her hand, and a right-handed desk. He was outraged on her behalf that he's paying for a university experience and the classroom she was in to take a test didn't have enough left-handed desks. A mother declared that she was going to serve as her "son's secretary," a title she proudly gave herself so she could regularly access the online learning management system to log all due dates and send him reminders and weekly printouts. She was adamant it was the only way to help him bring up his GPA given his ADHD. Another mother wrote that she desperately needed to find a ride for her son for the weekend. Another posted that her daughter was doing research for a psychology class, needed respondents for a survey, and hoped other parents would participate. Another mother was angry that the school didn't provide rides to and from the hospital when her daughter was sick and asked how her daughter could possibly get to medical appointments. Other parents expressed impatience and frustration with professors who aren't meeting all their expectations or awarding the grades they want their children to have.

Do you notice in these examples how one seemingly simple text or complaint from a student leads to a domino effect where some parents become overly worked up and start a virtual feeding frenzy among other parents? In these moments, I trust parents have good intentions, want the best for you, and are trying to show compassion for your experience. Yet at the same time, by engaging like this and egging others on, they're fueling their own negativity and yours in such a way that leaves everyone taking a more adversarial stance than the situation usually warrants. On these groups that aren't anonymous and rather easily accessible, it's all too easy for your privacy as students to be violated. The worst example of this creates safety concerns, and that's when parents post photos revealing the name of the residence hall where their student lives and even go so far as to mention room numbers. Having frank conversations about your expectations for boundaries is crucial for your own adulting.

Students often rely on their parents to solve problems, even from miles away at college, and many parents are capitulating to every demand, no matter how big or small. But here's the thing. If you send a screenshot of undercooked chicken in the dining hall or a complaint about how the soy milk and almond milk were never replenished, there's nothing parents can do to fix it, especially states away. Most importantly, it's better for you, as students right there in the midst of the lived experience, to approach dining hall staff in person to ask questions and make requests.

This screenshot culture in which students send pictures to parents or post on social media documenting every little and big thing is stealing something important from you. And that is the skill to continually strengthen your self-advocacy muscle to initiate and follow through with communication on your own, in a way that has integrity and humanity and is not simply rant-like or passive-aggressive online.

Generally speaking, students want to vent and move on, and parents want to fix things and linger a bit until they're sure everything is better. But when you indulge your parents in constant play-by-plays of what's happening on campus, it winds up being counterproductive both for your ability to do what you're there to do in college and for the overall well-being of both you and your parents.

Parents who remain deep in the mix in college, knowing everything about what's going on at all times, may have good intentions but the result is one in which young people become less and less comfortable, secure, and confident in finding out answers for themselves, relying on their own inner resources, and advocating for themselves. In the short term, the parent might be helpful and the student might appreciate it, but in the long run, it's damaging. I see the effects of this every semester. We have a generation of college students who aren't coming of age in college by themselves and with their peers. Rather, much of the experience is mediated by parents who seem to think they, too, are enrolled in college. This is evident even early on in conversations about preparing for college when a parent says, "*We're* applying to ______," or when asked which residential halls their student ranked as their top choices on their housing application, they say: "*We* like ______ and *we* hope *we* get ______." It's great when parents are part of the cheering squad. The problem is such blurry boundaries that it's like the student and parent are going to college together. Part of the point of college is for students to see the world larger than themselves and to cultivate a sense of independence and agency to make a difference.

The more neutral your parents are able to remain about classes and professors, the food, and anything related to campus life, the better for everyone and for reducing aggravation. It's normal that you'll freak out about stuff, and it's normal for parents to freak out in return and glom onto anything they're told, no matter how partial and decontextualized it might be. But the more upset and agitated your parents become, the more the focus is on the distress in the context of how expensive college is and if one is getting their money's worth, and the more you'll experience negative self-talk and hostility.

The more you conceptualize your role as a student in a learning process, rather than as a customer in a transaction, the better off you'll be, and if you can help your parents see this too, the better off they'll be. Trust me when I say, after more than thirty years of teaching, that the customer service attitude in higher education is driving out amazing educators and creating lower education.

Even though parental involvement is highly encouraged throughout elementary school, junior high, and high school, and parents who know what's going on in those years tend to have children who succeed, this simply isn't a thing in college. Professors cannot be involved with parents, and for good reason. And there's even federal law that backs that up known as FERPA (Family Educational Rights and Privacy Act, similar to HIPAA in the medical arena). Faculty like me want to engage with students like you as young adults and encourage your own self-efficacy. We'll be thrilled to celebrate with you and your family as you dance across the graduation stage, and we love it when students introduce us and want pictures together.

The moral of the story here is if you want to end the negative spin cycle, hit the pause button before asking your parents to solve a problem for you.

Lesson 75: Practice Disconnecting to Reconnect

"I won't tell you how you gotta be
You're old enough to make a choice
It's just that in between all the words on the screen
I doubt you'll ever hear a human voice"

—James McMurtry, "Walk Between the Raindrops"

My student, Jillian, told me, "The pandemic made my anxious and nonsocial self extremely more anxious and nonsocial because I don't know how to talk to people or strangers. I don't know how to make friends or how to start up a conversation. I don't even know how to small talk. It has kept me small minded." I'm not so sure we can blame all of that on the pandemic though. The thing is that pre-pandemic interactions and conditions paved the way for pandemic and post-pandemic ones. In fact, in 2012 on a TED stage, the social psychologist Sherry Turkle shared this alarming story: "An eighteen-year-old boy who uses texting for almost everything says to me wistfully, 'Someday, someday, but certainly not now, I'd like to learn how to have a conversation.' " The title of that talk was "Connected, but Alone?" and her book that came out a year before that is titled *Alone Together*. Surely, Turkle was onto something juxtaposing words like connected, alone, and together. It turns out her insights were prophetic in terms of articulating a certain agony around this social psychological paradox: feeling lonely in a hyperconnected world.

Similarly, in the past ten years, I've been working with more and more students who report struggling with social anxiety and loneliness, who have little to no understanding of what healthy intimacy and healthy solitude might look like, and whose parents are more perched on their shoulders than ever before. I regularly talk with students about the connections between technology, the self, identity, friendships and intimate relationships, and the larger society. Many students claim they sleep and shower with their phones, that they consider them "warm blankets" for "safety" and "security" and "to be sure they don't miss anything." Nicole told me she often rejects social plans with friends in favor of "staying in with my phone." Greta referred to her phone saying, "It's my baby! In fact, I even dress it up in new cases with different designs." All of this perfectly captures what Turkle so aptly refers to as "intimacy with our machines."

Students reveal to me that any time they have a feeling, especially a negative one, they reach for their phones rather than reaching inward. I try to remind them that sometimes we'll be sad, and that's okay and part of life. I remind them that feelings come and go, and the way that we feel in one moment isn't the way we're going to feel forever. It's crucial to discern when to rely on technology to communicate and when not to. For example, students need to learn how to handle difficult or painful conversations, like a breakup, through actual talking. It's in those risky, vulnerable moments that depth of connection can be felt with others.

What deeply saddens me is seeing a generation of young people, with seemingly so much to offer and so much to gain from peers and older adults, shy away from opportunities mainly because they admit to feeling ill-equipped to handle those interactions. While I find it heartbreaking and do everything in my power to help my own students conquer this, I certainly get why they're finding it so hard, and why you might as well. A generation like yours—that emerged from contrived playdates arranged by parents and who later become tweens and teens saturated in social media and nestled in a highly divisive and alienating culture—were bound to have these issues. It's the rare student who comes to college these days feeling relatively at ease approaching people face-to-face, talking on the phone, and sending clear written communication. The thing to remember is that no one is born knowing how to do any of this. This is good news as it means these are learned behaviors that can be practiced and fine-tuned.

While many students convey a deep fear of missing out on something—anything—there's a small number of students, more typically young men, who report that they barely check their phones, and those students describe it as "liberating." Noteworthy is this connection between gender and social media. Social media generates a great deal of envy and a sense of inadequacy that often emerges around body image and perceptions of attractiveness, leading young women to be particularly vulnerable to the intense weight of these impossible beauty standards, leaving them feeling worse about themselves and more isolated in their feelings.

When I went away to college, it was in the days when people had Walkmans, where you could listen to the radio or a cassette tape with a headset that had soft foam padding over the earpieces. You might think of it like the 1988 version of Bluetooth headphones and Apple music but with only one artist on that lonesome cassette tape. I thought it was cool to be able to walk around listening to music, and I happily blasted Fleetwood Mac, Elton John, and Tracy Chapman. But when my parents dropped me off at college, my mother warned me, "Don't walk around campus with those headphones on." At the time, I didn't appreciate what she was trying to tell me. It turns out she had been observing students everywhere moving about alone with headphones on, and she was concerned how I'd get to know people if I did that. It turns out her warning was prophetic as I now look around on my campus and others I visit and see young people buried in their phones. Even the expression "in their phones" is telling for how absorbing and constraining this activity can be even when, and especially when, it often gives us so little in return. Yet, college is about looking up, waking up, and paying attention. It turns out these are prerequisites for a more fulfilling life.

Relentless tethering has a significant impact on people's ability to have and enjoy solitude as well as intimacy. Logan told me:

"I think one of the worst habits I've picked up is recording events that are taking place. A number of events are stored on my phone and, in many cases looking back on it, I feel that I didn't even see it with my own eyes. I feel as if capturing the moment on my phone took priority over actually being part of the moment and enjoying it. I felt the need to be able to share it with my 'friends' on social media and think that in the future, whether it be concerts or sporting events, I'll be leaving my phone in the car."

Logan's friend, Tyler, agreed:

"Speaking of being tethered and isolating myself, just a few nights ago I went out to eat with my friends and half the time we were at the restaurant I was constantly checking my phone; in fact, I was too busy checking my own to even notice if anyone else had been looking at theirs. For some parts of the conversation I just gave short replies or nods to the conversation because I was missing what was actually being said."

Another student Caroline told me, "My attention is broken. I can't even watch a full-length movie. My sister and I tried to see one over the weekend and when it ended we realized we hadn't been watching it and had no idea just how long we had been scrolling on our phones." Logan, Tyler, and Caroline prompt us to at least consider occasionally ditching our phones for the gift of the present moment, perhaps when enjoying a meal, a movie, or a long drive with another person.

As we can see through stories like these, students are often overly tethered to technology which can result in an impoverishment of the imagination and disconnection from the things and people we most cherish. As individuals, we have so much to lose from this and our society even more still.

Take a moment to evaluate the impact of all of this on your sense of autonomy and freedom. Do you screenshot everything? Are your parents involved in tracking? Does life feel like one big post? How tethered must we be? How tethered do we *want* to be?

Maybe you can try to turn off your phone at night. Maybe you can leave it in your room and socialize without it. Think about how much you rely on it for the sake of safety, or the illusion of safety, both physically and emotionally. Does it deliver all it promises to? How can you deliver more to yourself without it?

Lesson 76: It's About Time—The Importance of Calendars, Schedules, Routines, and Spontaneity

In today's world, the experience of being tethered to technology is connected to how we experience time and how we structure our days. Students have many more options available to them for managing this than those who attended college more than a decade ago. Regardless of the methods available or employed, the human struggle remains the same, which is wrestling with how we want to spend our time and structure our days.

Before starting a new school year, consider what sort of organizing tool you'll use to keep track of appointments, meetings, due dates, exam dates, and other commitments that are extracurricular and social. There are numerous electronic ways of organizing, and a paper calendar still remains a terrific tool. Experiment until you find what's right for you. It's helpful to ask your friends, older siblings, aunts and uncles, family friends, and anyone else you can think of, about some of the strategies, tips, and tricks they use that work well. Gather information and take aspects that might work best for you. Don't feel funny about asking. How we keep ourselves organized and motivated, and how we get stuff done, is the subject of so many books, articles and businesses. It's the stuff of life and something we're all continuing to learn.

Related to this is that the more you learn to "chunk" or "block" your time, the more effective you can be. This involves thinking of time in shorter, more manageable frames so that when you're working, you can be most productive, and when you're playing, you can truly have fun and let go. It's important to not over-emphasize things that feed into the mindset of busy culture where busyness gets tied into feelings of self-worth. As necessary as it is to mindfully structure our days, it's equally valuable to have time to pause, reflect, get still, and touch down into our deepest wellsprings of creativity, flow, and joy.

The habits you develop in college will likely reverberate throughout your lives. We know this to be true with habits that get in the way such as binge drinking and how students who do this are more likely to struggle with alcoholism and other addictions after college. The same is true for good habits—these can blossom into survival skills for life. Perhaps it's daily meditation, journaling, exercising, or organizing—any of these habits can serve you well during college and far beyond.

College gives you newfound freedom to get to make your own schedule. For example, it's not unusual or inherently bad to stay up until two or three a.m. and to wake up at eleven a.m., but it might be better to not make a habit of it every day, and mainly because so much decreased daytime, especially in the winter months, can be depressing. Freedom to craft your days and your life as you wish is truly one of the best parts of college. In thinking back to what he loved most about college, Cody said, "I loved the freedom. The freedom to choose who I wanted to be, the freedom to choose who I wanted to be friends with, who I wanted to work with, if I wanted to attend class. It was refreshing to feel like I could finally make my own decisions about things."

When thinking about your schedule, try to lay out everything you're intending to do in order to visualize the big picture and any implications of these choices. For example, are you enrolling in four or five classes, and might you choose a section that is taught at a time in better synch with the rhythms of your particular body? Are you intending to get a job and/or internship, play a sport, join a club or fraternity or sorority, assume a leadership role in a student organization, or stay connected with a long-distance boyfriend or girlfriend with plans to visit each other once or twice a month? How will all of this fit together in a way that helps you craft the most satisfying life possible? Almost everything takes much longer than you think and hope it will, but it's not a race, so try to enjoy the process.

When thinking about these issues of striking a good balance and using your time well, consider whether or not getting a job during the academic year is a must. If you don't need a job financially, it might be best not to have one at first and instead use the time to get acclimated to the campus community and involved in the surrounding environment. However, a work-study job on campus can help defray costs and provide students with valuable connections. It's worth noting that for many of us, the more we do, the more we get done, and juggling school, work, and a social life can be a way for students to engage in social connection, project management, time management, collaboration, leadership-building, self-reflection, and goal-setting.

CHAPTER 17

THE MIND/BODY CONNECTION

Lesson 77: The College Mental Health Crisis Has Been a Long Time in the Making

These days we speak about mental health issues among young people as though it's a relatively brand-new phenomenon that urgently needs to be addressed. People are quick to blame the pandemic in particular, as well as technology and anything else they can think of for why this is so. Much has been done to remove the stigma surrounding mental health issues. As a result, it should come as no surprise that young people are more vocal about their struggles than ever before, whether that comes in the form of TikTok videos about their state of mind or announcing to a whole class that they're bipolar or attempted suicide in high school.

In 2004, Richard Kadison, the now former Chief of the Mental Health Service at Harvard University Health Services, sounded the alarm about this in his groundbreaking book, *The College of the Overwhelmed: The Campus Mental Health Crisis and What to Do About It.* In it, he stated: "If your son or daughter is in college, the chances are almost one in two that he or she will become depressed to the point of being unable to function; one in two that he or she will have regular episodes of binge drinking (with the resulting significant risk of dangerous consequences such as sexual assault and car accidents); and one in ten that he or she will seriously consider suicide. In fact, since 1988, the likelihood of a college student's suffering depression has doubled, suicidal ideation has tripled, and sexual assaults have quadrupled."

Kadison wrote that more than twenty years ago, so it's safe to say that what we're seeing on campus then is actually not that new. This isn't to minimize or deny the current problems which are felt in a real way but rather it's to provide a framework and perspective for understanding the magnitude and depth of what has been unfolding. Did the pandemic improve mental health? Obviously not. Does social media help people feel better about how they look in a bathing suit? That would get the big nope. The point here is that things like the pandemic and much of social media are sure to have not made things better in regards to people struggling with mental health issues but nor is it the case that these are *the* sole culprits of the problem either.

I remember walking back to my office after teaching a late class and finding a student of mine in the stairwell, rocking back and forth and sobbing, with her knees pressed up against her chest, her arms wrapped around her legs, and there was blood coming from her arms; she had been cutting. I remember a young man I had in class who came to see me about a paper grade and proceeded to bang his fists on the table and raise his voice, and when I asked him to leave, he slammed a series of doors on his way out. There was the young woman who approached me right before class the first week of school to tell me she was sorry she didn't come prepared but she had just been raped. There was the young woman who had been homeless, had an eating disorder, and had been assaulted. I can still see her face, remember her name. Hell, I remember all the faces and names of students who shared these sorts of things.

As I type all this horror and pain, it's as though a movie is playing on rewind in my head tracking back through a long career of hundreds of encounters and disclosures like this. If you weren't reading a book about the entirety of the college experience, you might understandably conclude that the setting about which I write is a psychiatric hospital or some other sort of community healthcare center or outpatient treatment facility. In fact, on many days I feel like I'm running triage.

Of course, not all faculty hear about this extent of what students are struggling with; the research shows that typically women faculty bear the burden of this emotional labor more than their male counterparts and those of us teaching about topics that overlap with our students' lived experiences are more bound to hear these brutal stories. While a campus is fertile ground for things like depression and anxiety, it's also the case that many students come with those problems and are exposed to new ways of seeing them in their coursework that then can open up old wounds. Nevertheless, the vast majority of students report feeling grateful to have learned about those issues. I find myself honored to be on their path toward the healing that comes from this kind of learning and going with them to their farthest edge while trying to make sure they don't fall off.

Lesson 78: Destigmatizing Mental Health Issues Has Promise and Carries Unintended Consequences

In recent years, I've certainly noticed more of a trend of student disclosure that is not accompanied by the same level of intensity as it once had. Whereas years ago, students would struggle to tell and resisted labels, now I see increasingly where students seem relatively unaffected by the process of telling, they do so with little to no previously established rapport, they're often hungry to be diagnosed, and they embrace the medicalization of mental health issues. With students' self-presentations increasingly managed and curated via public media platforms, some of this is unsurprising.

Another challenge we are faced with is the unintended consequence of the de-stigmatization of mental health issues. It's certainly a positive thing that it carries less stigma and isn't so cloaked in shame, secrets, and silence. However, the problem is that more and more students are coming forth and saying they have something, anything, or that they want a diagnosis.

When students have a single question about an assignment, the common refrain is: "I'm totally stressed and confused." The language used by students, particularly women students who are generally more vocal about their feelings to professors and to parents, tends to be heightened, dramatic, and decontextualized, leaving parents understandably even more worried than they might already be. For example, students don't report that they're sad, they say they're "totally depressed." They're not concerned. They have "anxiety." They're not nervous about a test. They're having "panic attacks." They're not tired and worn down. They're "completely exhausted" and having "a mental breakdown." They're not finding that today is just a bad day. They have decided, "F*ck my life, shoot me now." But feeling sad is perfectly normal. Now, I see students extrapolate that if they're sad, this means, "I'm struggling with depression. My mental health isn't good right now." And they proceed to talk in terms of "my mental health" in ways that make it seem like it's something outside of themselves and akin to a pet that needs tending.

Coming of age at a cultural moment in which talk of mental health and self-care is pervasive means that students are more aware of these issues which, on the surface, is a positive step. They're well aware that there's a larger culture that's concerned, yet they're also individual agents acting on these societal messages. When I get a dozen emails in the span of a couple days all falling immediately before and on a due date for class work, and each email mentions depression, anxiety, breakdowns, and issues with psychotropic medication, I'm not only concerned about my students' well-being but I'm increasingly concerned about the cultural messages swirling around that they're capitalizing on that appear to render them more helpless and out of control than actually self-empowered. They've heard they need to prioritize their mental health and they're asserting this in a highly individualistic, untouchable, yet public way; however, when I ask what they're doing to work on this, the answer is typically nothing. For years, there was a time right around midterms when educators would speak of the week of the dying grandparents as a slew of students would produce excuses related to dying and dead grandparents. More recently, those excuses have been eclipsed by often long, drawn out emails referencing "my mental health."

I've spent decades teaching in a way that prioritizes emotional intelligence alongside intellectual rigor, and I've built my teaching around an ethic of care for the whole of the student so I hope you can appreciate the ways in which these aren't meant to be flip, callous statements minimizing the distress many students feel. Rather I'm gravely concerned about students with the most severe psychological issues not getting the help and intervention they need, and especially those who present public safety issues on campus.

When students do try to seek help on campus, the tricky part is that most college counseling services are severely short-staffed and under-resourced. This predated the pandemic, and the pandemic didn't make things easier by any means. Though the American School Counselor Association recommends a ratio of 250 students per one counselor, this is not at all what's happening in practice and in fact at many institutions the ratio is far worse with well over 400 students, and sometimes closer to a thousand students per counselor. For this reason and others, some students express interest in seeing a therapist off campus but unfortunately cite parents as the single most major impediment to this. This isn't necessarily even because they feel their parents did anything wrong but more about their reluctance to tell their parents what's going on because they still rely on their parents' health insurance. Having frank discussions with your parents about health insurance and how to seek good quality care will go a long way.

Students report that when their parents are well aware of struggles they faced in high school such as depression, anxiety, addiction, eating disorders, self-harm, or an abusive dating relationship, they're even more reticent to let their parents know of ongoing issues and struggles. When parents were unaware of issues in high school, students are especially concerned about worrying their parents, they're afraid their parents' perception of them will change for the worse, and they tend to be protective of their parents' potential feelings. Other students claim to not want to tell their parents for fear that the parents won't understand them, will force them to get outside help that they don't want, will prevent them from getting help that they know they do want, or will threaten to pull them out of school. Students regularly report the fear of being judged, or worse, disowned by parents, for experiencing emotional turmoil. Some students wish to be off medication because they dislike the side effects while others wish to see a therapist or to be on medication to see if that might make them feel better, and here again, many students report that their parents wouldn't approve of them being on medication.

Arianna told me she was afraid to share with her parents what she was going through because she didn't come from a family where these issues were discussed. She worried they'd be angry at her for being sexually assaulted by an ex-boyfriend since then they'd know she'd already been sexually active. I tried to help her see that they might better understand where her anxiety is coming from if they were more fully informed to help her. Additionally, I conveyed to her that whether or not she decided to tell them, she shouldn't ignore the effects of assault on her since that sort of thing rears its head again later in undesirable ways if it's not dealt with promptly.

Lesson 79: Know the Signs of Depression and How It Shows Up in College

It's crucial to remember that the sooner you seek help, the better chance you have of getting back on track, academically, socially, and emotionally.

- Skipping classes
- Describing only negative reactions and disparaging remarks about classes, professors, roommates, peers, and the area in which the campus is located
- A marked change in habits of daily living such as poor hygiene habits, not eating, or sleeping excessively
- Self-reports of panic
- Not using a calendar of any sort
- Not having any idea how they're doing in a class because of being so disengaged
- Not knowing the names of their classes and professors
- Persistent homesickness
- Unresolved crisis at home including a sick or dying relative
- Resorting to self-harm as a coping mechanism
- Trouble with sustaining relationships
- Violations of student codes of conduct
- Illegal behavior such as shoplifting and drunk driving

Lesson 80: Substance Use in College Is an Opportunity to Think About Choices and Habits That Last Far Beyond College

When thinking about cultivating a healthy body and mind, it's important to address alcohol and drug use and abuse. It's understandable and likely that you'll want to try and experiment with new things in college, perhaps including alcohol and drugs, and my hope is that if you do, it will be in ways that are as safe and careful as possible, where you're armed with knowledge and resources to greatly minimize risk, and where you can have fun.

Drinking on campus is nothing new, but the extent to which we're seeing binge drinking on campus, coupled with a level of excessive drinking that leads to a trip to the emergency room (or recurring trips as is sometimes the case), is a relatively new and disturbing phenomenon worth addressing. Sadly, all too often, young men and women rely on drinking and drugging to seem attractive and acceptable. The binge drinking that is prevalent on campus is linked to hookup culture as well.

You'll benefit from having open conversations and advance agreements with people closest to you in order to stay safer. Sometimes, you might want to say no to pressure and don't know how. You'll benefit from talking with friends or older siblings and practicing how to say no. Consider sharing contact information with roommates and friends. For example, in an emergency, if someone has consumed too much and is sick or unconscious, it's prudent to contact trustworthy adults for help including 911, campus safety, the resident assistant, and parents if things take a turn for the worse. Including parents in this loop is effective when you're assured that you won't get in trouble for reporting a problem. Now that many schools have implemented plans for students that ensure that reporting students will not face negative repercussions, it's important to talk with your parents with the hope they would follow suit and not create punishments such as threats to withhold money for tuition, room and board, spending money, etc.

Often, students have already tried some sort of alcohol and drugs prior to college, but college is a time when there's more freedom and opportunity to experiment further. As your parents might have gone on a frantic mission to stock up on anything and everything you might need in the event you have a cold or flu on campus, it's crucial to remember the dangers of mixing these sorts of over the counter medications and prescription drugs with alcohol and recreational drugs. Additionally, a large number of students are now on psychotropic drugs for anxiety, depression, bipolar disorder, panic attacks, ADHD, and other diagnoses, and all too often, many students mix these with substances. Frequently, students share these prescribed drugs with friends or sell them to peers. The results of all of this can be nothing short of tragic.

For young women, I know you've heard this before but it's true; when you're out, it's helpful to stay with your group of friends throughout the night and to not leave friends alone. Of course, rape and sexual assault happen when perpetrators and victims are stone sober. They also happen when both parties are inebriated. And they happen when perpetrators have had little to nothing to drink, and they seek and find potential victims who are drunk or high as a kite and at their most vulnerable.

Violence against women isn't something women ask for, and it's not women's fault. I empathize with the problems of relentless victim-blaming and don't want to perpetuate it. At the same time, it's crucial to urge young women to empower themselves to take measures that render themselves less vulnerable. Along these lines, it's a good idea to keep an eye on your drinks, or to toss them if you weren't paying attention, so you're not the victim of drinks that have been tampered with at bars and parties. Additionally, it's important to monitor your intake so you don't get inebriated and then too incapacitated to make wise and careful choices. It's critical to know your tolerance and to even consult a chart on weight-alcohol consumption guidelines so you can see for yourself how little it takes to create a problem. This is especially true if you have access to a car on campus in terms of the tragedies associated with drinking and driving and the legal consequences accompanying that as well.

Students may rely on substances and use them frequently as coping mechanisms and as ways to self-medicate for which there might be underlying reasons that reveal even larger problems such as depression, anxiety, trauma, etc. For example, after girls experience sexual assault, it's highly likely that they'll turn to alcohol and other drugs. Similarly, those who suffer from eating disorders of any kind are susceptible to substance abuse as a way to get high and drunk even faster without eating.

It's common, though risky, for students to try to obtain fake IDs. Some students get caught up in being part of a ring that makes and sells these to other students. It's crucial for students to see the life-altering ramifications of being charged with these sorts of crimes.

If there's one thing I hope you'll take to heart, it's this—the decisions you make now, whether healthy and ethical, or destructive and dangerous, can set in motion lifelong habits that are good or bad. Often, I find myself reminding students how binge drinking can easily become full blown alcoholism that results in a lifelong struggle for recovery for decades to come. I have friends who experimented a bit in high school, got fully immersed in college, and decades later are counting the days, weeks, or years of sobriety they've managed. What they have in common is wishing they had done things differently when they were in college.

It's the normalizing excessive amounts of alcohol that's the problem. We see that message all around us in the culture in jokes, memes, shows, products we buy, etc. Some of it may seem relatively benign until we look a little deeper. For example, one thing I've noticed over the years are the increasingly popular alcohol related birthday cakes that many students receive at college. There are the cakes with full-size liquor bottles sitting on top or wedged into the icing and there are the alcohol drip cakes. There are the shot glass cakes and beer bottle cakes typically geared to boys and the drunk Barbie cakes for girls. Do you want to eat a cake on top of which there's a half-dressed Barbie doll with her limbs flopping around, her legs spread open, and loads of sprinkles spilling out of her mouth into a toilet made out of frosting to look like she got sick from a night of too much partying. The thing is, if that's the cake being purchased by your friends or parents to celebrate your twenty-first birthday, it becomes hard to understand the dangers of binge drinking coupled with the heightened vulnerability of sexual assault.

I have too many students who report that their own parents struggle with alcohol and drugs, and some have parents in prison because of related crimes. Many of these students became parentified early on and wound up trying to assist their parents and younger siblings with basic life tasks and duties, helping their parent get clean and sober, or preventing and protecting their siblings from falling prey to addictive behaviors. If you see yourself in this situation, my hope is that your parents will do themselves and you a favor by working hard to seek therapy and support toward recovery. We know there's a genetic component to addiction and I hope that if this is part of your family's picture that you will take extra care and precaution.

Lastly, it can do you a world of good to find and create a social network that's less reliant on substances to have fun and where you can spend time with people who still know how to work hard and play hard. Here are some different things to try with your friends where you're not reliant on substances:

- Set aside time just to talk, perhaps meeting for coffee, going out for dinner, or taking a walk. Better yet, try this with no phones, televisions, or internet.
- Play a board game. There's nothing like an old-fashioned game of Twister.
- Each person is allotted an agreed upon amount, for example ten or twenty dollars, to go buy fun and funny gifts for the other person. Meet back up an hour later at a designated restaurant or coffee shop to hang out, eat, and exchange gifts.
- Take a day trip—or even just a long car ride—with no destination and just talk. Often, time in cars generates interesting conversations because people aren't looking at each other and start to say what's on their mind, or they get dreamy, daring, and more creative with self-expression and with questions.
- Discover a hiking trail or swimming hole together.
- Host a potluck dinner and movie night in your suite.

Lesson 81: Self-Harm and Suicide

There are a variety of forms of self-harm including cutting, hair-pulling, burning, hitting, and scratching, as well as eating disorders which fall under the larger umbrella of self-harming behaviors. Sometimes students are engaging in more than one of these harmful behaviors at a time or move back and forth between these. One thing to note is that these behaviors are generally not indicative of suicidal ideation or predictive of suicide. Rather, they typically begin as coping mechanisms to deal with gravely complicated situations such as trauma.

In a book about the college experience, suicide itself must be addressed. It's estimated that approximately 24,000 US college students attempt suicide each year and about 1,100 of those complete their attempt, making suicide the second-leading cause of death among college students. More women attempt suicide yet more men die by suicide, due in large part to the method used. Suicide is higher among students from marginalized communities, such as students of color and those who identify as LGBTQ+.

Because of the magnitude of this problem, I want to offer a few resources in the event this is something you or someone you're close to may need. This is yet another arena in which peer support in college can make an enormous difference. Some schools offer QPR training which stands for Question, Persuade, Refer and if you're able to participate in this, it can be an effective tool in raising awareness, knowing the warning signs, and engaging in suicide prevention.

If you or someone you love is in crisis, call or text the suicide hotline and consider contacting your school's counseling service and campus safety as they have people on staff equipped to deal with these issues. Even in cases in which the counseling center on campus is booked solid for weeks or months, you should still call or walk in as they'll do everything possible to be supportive in a life-threatening emergency. You won't be the first student needing this, and you won't be the last.

Another thing that has gained traction across college campuses is what's known as a student of concern report which any student or employee can submit via the school's website. What this does is document someone's concern about an individual's well-being, as well as if they pose any threat to public safety, and a committee of trained personnel meet to review and evaluate these and then follow up to check on the welfare of these individuals and provide them with resources. Some schools will offer confidentiality to the person filing the report while others don't. Other national organizations from which you can seek help include the National Alliance on Mental Illness and the National Institute of Mental Health.

Lesson 82: EveryBODY Is Beautiful

Most college students I talk to struggle with body image. On the first day of school, when I ask students to complete a questionnaire so I can get to know them as learners and people and be the best teacher I can be for them, I ask what qualities they like most about themselves and what they'd like to change. Nearly every student I've ever had wants to look different than they do; I have female students who invariably wish to be thinner and male students who want to be taller and more muscular, and if they consider themselves heavy, they want to be leaner. There's seldom any celebration of their bodies. Too many share a history or current struggle with eating disorders and other forms of self-injurious behavior.

I get it. I came of age amidst the release of *Jane Fonda's Workout Book* and Wendy Stehling's, *Thin Thighs in Thirty Days*. This was in the early 80s. I was just thirteen. By day, my mom and I attempted many of the exercises together in front of her bedroom mirror. By night, my mom crawled into bed with these fitness bibles to study them. I got clear messages that this was indeed a project, that it was something women undertook, often privately, painfully and obsessively, that mothers and daughters could bond, as well as compete and judge each other, over dieting and exercise, and that these images of perfect, slender bodies were the ones to which I would need to aspire.

In college, it seemed as though every woman around me was struggling with eating problems. My roommate suffered from bulimia and its rampant destruction of her body for years until she was forced to drop out of school when the repeated cycles of binging and purging finally did damage to her internal organs. In the suite of four women across the hall, one had anorexia, one was a compulsive overeater, and the third suffered from both anorexia and bulimia. The parents of the one with anorexia threatened to pull her out of school if her weight fell below a hundred pounds. All around me, women were waging war against their bodies.

In doing research for this book, I wanted to interview someone who I knew had recovered from an eating disorder and would be uniquely situated to help you understand the depth of this problem in college and remind you that healing is possible. To this end, I interviewed a woman named Bari who is now fifty-six years old and was able to look back on how her struggle with eating problems and body image tormented her through much of college, permeating her everyday life. This is what she had to say:

"Anorexia and bulimia plagued me all of high school and most of my college years. I would have what I considered to be 'good days.' These consisted of a long run, some strength training and eating only what I considered to be safe. Safe food for me was a starvation diet of yogurt, fruit, and salads. I would allow myself a peanut butter sandwich for lunch since I needed something to sustain me while I studied. Then there were long strings of 'bad days.' Bad days consisted of no workout and massive binge eating and purging cycles. Sometimes I would do this three or four times per day. My head and heart were pounding due to electrolyte imbalances. It was hard to focus on my studies and it deeply impacted my social life. I became isolated in a sea of shame. I was so ashamed of myself. I didn't want anyone to know my truth. My behavior was not well hidden. My boyfriend was acutely aware of what was going on. He once wrestled me to the ground out of love to stop me from making myself vomit! I assure you there was no ill will or violence, he just wanted me to respect my body. I am certain it was difficult for my friends and boyfriend to find a way to intervene. There are a lot of dishonest and manipulative behaviors when you live in shame. You just want to put on an invisibility cloak. What I learned is you can run, but you cannot hide. You will always have to face yourself. I was lucky that my dear friend mustered up the courage to confront my parents. At the time, I was embarrassed and that was expressed as anger toward her. That being said, it needed to happen and was the one point in which I voluntarily sought a program for eating disorder recovery. Fast forward to many years later, I have had the pleasure of being able to thank my friend. She saved my life. Just like any other self-destructive behavior, an intervention can be a crucial turning point. I encourage anyone who has a loved one engaging in destructive behaviors to find a way to let them know you're worried and want to help them to help themselves."

It turns out that the friend that Bari references who seemingly betrayed her by calling her parents was indeed me. What prompted that was running into her on the sidewalk when I was headed home from a class and saw her bundled up, looking a pasty white green color and coming out of Unos restaurant. She looked caught in the act of doing something she knew she shouldn't be doing. Most of all, she appeared sad and unwell. Her fear and desperation were palpable, so much so that I, too, felt scared and uneasy, unsure of what to do, and how, if at all, I could ever help her. Somehow, thankfully, I intuited that I was in way over my head and needed to reach out to people in a better position to be able to get her the help she needed. I was aware that she might hate me or stop speaking to me, and yet I was conscious of the fact that it's hard to feel close to someone who is that preoccupied with mass destruction of their own body, and that things like this and other addictive behaviors as well, strain friendships.

I wanted Bari to feel better and to reconnect with the vibrancy I knew was within her, and I was scared she could wind up like my freshman roommate, damaging internal organs and having to leave school. I recognized how humiliating it would be for Bari if I called her parents, and for that I felt badly, but I knew I'd feel far worse if something tragic happened—which given the way things were progressing, seemed entirely possible. I took the risk of thoroughly pissing her off and alienating her and called her parents out of deep love and concern. It's true she was angry with me, felt betrayed and embarrassed, and it all took time. Still questioning myself decades later, worrying that I could have done better by her, I asked Bari what else I could and should have done, but her response of open-hearted forgiveness and gratitude helped me forgive my younger self. If a friend or family member struggles with problems like these, I encourage you to take the necessary risk to help the life of someone so dear.

My women students struggle with the ways that beauty standards make them walk a tightrope of feeling hyper-visible and harshly labeled and judged for the body they're in and feeling invisible. It's understandable at an age where people's self-concept rides heavily on how they feel seen or ignored. So many women students, especially white women, express a deep desire to be smaller, to take up less space. Today, we see girls and women aspire to be a size zero or double zero. Every semester, I ask them, if zero is nothing, why aspire to be that which doesn't exist?

Students routinely disclose painful stories of what it's like to live in their bodies—bodies that weren't always safe spaces for them or that ever felt like home. They describe intense, overwhelming family criticism and cultural, racialized, and gendered pressures to look a certain way, as well as the ways that their bodies stored trauma, fear, grief, rage, betrayal, and obsessions. It seems that a war of sorts has been waged against my students' bodies and some resisted and fought back by waging an internalized war on their own bodies in the form of compulsive overeating, anorexia, and bulimia.

Jody stated:

"Since moving away to school, my parents remind me I'm still 'chunky' and they wanted me to join the college track team so I could lose those extra pounds. When I told my dad the coach put me on the sprinting team, he said to me 'Why would your coach do that, doesn't she look at you? You're not fast enough, nor are you skinny enough.' I remember when I got a C+ on a test in one of my science classes and my dad said 'That's not good enough if you want to become a nurse, nurses don't get C's, so you can do either two things—study hard to get a higher grade or lose a good thirty pounds so that a wealthy man will find you attractive and support you for the rest of your life.' "

Another student, Carla, explained the impact of race and culture on her sense of her weight:

"I've been ridiculed most of my life for so many things because I embraced a white culture. But the one aspect of my Hispanic heritage I could never escape was my body type and that means I'll be stuck with these big thighs and butt for the rest of my life. My weight constantly fluctuated and there were many times when I was called fat to my face. Needless to say, it hurt me a lot because I didn't see it, but apparently, I was offending people because I couldn't restrain my obesity. I'd cry myself to sleep, and I'd always put my friends in these horrible positions when they were posed with the question, 'Am I fat?' I don't regret losing weight because I'm happier now but I do regret letting other people get to me."

Michelle described how she came to view her own body vis-à-vis interactions with others and how it led to her own self-loathing until the moment when she ultimately came to regard beauty in other women's honesty about their bodies. She said:

"When I was in sixth grade, I starved myself for weeks with only water and juice so I could look like this new girl in my class who was Brazilian and thin as could be, but then one day, I had my period and was at basketball practice and passed out. After that, I decided to not let my weight get to me until college when I gained a massive amount of weight freshman year so I started to lose again, but this time it didn't work because still today when I go home for the weekend, church members will say 'You're getting bigger by the minute' and my doctor says I'm obese, and my family says I look pregnant or like a two-family house. Those girls in our class who are able to discuss their struggles with their bodies, well, to me they're pretty."

Lesson 83: How to Love Your Body—Befriending the Skin You're In

- See if you can bravely stand in front of a full-length mirror naked and observe your body, focusing on even just one part you admire and for which you feel grateful. Continue to do this until you can find more and more. Think of a mantra that might help you accept your body just as it is, regardless of how flawed you might perceive it. If this was the body of a friend you love, what would you say?
- Write a letter to your body. Think about your hopes and fears for your body, what your body has held onto, what it has done for you in spite of everything and because of everything. Think about how and where emotions are located in your body whether it's joy, anger, grief, anxiety, etc. What sort of gratitude do you have for your body? What sort of intentions do you have for your body? Save whatever you write so you can reread it years from now.
- When kind sentiments about the body radiate outward into the community, it can be a powerful experience. Several years ago, my Sociology of the Body class started writing affirmations on Post-It notes about body love and self-acceptance and sticking them all around campus, in hallways and classrooms and on bathroom doors, mirrors, and kiosks. Who knew a trip to the bathroom could become so affirming? It made people smile and spread good, healthy energy.
- Instead of meeting friends for meals, arrange to be together moving your bodies out in nature, hiking, swimming, or biking,

or go lift weights or take a yoga class together. Sweat together, release endorphins, and reset!

Lesson 84: Let's Talk About Sex

College is a formative time when students develop a sense of self, and in particular, it is when one's sexual self is likely to develop. Human beings are sexual beings. Regardless of parents' views on premarital sex or on their adult child becoming sexually active, chances are likely that students enter college having already experimented sexually in some ways and will continue to do so more fully and deeply in college.

Sex. What a loaded word. It's something most people get excited about and are often reticent to talk about. This can be related to family upbringing, peer socialization, religious constraints, conflicting media messaging, and many other reasons that leave people feeling ashamed, muted, inhibited, and vulnerable. Yet these are the exact qualities that do *not* lead to a fulfilling sex life. Add to all of that the fact that most people haven't benefited from positive and comprehensive sex education.

Almost forty years ago, psychologist Michelle Fine wrote about the severe limitations of sex education in schools, explaining that when it takes place, the focus is overwhelmingly on these aspects: morality, the potential for disease, pregnancy, and violence. Fine identifies that the thing that's sorely missing, to our peril, is an honest discussion of desire and pleasure. She's right. Sex is more fun and pleasurable when the worry is taken out of it. This means that part of true self-care involves responsibly taking care of your sexual body including taking precautions against sexually transmitted diseases (STDs), getting regularly tested for STDs, knowing your status (meaning if you're HIV+ or not) and having plans for contraception, assuming that having children is something you may want further into the future, if at all.

I think about some of my students who have approached me for feedback about how to let a new boyfriend or girlfriend know they have a STD. Remarkably, though they had been made to feel dirty and ashamed, these are all people with a strong sense of self and at peace with who they are, but their concerns were in regards to others' potential reactions. They knew that desire and pleasure were still possible but were worried that their partners wouldn't easily understand. In addition, countless students have approached me, worried they were pregnant and contemplating what they would do. Though none of these students chose to have these problems to worry about, they all recognize that they wished they had chosen to use protection to at least prevent whatever they could.

It's rather stunning and horrifying how few students seem to understand the significance of using protection. Research by sociologist Lisa Wade backs up this assertion. In her book, *American Hookup: The New Culture of Sex on Campus* (2017), she shows that hookup culture accounts for the cavalier ways in which students today regard their sexual health. A hookup isn't much different from a one-night stand except that with hookups, these may occur over time with the same person, and typically while a one-night stand is with a stranger, a hookup is typically with someone at least somewhat familiar if not an acquaintance, classmate, or friend. Unsurprisingly, hookup culture is linked to the use and abuse of alcohol and other drugs. It's perfectly normal to want to experiment with your newfound sense of self in a new place, but using your sexuality as the primary way to connect with others usually results in a downward spiral, for both men and women students. Try to cultivate a social life and sexual life not wholly dependent on substances and sex.

Perhaps the two most interesting findings in Wade's book are these: 1) hookup culture doesn't create a climate of happy, carefree college students, and 2) hookup culture regards women's desire and pleasure as subordinate to that of men. Wade quotes women students who told her, "I was just a warm body being used to give a guy an orgasm" and who felt treated "like two hands and three holes." Men reported being disinterested in women's orgasms in the context of hooking up and only cared about that if the person was an actual girlfriend. So many women have clearly internalized this disregard as Wade references women students who said, "We don't ask for anything in bed," and "I don't feel like I've had a sexual experience if the guy doesn't come," and "My sexuality was filled with anxiety and my need to please the guy instead of worrying about my own pleasure." The fact that in a hookup the two people are more likely to have known each other and had some connection makes the lack of regard of women's pleasure even more disturbing. Furthermore, at a time of heightened vulnerability around their sense of body image, it seems even more disconcerting for women to be cut off from their own experiences of pleasure.

One thing that people can do to create pleasure for themselves is to engage in sex for one. That can make sex for two even better. When we know what turns us on and how to make that happen, we can better communicate that, in words and in touch, to another person. I remember some years back, my friend Helene shared with me over dinner that she bought a vibrator for each of her two daughters on their sixteenth birthdays. Talk about a sweet sixteen, right? Trained as a psychologist, Helene wanted to be sure her daughters never ignore their own desire and pleasure. Just as she had purchased other toys and fun things for them throughout their childhood, I think she saw this gift in adolescence to be no different, and in so doing she normalized desire and pleasure for them.

At its best, sex is a creative act. When it's wonderful, it has art and soul. The problem is that we live in a culture so mediated by formulaic, pornographic images that it takes a certain amount of going inward and truly connecting with another person to make it original, meaningful, and fun. Feeling open and free are key ingredients to a more exciting and fulfilling sex life. As scary and hard as it may be, communicating with another person about our desires, expectations, and fantasies, and finding out about theirs, is a surefire way to enhance intimacy. We deepen *any* intimate experience when we take time to get curious and listen to another person. We become more intimate through exploring questions and answers with sensitivity, curiosity, gentleness, and humor. This is true in a new relationship and in a long-term relationship, even when we're already convinced we know all there is to know about someone.

Lesson 85: What to Do When You Have the Flu

On campuses, illness spreads like wildfire. I've always joked that teaching is like living in a petri dish. But truly, it is. People are living and working in close quarters, stress is on the rise, sleep is minimal, and healthy habits aren't always in abundance.

In our 24/7 culture with everything on and buzzing all the time and with work schedules that bleed into home schedules, it's no wonder students often repeat what they've seen modeled all their lives—adults who've been self-sacrificial, who've pushed themselves to extreme exhaustion, who've gone to work regardless, engage in little to no self-care, and who've traipsed around sick kids to accompany them at work when they couldn't stay at daycare, further infecting their own workplaces.

Long before the pandemic, I've routinely asked students to leave class who are visibly and audibly ill. I've had students come to office hours presenting in the same way and I've turned them away, requesting we reschedule. Sick students simply get sicker and put others at risk of becoming ill when they come to classes and appointments. Somehow, the more disembodied our decisions and the less we honor our bodies in health or in sickness, we think of ourselves and others as heroic and ambitious. I'm reminded of how important it is to think about these things when I reflect back on one of the most interesting human beings I've ever taught. Jo-Ann is an older, returning student I had for six different courses. She's HIV+ and otherwise healthy and vibrant. But the fact of the disease makes her body more susceptible to colds and flus. A student who's running a fever and coming to class coughing puts a student like this at terrible risk, and everyone else is still vulnerable as well.

It's almost inevitable that in the years you're working toward your degree you'll occasionally feel unwell. When you find yourself sick at school, consider these suggestions:

- Stay in your room. If this means you must miss classes, email each of your professors to inform them if they have asked that you do this. When you return to classes, get all missed notes and announcements from several other students (you will have more perspective on what you missed if you consult with more than one student).
- Ask a roommate or friend, or contact a delivery service, to drop off food items and medications as needed.
- Get a box of facial masks for your suite. These are good to have on hand anyway in this day and age. When you feel better, you can get creative with the leftover ones next Halloween!
- Arrange for an appointment with Student Health Services. If your campus doesn't offer this, seek care at a reputable urgent care clinic. You can find reviews online.
- You might try in advance, when you're well, to find a primary care doctor in the community since you're likely to have medical needs during the years you're away at college. If you face any sort of injury or require medication for anxiety or depression or have other issues such as gynecological or gastrointestinal ones, you

have your own doctor with whom you've established a rapport who can then get you in when you're ill. This will provide you with more continuity of care which is always helpful.

- Use the time when you're ill to catch up on much needed sleep and rest, listen to music, watch a series, read, and daydream.

- Use the time to make a list of self-care practices you can employ when you're better that can help you stay healthy. This might include making commitments to: eat better, practice meditation and yoga, exercise, take vitamins, etc. Being sick gives us an opportunity to think about how we want to be well and what it might take to get there in terms of cultivating habits that best honor our bodies.

- Always try to have basic nonperishable items on hand for sick days such as broth, soups, teas, ginger ale, and rice, as well as echinacea, acetaminophen or ibuprofen, anti-nausea medicine, band-aids, medicine for coughs and congestion, etc.

- Wash your hands often! Keep hand sanitizer with you.

- As soon as you're better, go on a cleaning rampage. Wipe down surfaces, faucets, doorknobs, and keyboards. Change your toothbrush. Wash your sheets, duvet cover, blankets, towels, hats, gloves, scarves, clothes, etc. We all know what the floors look like in students' bedrooms. All the advice about sneezing into your elbow is great as long as you promise to wash your sweatshirt!

Lesson 86: When Your Heart and Mind Are Someplace Else—How to Cope with Stressful Situations Going on at Home

As we've seen, the college experience is a complex time with lots of puzzle parts, some fitting together more easily than others. For a sizable number of students though, the college experience has additional loose pieces that add anxiety, stress, and confusion. I've worked with many students who've shared with me that they're simultaneously having to think about and navigate intense and difficult things happening back at home such as: a parent's or sibling's mental health, an addicted parent or sibling, infidelity by one or both parents, their parents' constant fighting or sudden announcement of divorce, an incarcerated family member, ongoing family violence, family members struggling with new diagnoses, chronic illnesses, severe disabilities, multiple hospitalizations, terminal diseases, deaths of loved ones, family members killed in accidents and murders, and their younger siblings still at home who may be going through any number of these things. These students are understandably distracted and worried by these added layers of complication. Likewise, parents who find themselves mired in painful and nerve-racking circumstances at home, while at the same time trying to honor their student's transition to college and celebrate with them on this journey, face their own challenges.

Back in February 2020 when I was on a stop in Cleveland for my last book tour, I reconnected with an old, dear friend, Kate, and it was magical. Within just a few months of that trip though, Kate found herself abruptly and cruelly shipped off to a world of hospital stays, tests, diagnoses, medical nightmares, and hospice scares for her youngest daughter, Margaret, who was suddenly diagnosed with cancer and later suffered complications from chemotherapy that left her in a minimally conscious state. I was worried about Margaret. I was worried about Kate. I was worried about her husband and their other two kids, one of whom has autism and severe mental illness. But as a college professor, my mind kept going to their oldest daughter, Sarah, who was headed for college in fall 2020, a semester that was already promising to be a doozy of epic proportion given the COVID-19 pandemic and the upheaval it was creating on campuses across the country. I kept thinking about how the transition to college is challenging enough for any student in any given year, that the pandemic would make it that much harder, and this newly added fear and anxiety about her sister and how her family would fare would just be too much.

Kate shared with me the agony she felt not being able to be as present and active in the preparations for Sarah's move to college as she had always imagined:

"I didn't have the chance to do what I saw and heard so many other parents doing: going through things in their child's room with them, shopping, packing, making memorable 'lasts.' I felt tremendous guilt when I did things like ask my sister to help Sarah get her bedding and other supplies. I felt numb, like I didn't get to grieve my child leaving this stage of life. Or process the fact that I was myself moving into a new stage—no longer the parent of three little girls."

Since Kate didn't get as much special time with Sarah as she hoped, she got creative with what she did have available:

"I turned on the hose and set up the slip-n-slide. And even put on my own bathing suit! She thought it was so cute when she pulled in the drive, and was totally game for a run. On our last sunny August afternoon at home, we ran across the backyard and belly-flopped onto the yellow and blue plastic slide that had been rolled up in the garage and almost forgotten. Another thing I'd thought of the week before worked as something special I could do. When Margaret was in the hospital for so many months, and Sarah was at home on her own a lot and the world was locked down from the pandemic, she decided to try and learn how to sew. She got out the little sewing machine that was a Christmas gift years ago and tried and tried, to no avail. She had wanted to sew a heart-shaped pillow for her sister. She'd cut and pinned and found stuffing, but eventually got too frustrated by the machine and abandoned the project. I found the pieces and decided to go ahead and hand-sew the pillow…and give it to Sarah for college to remind her of the love between her and her sister. Sarah had cut the heart-shaped pieces from a mismatched set of white percale sheets with pink polka dots. At night while I was sitting by Margaret's hospital bed I worked with my needle and thread, and finished the pillow just in time. I even wrote a little phrase along the bottom seam: 'Safe and Loved.' It was something I used to say to Sarah when she was anxious, especially at night, trying to go to bed. I hid the pillow in my bag for our trip to school. After we'd unpacked and set up her room and walked outside to say goodbye, I told her I forgot something up in the room and sent her to get the car while I ran back up. I put the pillow right in the center of her comfy new twin bed. She called me in happy tears before I'd even reached the highway home to tell me how much she loved it."

I had the unique privilege to be in touch with Sarah to get her perspective on things now. She said:

"After my sister went into the hospital, I stepped into a caretaker and entertainer role. I waited up for my parents to get home from the hospital each night, I put dinner together, I cleaned the house, took care of my other sister, tried to make light of bad situations by cracking jokes or singing around the house, etc. I tried to act as normally as possible, so I didn't add one more thing onto the teetering pile of chaos that surrounded us. I was worried that things would fall apart at home when I left for college. I felt like I was a vital cog in the way that our house ran. I felt underappreciated for how much I helped out at home. It felt sort of good at times that things might fall apart when I left for college though because then I might finally be recognized and seen... I absolutely feel pressure to be the perfect one. As an oldest daughter, I know that this feeling is common amongst other oldest daughters. But there's an extra layer for me. I have two younger sisters, one who has autism and schizophrenia and the other who survived a cancer diagnosis and is now living with a brain injury. I am the only one of my sisters who can have a 'normal' life. I feel extreme pressure to live my life to the fullest but also extreme guilt because I know that my sisters will never get to experience life in the way that I have and will continue to. These conflicting feelings paralyze me. I struggle to make decisions for myself because I want to make everyone else happy and proud."

I wanted to know what sort of advice Sarah would offer you as readers in balancing the complexity of life at home with the college experience. I believe her suggestions transcend the particularity of her experience and could apply to students with all sorts of heavy things happening at home. Sarah said:

"My advice for other people who might find themselves in a similar situation as mine is to make sure you don't talk about the challenges you're facing 24/7. Communicate at the beginning of a conversation, meal, or activity that you don't want to talk about your challenges, you just want to be in the moment or talk about anything else. You deserve to take a break from the hardship... When you intentionally do something for yourself every day, you honor so many parts of you that need attention, love, care, or release. This teaches you that you can lean and rely on yourself to care for your needs—something that I struggle with. I outsourced all of my comfort or needs in other people, which often left me disappointed and unfulfilled. This is not to say that you can't rely on others. You absolutely can and should (connection is everything)! But always reserve something for yourself; you are your own greatest ally, friend, advocate, lover, and so much more."

Lesson 87: Self-Care Is a Radical Act

The act of engaging in self-care has the transformative possibility of freedom, connecting us back to ourselves, our own creative process, and the relationships we most cherish. Through reclaiming our time, our priorities, and ourselves, we can move further along the path toward clarity, wholeness, and survival.

- Perfect the art of saying no, and practice setting boundaries.
- Pause and reflect. Ask yourself if responding positively will serve you well and benefit your life trajectory. Discern when to say yes and when to say no. Both can be done with heart.
- Reflect on what truly sustains you.
- Honor the power of sacred solitude and silence. Constantly being tethered to devices can be draining.
- Get into nature, connect to the world beyond yourself, and relish in wonder and hope. We all need to do that more. It's a way to be kinder to ourselves.

CHAPTER 18

VIOLENCE AND RECOVERY

Lesson 88: How to Know If You or a Friend Is in a Controlling and Abusive Relationship

In the last section, we explored self-care and extending kindness to ourselves, and I want to emphasize how crucial all that is when it comes to approaching our next topic about violence. Learning about relationship violence is a way to rethink complicated family dynamics, to re-evaluate past and current intimate relationships, and to imagine a future free of violence. I've designed this primer to support you if you're personally faced with this situation or if you want to help someone you care about.

I teach about intimacy and violence. Every. Single. Semester. Consequently, I'm faced with many students—too many—disclosing about witnessing and experiencing violence and trauma. I've worked with countless students who have been raped, harassed, stalked, manipulated, beaten, and threatened, and I've had students who lost their mothers, aunts, and grandmothers to domestic homicide. There are many lessons I try to impart both from my research and from my work in the field. For many years, I co-facilitated groups for male abusers, and I was the clinical supervisor of a battering intervention program. In addition, I spent years working with female victims/

survivors of violence, adolescent perpetrators, and children who had witnessed and experienced violence.

While I recognize that men may be victims of sexual and domestic violence, my primary focus here is on women's experiences of being hurt in these situations and men as perpetrators. This is for two reasons: 1) my research and work experience focus on men's violence against women, and 2) statistics bear this out. It's estimated that approximately one in three women experiences some sort of abuse in the course of her lifetime, and on the college level approximately one in four women will experience sexual assault.

Instant intimacy is often followed by disillusion, so tread carefully. Those who are abusive are experts at zeroing in and preying on vulnerability. This is one more reason why hookup culture can be detrimental to people's well-being. When an abuser tries to get too close too quickly, it's usually because they're preventing you from being more fully informed about their personality and behaviors, knowing that if you knew them more extensively you might not get involved.

Violence consists of acts and beliefs that rupture human connection and trust. Just as entrapment encapsulates the experience for victims/survivors (I use both words to recognize the power in survivorship while acknowledging both that someone was victimized and that indeed, sometimes, not all victims survive), entitlement characterizes the experience for abusers. As a society, we tolerate abusers' excuses that perpetuate women's entrapment, excuses that include the perception of victim provocation.

Abuse can take on many forms including:

- **Physical:** hitting, slapping, punching, kicking, biting, spitting, pulling hair, pushing, grabbing, blocking exits, destroying property, precious objects, and gifts like family photos or jewelry.

- **Emotional:** name-calling, mind-games, threats, blaming, criticizing, gaslighting.

- **Sexual:** includes assault and rape as well as coercion, pressure, threats, sexual bargaining for things in return, and pressure to reproduce acts derived from pornography, especially violent pornography. Since the damage of this form of abuse is often invisible, it's helpful to be able to recognize signs that sexual abuse may have occurred. These include, but aren't limited to, the following: disordered eating patterns, for example binging and purging as a way to claim control of what goes in and out of one's own body; other forms of self-harm such as cutting; binge drinking; using alcohol and other drugs to numb out pain and trauma; perfectionism in school and other activities; chronic absenteeism and a lack of interest in activities that once brought pleasure; chronic illness and specifically complaints of frequent vaginal and urinary infections, headaches, gastrointestinal issues, TMJ, etc. While the idea of the "Freshman Fifteen" is nothing new, sometimes this weight gain, and much more, can reveal a young woman trying to create a sense of body armor to shield herself from further violation.

- **Financial:** putting someone in debt, borrowing money and not repaying it, stealing, and closing accounts without consent.
- **Neglect:** withholding affection and attention.

Abuse is damaging on various levels—to the body, the psyche, the heart, the spirit, to one's moral core, to the wallet, etc. Abuse and violence aren't natural, inevitable aspects of intimate relationships. Abuse and control are embedded in the fabric of our society and in patterns of social relations as to only seem natural. Abuse is not episodic; it's patterned. What exists between what we call "episodes" is what keeps the victim/survivor seduced into the pattern of violence. What exists between are often the apologies, gifts, quick fixes, and promises. In an abusive relationship, one person is treated as being less valuable than the other with their needs, desires, and interests subordinated to the other.

Abusive relationships involve power and control; abuse is not so much about anger or conflict tactics but about control tactics. Abuse is about forcing someone to do something against their will as well as preventing someone from doing what they want to do. Violence exerts social control, meaning that even those who have never been victims of violence know to fear it. This is most certainly the case with rape and sexual assault, particularly on college campuses.

One of the primary tactics of abuse is isolation, making it difficult or impossible for someone to see and talk with their friends, pursue goals such as school, or travel and get where they need to go, for example, slashing tires so a person cannot leave. Other examples of isolation include not conveying messages, intercepting mail and voicemail, etc. Being jealous of someone or something is a normal emotion, but acting on it by being possessive is not. The story of my former student, Blair, illustrates many facets of enduring an abusive relationship; she was a senior who had been married to a fellow student, and when she decided to separate from him, he made it so she was trapped. He stole her phone, destroyed her laptop, made it impossible for her to complete schoolwork, and threatened to kill her saying, "If I can't have you, no one will."

An abuser frequently carries out the violence at his partner's school or workplace and that reveals a great deal about how he sees and regards women. This harassment often causes women major disruption when pursuing an education or causes them to lose their jobs. When men who are abusive intrude on their partners at school and work, they violate their partner's independence and restrict her movement in organizations in which she could have access to power and resources. Abuse creates a web of fear and the feeling of walking on eggshells, and it creates low self-esteem and ambivalence.

Girls and women are socialized to forge and maintain relationships, almost at any cost to themselves. So, it's a particularly cruel irony that at the time a woman is most vulnerable in an abusive relationship, we ask questions such as: why does she stay, why doesn't she leave? But in actuality, she has done what good women are taught to do—she has conformed, maybe overly so, to societal standards. The point at which women try to leave abusive relationships is the riskiest time and when there's the greatest chance of being killed by a partner or ex-partner, just as we saw with Blair's experience. The problem is that we insist on asking these questions about why women stay, and we insist on her resisting and going against all the socialization that has been imposed on her.

There are many reasons why people stay in abusive and coercive relationships—love, fear of danger, fear of not being believed, health or disability of their partner or themselves, immigration status, religious upbringing, threats that the abuser may have made regarding killing her or himself, racial loyalty (Black women often report that given the rate of incarceration of Black men, they don't want more dirty laundry to be aired), finances, etc.

I'm often asked why survivors of violence recant their story. This gets at how victims are trapped in abusive relationships. A vicious cycle is perpetuated, because once the victim/survivor recants, the sense of the brutality of what was endured gets minimized in the relationship and by those outside the relationship. The experience gets reduced to: "See? It wasn't that bad. It's never that bad." A dynamic ensues such that survivors aren't seen as trustworthy with the experiences they've faced. Survivors already have the sense that they won't be believed, because they've been told so by abusers over and over again, and society reinforces this through victim-blaming, tolerance, and excuses for violence. In essence, the reasons survivors recant their stories are often the same reasons they stay in abusive relationships—a torturous combination of love and fear. Most survivors face a tremendous sense of ambivalence—wanting the controlling behavior and abuse to stop and the relationship to continue, though these may be incompatible goals.

Most people want to believe that the person they love loves them back, and that when he says he's sorry, he means it. Though women may wind up scarred and scared from the experience, and often not presenting well, seeming angry, depressed, and anxious, while abusers can present better and calmer, it's crucial to understand that victims do resist. Sometimes resistance may be subtle and less explicit. In fact, resistance is always present, because violence is unwanted.

If you or someone you know is being abused, the following suggestions might offer a helpful, healing path:

- Help the person identify and name the abuse.
- Help create a timeline of the abuse so they can see the patterns and cycles of it.
- Ask specific questions, in nonthreatening ways, to show them that this behavior is abusive.
- Ask what their concerns are.
- Help to identify reasons for abuse as excuses.
- Consider the victim as an expert.
- Talk to the person in private and away from the abuser.
- Let the survivor of the abuse set the pace and tone.

Here are helpful and supportive resources:

- Seek medical help right away at university health services or the closest emergency room where a SANE nurse should be assigned to meet with you; this stands for Sexual Assault Nurse Examiner. This person will have had additional training to be best positioned to help and to arrange for a rape kit to be performed to test for STDs, pregnancy, etc.

- Consider reporting this to campus police or another official person on campus, and the local police. All colleges and universities receiving federal assistance are required to have Title IX administrators with whom people can and should talk and report what happened. These people can provide you with a range of options to help you feel most empowered, and they can make good referrals.

- Many colleges and universities have offices of sexual assault prevention and response or some sort of victims' services and advocacy. The school's counseling center, while helpful, doesn't necessarily offer the specific expertise that comes with therapists who are highly skilled in the dynamics of abuse and control. If your school doesn't have a dedicated office that deals with dating violence, domestic violence, and sexual violence, be sure to ask if anyone in the counseling center specializes in these issues.

- Many schools have partnerships with local programs in the community and with hospitals to help students access free services such as counseling, support groups, etc.

- Every state has a coalition to end sexual assault and domestic violence so if you type those words and the name of your state into a Google search, you'll be able to easily access the resources that are geographically most convenient for you. You will find hotline information and extensive supplementary programming offered. Two excellent resources include RAINN (Rape, Abuse, and Incest National Network) and the National Coalition Against Domestic Violence.

- In time, it might be empowering to explore self-defense classes offered on or near campus.

Lesson 89: College Interrupted—Sexual Violence and the Crisis of Disclosure

"Self-preservation is a full-time occupation."

—Ani DiFranco

Higher education is an important pathway to success in the public realm. Sexual assault and the aftermath of trauma significantly derail young women and sabotage their success. Sexual abuse encompasses assault and rape as well as coercion, pressure, threats, and sexual bargaining for things in return. Young men who are sexually violating on campus are also violating and undermining women's chances for independence and success, academically, professionally, and personally. Research repeatedly demonstrates that first-year female students, especially, are at the highest risk of sexual assault. Particularly noteworthy is the fact that much of this occurs in what's known as the Red Zone, a term coined by psychologist David Lisak, to describe women's heightened vulnerability especially between orientation and winter break when they're new and adjusting to campus. This means that some young women are entering their first weeks of classes already disoriented from violation so soon after campus orientation. This fact alone helps to reveal the tremendous disruption and sabotage occurring here, right as someone is trying to establish a sense of a new home.

New students on campus, hoping to make friends, to connect with a seemingly "in" crowd, who are unfamiliar with the campus and local geography, who have no idea where help would even be available, who are reticent to vocalize their own needs and wishes, who feel lonely, who may imagine any form of potential sexual closeness to be a path toward something romantically desirable, are especially vulnerable. Sexual assault in residence halls needs to be simultaneously conceptualized as domestic violence since the dorm and the new college environment are, indeed, home. For survivors, this experience is not a death sentence, but it's certainly debilitating until treatment is sought.

While men can be victims of sexual violence, the overwhelming problem on campus is that of male perpetrators and female victims. Sadly, those women that come to college already having been sexually victimized in their families of origin and/or in their communities while growing up, run the greatest risk of multiple victimization. Some research, such as that by Lisak, has shown that the majority of sexual assault on campus is perpetrated by a small group of predatory males who are doing this over and over to multiple women. Mary Koss, another prominent scholar in research on sexual assault on campus, has taken that serial rapist theory to task demonstrating that these heinous acts are done by much more than a small group of predatory men.

Amputated from empathy, bloated with perceptions of being disenfranchised from a dominant sense of masculinity, and loaded up on virulent misogyny, men who commit these acts showcase what's broken in our society. If young women aren't free to move about in their bodies, in their relationships, and in the world, they cannot operate as full human beings.

Lesson 90: Breaking the Silence— Up Close and Personal

"The bud
stands for all things,
even for those things that don't flower,
for everything flowers, from within, of self-blessing;
though sometimes it is necessary
to reteach a thing its loveliness,
to put a hand on its brow
of the flower
and retell it in words and in touch
it is lovely
until it flowers again from within, of self-blessing"
—Galway Kinnell

I had a lovely first-year student named Hannah who confided in me that she had gone to a party with her friend who was her suitemate, and her friend was flirting with a young man there via an app but not yet actually talking with him. Later, they all wound up meeting up and went back to the dorm, and the friend and the man fooled around, but she didn't want sex and asked him to sleep on the couch in the common area of the suite. Instead, he wound up barging in Hannah's bedroom and raped her. It's no wonder why Hannah struggled that semester and left campus. Sometime after, Hannah wrote to me, "It's crazy how that one night changed my entire life... Rape is very real and should be talked about more openly, I don't know why we feel as though it's something to hide or be ashamed of. I know it happens a lot more than it's reported and I hope one day soon that statistic is different."

I look at this problem not just as a researcher and writer but as a survivor of an attempted sexual assault. Just as Hannah's experience was consistent with the research, so too was mine. During the first semester of my first year at college, I was studying in the basement of my dorm—*my then home*—and a young man named Jason, with whom I had been socializing, suggested that we head upstairs to his room to make coffee so we could stay up later to study. When we got to his room, Jason didn't have coffee on his mind. Instead, he threw me on the bottom bunk and proceeded to take my shirt off and had my bra almost undone. His moves weren't romantic; they were forceful, hostile, and aggressive. I was cornered and pressed down. With all the strength I could muster in my legs, I pushed him off of me and ran out of his room and down nine flights of stairs with only my pants on and a light blue bra half on and half off. I now understand that Jason's strategies and tactics in the study hall were predatory, acting on his perceptions of my naiveté as a new freshman.

I'm convinced that had Jason and I been drinking with friends or out at a party, rather than going to his room stone sober, this attempted assault would have easily become full blown rape. The pace at which he tried to seduce me into positions of entrapment were so accelerated that had I been drunk (and likely significantly more drunk than a male peer given physical size and tolerance), my ability to respond emotionally and physically as fast as I actually did would have been greatly compromised. It's not that I would have been asking for it had I been drinking or wearing something super provocative rather than the maroon leggings and maroon and cream-colored striped sweater with the little pocket at the bottom. It's not that my casual get-up protected me from advances. Clearly, it didn't. But being as clear-headed as I was in that moment—being sober and intuiting something felt too rushed, too rough, too-not-even-interested-in-me but-in-what-my-body-could-do-for-his, and knowing I needed to get him off me immediately—protected me.

Looking back on that event and how it unfolded, I think my eighteen-year old self was initially happy to know someone was expressing what, on the surface, appeared to be the beginning of romantic interest in me. In accepting the invitation to join him at his room for coffee and to study some more, I was obviously naïve about what I was saying yes to. If I could meet him again now along with his eighteen-year old self, I'd want to ask if he was aware that this wasn't an appropriate way to show interest in another human being. I'd want to ask to what extent did he know he was taking advantage of me and to what extent he ever thought about it after. I'd want to know what went through his mind as I bolted out the door. In 1988, getting in trouble may have never crossed his mind. If this happened now, would it? I would bet he has no memory of this or of me. Looking him up on the computer, I can see he has a career working with high school and college students, and my hope is that he evolved into a much gentler and more compassionate role model.

I want to live in a world in which women feel liberated to do whatever they want to do, whenever they want to do it, and that screams loudly and clearly to young men, "Don't rape. Period." That would be a much better world but it's not the one we're living in. The world we're living in is grayer than that. Sexuality is grayer than that. Intimate relations are grayer than that. Of course, this isn't to say that sexual assault is love gone wrong, a date gone wrong, or just a lot of miscues and misfires. Sexual assault is about wielding power and control and about using sex as a sort of weapon, as a way to get nonsexual needs met. A lot of time is spent, specifically at school sponsored sexual assault trainings or in required online modules, suggesting that rape is not about sex, that it's only about violence, but in fact it's about both, about some people's violently skewed sense of sex.

The heteronormative script that Jason learned as a young man was one of pursuing women, getting them to say yes in one way or another, or at least to say maybe, since the perception is that maybe can turn to yes. And, in turn, the script I learned back then was to wait for a young man to make the first move, to not pay as much attention to my own sense of desire, pleasure or lack thereof, to acquiesce, to not say yes too fast to avoid being labeled a slut, to not lead him on, to give off the perfect balance of a sense of a yellow-to-green light so he'd be assured that a bit of slow down would eventually lead to yes.

Interestingly, I didn't experience UW–Madison as a dangerous place because of this experience. The entitled attitudes of predatory young men like Jason are what's dangerous, and the society that tolerates and supports misogynist attitudes and behaviors is what still feels most dangerous to me. Actually, it's UW–Madison where I learned to feel more safe, empowered, and free. It was there that I became me. It was a formative, lush time in my life. Most specifically, it's where I became a sociologist committed to understanding social inequalities and structural oppression, where I learned concepts and terms to name grossly unequal social arrangements and conditions, like those related to violence against women. It was in classrooms focused on those issues that things began to make sense and have meaning, where I could reflect on that October night with Jason, one that began as seemingly sweet and innocent and quickly turned confusing, lonely, and scary. At that tender age, I could begin to understand that the devastation of violation will always feel personal yet the origin of it is sociopolitical and so must be our proposed solutions. Now, as a faculty member, I firmly believe that we must cultivate a campus culture in which it's possible to end rape and imagine freedom, where we can have the hard conversations, where faculty and students can collaborate to consider creative pathways toward peace and healing, both essential elements for a meaningful life that's not overrun by despair.

Like most women, I didn't report what happened, and in fact, I never told anyone, neither my friends nor my parents. It wasn't until many years later standing in front of a classroom that I found myself more willing to be open about my own survivorship and carefully disclosed this story to my students, sharing in their newfound outrage and in the courage to break the silence. As I see it now, the classroom was and is transformative: it was first as a student in a classroom that I learned to make sense of sexual assault, and then years later, again in a classroom, this time as a professor, that I offered to others a place for finding language, meaning, and voice.

At the essence of traumatic experience is silence. Trauma informs and shapes the identities not just of individuals but also of whole communities. We even notice this when we hear people reference certain towns, cities, or universities, and it is trauma that's often remembered first. When people mention places such as Littleton, Aurora, Charlottesville, Newtown, Highland Park, Virginia Tech, Buffalo, Minneapolis, and Michigan State, certain images come to mind. Places, like people, carry devastation, pain, and horror. This is true with the skyline of New York City or the Lower Ninth Ward of New Orleans. For college students, the campus often becomes a second home. For faculty, the campus becomes a sort of intellectual home. When a space is invaded and violated, as is the case with mass shootings that have a proven connection to violence against women, it's akin to a person's home and self being robbed. Similarly, when a person is invaded and violated, they may feel homeless in their own body and that they lost a part of themselves.

Hannah shared with me the ways in which the space of her room, suite, and the entirety of the university became contaminated, tainted space and where it felt impossible for her to thrive. She said she thinks about:

"...how differently my life would be had that night never happened to me. I know I'd still be at the University of South Carolina Beaufort. I absolutely fell in love with it. I knew all along that's where I wanted to go to school. But after that night it wasn't 'home' anymore, it was more like hell. I literally lived in the same room it had happened in the whole time I was there. It's completely traumatizing how someone you don't even know can have such a hold on your life. How he's probably had sex (I pray consensual) with tons of other girls since that night, but yet I still have a hard time getting into it with my boyfriend of nearly two years. (Thankfully he's extremely understanding toward me.) It disgusts me that I can't go a day without thinking about the worst night of my life and it's all because what? He felt that 'I wanted it' lying there in my bed nearly passed out but conscious enough to feel him climb onto the bed and have his way with me? It doesn't matter how many sexual assault prevention classes you go to (I went to two) and that's the first thing my mom said to me 'What about the things we learned in those classes?!' Learning in those classes and actually being the victim are two completely different things because during the classes you're not numb like you are when you're being assaulted, you have the whole adrenaline rush of 'Hell yeah, I'd beat his ass if that was me!' And yes, now I can think of the million different things I could've done differently to get myself out of the situation but I was literally numb. I felt like I couldn't do anything."

Lesson 91: How to Be a Good Bystander and Ally in Working to End Violence

Peer groups have a significant effect on how young people perceive and respond to sexual violation; having friends who are proactive bystanders is helpful for both men and women. A few of the men referenced in this book sought me out when they were in college to talk about how they observed the effects of sexual abuse on girls and women they cared about, and they clearly demonstrate how powerful it can be to have compassionate and outspoken allies who share the rage.

When Cody was taking classes with me, he emailed me late at night, more like the wee hours of the morning, to tell me what was on his mind while learning more about violence against women. His messages struck me for how much he embodied and practiced what good allies do, and I appreciated that he referenced incest as another way in which he observed girls' vulnerability.

"Where I went to high school, when you got to know a female it wasn't at all uncommon to find out that they'd been sexually abused, most often when they were younger, and most often by a family member. You almost can't find a family who doesn't have a female member who hasn't been through it at some point… I want children one day but this isn't a world I feel safe to raise them in… I cannot even begin to express how deep and harsh of an anger and extreme mix of other emotions I feel toward this entire thing… I hate this with a passion, I hate that people joke about it. I have a friend who cried her fucking brains out the night after her assault and told me she'd rather be dead, I had another who after years finally had enough and tried to kill herself. I don't think people get that, I don't think people understand the mental effects of going through something like that. We joke about death and it's accepted by almost everyone and…that's because we know for certain that it's coming and we can't avoid it, so we joke about it because we all have it in common and it's inevitable. People joke about this and don't understand why it isn't the same, this isn't an inevitability, this [sexual abuse] isn't something that is supposed to happen, it's not this big unavoidable event that comes with life. I sometimes wish I could show people the memories of these conversations I've had with victims, somehow show them on projector screens. Memories of a friend coming to school one morning, eyes dark, arms covered in fresh wounds, cheeks stained with tears after her cousin and friends decided they were entitled, and how she said she'd rather die than go through that again or deal with the fear of it. Or a memory of a girl who was repeatedly met home alone by her uncle starting at age eight, or how she cried every day in the car line but no one knew why or cared to ask, or how I looked into her eyes as she told me 'No, it stopped' so I wouldn't call her mom and finally let someone know because she feared for her life, and how I put my phone away and chose to believe that though she was clearly lying, or how she came back the very next day with a new story and a little less of herself, or how after the attempt on her own life and his eventual death she still shuddered and sometimes hid and cried at the sight of any red truck.

Or a cousin of mine who decided to share with me her story of her stepdad and of another recent attacker, and how she acts like she's fine but doesn't eat much and gets smaller every day. Thank god for those who have never been and never will be affected by this, but I wish they understood the amount of mental pain it causes. It's not a one-time physical ordeal that goes away once time heals the physical wounds."

About ten years before I had Cody in class, I had a student, Michael, with whom I shared a conversation that seems to have made an indelible imprint on both of us. He came to my office hours to express his concerns about his girlfriend who was in the same class and his confusion and sadness about violence against women. In reflecting on that meeting years later, Michael said:

"I came to you when my girlfriend at the time thought she may have been raped at a college party that she could hardly remember. It made me think about details. How can you deal with something properly when it comes to violence if the violence itself is ambiguous? Is that worse? It hurt me as her boyfriend, knowing there was very little I could do but be there for her. Listen to her. Offer support. I just keep remembering that it must be so hard not to remember an evening where you *think* you may have been raped. Does the lack of information, or the lack of certainty make the healing process easier or harder? I remember you pointing out how interesting it was how it affects men, and the emotional reaction men can have as a result of violence against women."

In thinking back to that email with Cody and that conversation with Michael, the only way I can describe those exchanges is to say they looked like love, a love borne out of profound care: Michael's for his girlfriend, Cody for his dear women friends and family members, and mine for both young men. Notice that neither Cody nor Michael tried to be a knight in shining armor swooping in to fix anything, and they didn't say or do what is most common among men which is to threaten to beat the other guys up; rather, they each let the woman have their feelings, whatever they were, and stayed attentive to what she needed and wanted. And quite noteworthy is the fact that they processed their anger and grief with someone other than the victim so as not to further burden her. They both intuited some crucial things that are key for young men to remember who want to support friends of their own:

- You might find it empowering to enroll in classes that explore these issues.
- Attend and support events offered on your campus, most often in October for domestic violence awareness month and in April for sexual assault awareness month. You might find poetry slams, films, special speakers, discussions, self-defense classes, candlelight vigils, Take Back the Night rallies, art exhibits, etc. These are usually highly informative and inspiring.
- Even if you cannot imagine laying your hands on a woman, or if you cannot fathom refusing to take seriously a "no" for an answer, remember that unfortunately you still pay a price for the ways that others have violated her trust.
- Aim to be part of peer groups that resist violence against women. Connect with men on campus who are good peer mentors and leaders. Among other things, this means having male friends who aren't making sexist jokes, regarding women as objects, or relying on pornography.
- Think of a time when someone treated you as less than, disregarded your feelings and requests, or bullied you to do what they wanted you to do. How did that make you feel? What effects did it have on you?
- If you feel strongly about working to end violence against women look into organizations that could benefit from your time, energy and support such as an office of sexual assault prevention on campus or a local rape crisis center.

CHAPTER 19

THE COMMUNITY OF COLLEGE

Lesson 92: Creating Community in College

"I wish the world were set up like universities: walkable, community-oriented, a group effort. I only wish that one day we, as a society, can get to a place like that."

—Chris, a former student

A quintessential element of college is how individual pursuits and ambitions rub up against communal responsibility and obligations of social solidarity. Yet, students and parents approach college in increasingly individualistic ways and this runs counter to the uniqueness of the college experience which is that it's based in community.

It's a rare and unique opportunity to be in a setting in which you're living, working, sleeping, eating, and playing with others, many of whom are your friends. This is no time to hole up alone. If you're just trying to check off boxes to finish classes and graduate, you miss out on this once in a lifetime opportunity to expand and learn about yourself, relationships, and the world.

The communal aspect of college is designed to be to your advantage. Students who do best stretch themselves beyond the classroom, beyond themselves, and beyond what they originally thought possible. A good deal of that stretching involves getting connected with the campus community and the larger community in which the college is situated, and it means finding and forging your own sense of community from this vast landscape. I still remember when I was deciding on where to apply to college, I felt confused as I found aspects of small colleges and aspects of large universities to both be compelling in different ways. Everyone raved to me about UW–Madison so I figured I would go ahead and apply but I admit I felt intimidated by any place that size. One day I told my dad I didn't think I could attend a school larger than 10,000 or 15,000 people max. I'll never forget his response because he tried to get me to understand that once you get past a number like that, it doesn't matter if a school has 25,000 or 45,000 and that regardless of where I would eventually go, what would become most life-changing was landing in a place with an endless array of stimulating offerings in and out of the classroom and then engaging with those to simultaneously enlarge the scope of my life and perspectives *and* make the school feel smaller. I see now that my dad was preparing me for the idea that college is all about community.

The great thing about being part of a community is that it takes the pressure off of just you. In a college community, you learn to work with others in and out of the classroom, you figure out how to combine efforts, how to borrow from others the skills and strategies to help you become who you want to be, you get exposed to worlds you've never experienced in terms of books, art, food, and music, you can try your hand at leadership through clubs and organizations, and you can contemplate what it means to be an engaged citizen.

The community of college is about connection and touch and flesh and the body and the mind and the heart and the voice and the spirit. That's how it's most joyful. Sheer ecstasy, in fact.

Lesson 93: It Takes a Campus—Community, Identity, Place, and Belonging

You've heard the expression, "It takes a village." Well, in this case, I can say with great certainty that it takes a campus. There are so many things on campus designed to support your needs and interests. There are a range of offices dedicated to providing services that both buttress your success in the classroom and enrich your life and well-being out of the classroom. Take some time to think about your strengths and talents and then consider the people, places, and resources you can seek out on campus or in the larger community to maximize these. How will you follow your passions?

In this section, I'll highlight for you the places on campus and the activities you might find that can become real bright spots in your life and that might lead to life-changing relationships as well as greater awareness of your own capacity and strength. These are the things that make a campus a community and that make a college feel like a home you're making for yourself. You'll find plenty of opportunities for getting involved and growing your leadership skills. *You* have the chance to shape your campus! In terms of involvement and the many ways it can be meaningful for you, I hope you might take to heart something Cody shared with me: "I suppose the biggest thing I wish I would have done differently would have been to get more involved with on campus groups for the professional connection it seems to have brought others that took part in them."

Students who hit the ground running in their first year are the ones immediately trying to find ways to get involved on campus, and as a result, they're doing something important for themselves. Rather than preoccupying themselves with gathering every creature comfort for nesting in the room and waiting until a campus feels like home to venture out to be involved, the students who distinguish themselves intuit that it's involvement itself that helps to make a campus feel like home. That's a worthwhile distinction to understand and experience.

If you're a commuter student, you might consider taking advantage of dedicated spaces and lounges on campus where commuters hang out and socialize. Additionally, you might consider specific days when you can stay later for special events or evenings when you can stay overnight with friends living on campus so as to bolster your social experience of college.

There are countless benefits to extracurricular involvement outside of the classroom, and I want to elaborate on these for you. But first, let me share with you a story that got me thinking about this. I was texting with a fabulous former student-turned-friend named Bella, and as conversations with her have always gotten me thinking, this one was no different. She let me know that earlier in the evening she had attended a tense meeting for an organization she's part of; Bella is now a college junior, but before gaining admission to her current university, she participated in dual enrollment at age sixteen and was in my Introduction to Sociology class at the university. Even then, it was plainly obvious to me that this was a student who would get to college and hit the ground running and would know to get involved in as much as she could outside of the classroom to continue to stretch herself as a leader. Growing up near Hilton Head Island in South Carolina as a mixed-race girl who identifies as Black, Bella was no stranger to issues of inequality and social justice, and even in the tender ages before entering my class, she joined forces with others in the community here agitating for change to the word, "plantation" that is attached to far too many residential neighborhoods near where we live. So, it's no surprise that as a college student, Bella is concerned with issues of gentrification. I watch her as these interests intersect with her passion about the well-being of youth, especially ones labeled and stigmatized in the juvenile justice system, environmental racism, access to educational opportunities, poverty, and crime.

When Bella shared with me how stressful it was to endure the recent meeting of this student organization, I remarked to her how experiences like this will serve her well in college and far beyond. I can say with great certainty that so much learning happens *outside* of the classroom, in moments with friends, at campus events, in intimate relationships, and in clubs and student organizations. This got me thinking about the myriad benefits of campus involvement which include:

1. Countering feelings of loneliness, boredom, or feeling lost.

2. Exposure to difficult meetings like what Bella experienced gives you the chance to navigate challenging conversations about sensitive topics. The complicated interpersonal dynamics that often arise in student organizations serve as foreshadowing and great practice for what that's like to deal with in future work settings.

3. You have a chance to meet like-minded people who might share your worldview and at the same time are likely to be quite different from you, opening you up to new ways of seeing things. For example, when I was a student at UW–Madison, I joined an art organization, and we selected and curated exhibits and sponsored A Day Without Art to create awareness on World AIDS Day. I interacted with students who shared similar values about art-making and social justice and that was a formative experience.

4. Participating in groups like these adds shape, meaning, and purpose to your days. The result is a richer, deeper, and more meaningful college experience.

5. Getting involved in something about which you know little but have some curiosity can be a great way to stretch yourself and expose you to new vantage points. This strengthens your muscles for risk-taking that are essential for growth.

6. These groups are typically populated by students of all years in college, which then provides students with the chance to become peer mentors.

7. Remember that student organizations should be about inclusivity and belonging. If for any reason you witness or experience hazing and bullying behavior, you should report this to school officials. Those behaviors contaminate the experience and can have fatal effects. Anti-hazing laws are evolving, so do your part to stay in the know and hold yourself and others accountable.

Lesson 94: Locating the Vast Array of Support Services and Resources for Enrichment

At orientation, through word of mouth, and via the school's website, you can get a good sense of the myriad support services typically offered on campus. Here's a list to get you started:

- Student Success Center (includes tutoring services)
- Library (often includes private study rooms and media labs you can sign up to use)
- Writing Center
- Counseling Center (offering individual therapy and support groups)
- Office for Students with Disabilities

- LGBTQ+ Center
- Health Services (may include access to birth control and STD prevention and testing)
- Office of Sexual Assault Prevention/ Victim Support Services
- Office of Substance Abuse Prevention
- International Programs Office
- Office of Career Services (staffed by experienced professionals excited about connecting students to jobs, volunteering, and internships, and they regularly organize campus-wide job fairs)
- Cultural Centers, for example the Black Student Union or the Puerto Rican Latin American Cultural Center
- Office for Religious Life
- Hillel, largest Jewish student organization worldwide
- Office of Fraternity and Sorority Life

Activities

Be sure to regularly check the school's website which often has a calendar of events. This is another reason to consistently check your school email as you're likely to receive lists of weekly events. And, by all means, pay attention to signage. Kiosks and bulletin boards with posters and advertisements are everywhere on campus and can tell you so much about what's happening around you on a daily basis. Contained in these various announcements is valuable information about an assortment of terrific activities, all of which contribute to both the vibrancy of campus life and your own individual lives. All of us enjoy where we are much more when we're grounded and connected and have a sense of purpose to our days. Chloe pointed out, "Take advantage of the resources at your school before you graduate. You're paying for them in your tuition! Use the amenities!"

Here are things you can attend or become involved in planning with your peers which foster a sense of belonging and help to strengthen your sense of identity. The bonus is that with all of this happening around you, there's no excuse to be bored:

- Special campus lectures by interesting people from all over the globe including authors, poets, activists, actors, musicians, artists, and entrepreneurs
- Intramural events
- Sporting events
- Sponsored excursions
- Movie nights
- Art exhibits
- Performances including: music, dance, theater, and spoken word events
- Boating adventures
- Religious offerings
- Hiking and camping trips
- Gaming events
- Beach or mountain getaway trips
- Politically oriented talks; for example, during an election cycle, candidates frequently come to speak on or near campuses
- Awareness events, rallies and demonstrations, for example, related to autism education, the climate crisis, or Take Back the Night about sexual assault

- Events sponsored by organizations that are religiously, racially, or culturally specific such as the Buddhist Student Association, the Muslim Student Organization, or the Asian Student Alliance to name a few (there are so many more for you to check out!)
- Yoga and meditation
- Concerts
- Dances, parties, and socials

In addition to finding out about amazing and fun activities, it's through campus communications and flyers that you'll learn about opportunities for how you can become more involved on campus. The trick is trying out various things to see what best suits you. Be sure to experiment with things that take you out of your comfort zone. Once you've found things that speak to where you feel most called to be involved, then assess how everything fits together timewise; be realistic about your commitments so you don't spread yourself too thin. It's a good opportunity to reflect on your sense of mission that I brought up earlier in the book. Where are you wanting to direct your time and energy? What are you most wanting to say yes to, and what might you say no to?

Here are things commonly found on campuses where you can try to get involved, but remember that if there's something you'd love to see that doesn't yet exist, talk with peers and officials at school about starting it!

- Brand-new clubs and student organizations
- Student activities committees where you can become involved in planning events and exhibits for the campus
- Student government
- Fraternity and sorority life; depending on your campus, rush is scheduled for the fall or spring. It's worth checking out the percentage of students involved in Greek life at your school to determine how essential this feels to pursue. For some

students, it's a way to be involved socially and philanthropically. The decision itself presents an opportunity to do some soul-searching.

- Opportunities for volunteering, service learning, internships, conferences, peer counseling, research, scholarships, and contests
- Student newspaper, literary magazine, or creative journal; this can provide a great opportunity for writing and publishing
- Audition notices for campus performances
- Major fairs, where you can learn about the variety of majors to choose from
- Gatherings sponsored by academic departments to introduce you to older students with that major, professors in that field, and returning alumni who come to share their experiences and wisdom
- Clubs based on your major, for example the Psychology Club or Economics Club
- Support groups for various issues including grief, addiction, self-harm, etc.
- Part-time jobs on campus and in the community

And if all that isn't enough, be sure to check out things that are often quite close to campus and provide much needed reprieve and joy. I'm still in shock that it took a return trip to Austin, Texas for me to venture to The Broken Spoke for country music and to see a concert at Austin City Limits after having attended graduate school there back in 1992–1994. It seems perfectly ridiculous to me now that I didn't participate in all that then. Of course, I did plenty of other fun things when I lived there, but it was easy to get into my own little routine and not expand beyond that.

Be sure to always have your student ID card with you because there are so many places across the country offering generous student discounts for tickets, food, and merchandise. Since you need not be a local student to take advantage of these deals, you should bring your ID when you travel to other places and when you head home.

Here are some places likely in close proximity to your campus that are worthy of exploration:

- Hiking trails
- Parks and green spaces
- Arboretum
- Farms for picking berries and apples
- Lake, pond, or beach
- Museum
- Botanical gardens
- Farmers market
- Funky independent coffeehouses to hang out and study
- Independent movie theaters featuring lesser known but incredible films
- Concerts and performances
- Interesting towns or major cities that could be a fun day trip with friends or somewhere to venture alone; this gives you a better sense of the area you're calling home

Lesson 95: Considering Issues of Identity and Belonging—Gender, Coming Out, and Coming Home

Because of the social change work of tireless LGBTQ+ activists and their straight allies, we are living at a time where it's increasingly more possible to talk openly about issues of gender and sexuality. Students and parents can benefit by asking questions, staying curious, and being prepared to be surprised as to how and where to find allies.

It's normal to crave peer acceptance. This is no different for LGBTQ+ students, except LGBTQ+ students perceive cultural hostility and silencing and may not be ready to come out. If they do, they risk being bullied. Some compensate by trying to be perfect in other ways, or by being a class clown, or some withdraw, risking profound isolation.

It's helpful to seek counseling to have a safe, open, and trustworthy space to talk with a trained therapist, preferably one who demonstrates friendliness to these issues. You might consider talking to your doctor if at all possible so health needs can be addressed holistically. Self-loathing, isolation, self-injury, and suicidal thoughts are sadly common among LGBTQ+ youth.

Some community-based organizations provide peer support, mentoring, and safe space for being out and/or gender questioning. Organizations like PFLAG (Parents, Families, and Friends of Lesbians and Gays) provide exceptional support for parents and families to facilitate parental acceptance. Here's a story of how life-saving it is for people to experience parental acceptance. Samantha took introductory sociology with me and then went on to enroll in more of my classes and went by Sammy. We enjoyed a good rapport, and Sammy revealed to me his identity as a trans man and his preference for being called Alex. I often ran into Alex with his mother, Leah, at Starbucks but she was still calling him Sammy and wasn't yet aware of his trans identity. Leah was undeniably cool, and I sensed her love for Alex would never, ever change, and given Alex's fondness for, and trust in, his father, I intuited the same would be true of his response. I was aware of how hard it was for Alex to reveal his true self to his parents yet I knew that their love would be, without a doubt, life-saving for him and so I urged him to initiate the conversation.

If you find yourself in the throes of these issues and reticent to talk with your parents, you may benefit from what Leah shared with me and may want to pass it along to your own parents. Her affirming advice could be applied to other situations as well in which adult children and parents find themselves in uncharted territory.

"If you need assistance working through this, get help and educate yourself. It's not your child's responsibility to educate you or to make you feel better or to help you accept them. Your child is not your therapist—find one—get help for yourself. Your child needs your support, unconditional acceptance, and most importantly your love… Use the correct pronoun, use the correct name, ask what you can do to be helpful and affirming and then do it… You don't need to 'understand' to be kind, to be caring, to be accepting, and most importantly, to love another human being especially the gift that is your child."

Lesson 96: Off the Page and into the World

"Education is the most powerful weapon which you can use to change the world."
—Nelson Mandela

"Do all the good you can, by all the means you can, in all the ways you can, in all the places you can, at all the times you can, to all the people you can, as long as ever you can."
—John Wesley

Colleges recognize the myriad ways students benefit from hands-on, immersive learning and, so too, they realize that such engagement typically reflects well on the school. Referred to by lots of different buzz phrases like service learning, experiential learning, activity-based learning, and applied learning, all of these have in common the principles of merging theory and practice, being community-connected, and fusing intellect with emotional intelligence. I identify three main areas through which you might gain this sort of learning experience:

- Work and community immersion through local internships
- Campus and community immersion through politics and civic action
- Cultural and world immersion through study abroad and study away programs

You can find these opportunities through campus offices designated specifically for these activities with names such as the Center for Community Partnerships, the Office of Civic Engagement and Leadership, and the Office for Study Abroad Programs or the International Center. You might find internship-based courses in a variety of programs of study, and some majors will require you to complete one or more internships to graduate. Some will provide financial compensation and others may not. Often times in these classes, you'll be asked to critically reflect on your experiences in the internship setting and the dynamics at play in the agency, organization, or business. The exciting part is gathering around the seminar table to exchange insights with your peers about their internships and gaining exposure to the needs of the community in various settings, the missions of these agencies, aspects of fundraising and management, community building between agencies, victories they have, and challenges they face.

You might ask yourself: where do my interests and talents match up with a community need such that I can do the most good and be of the most service while learning a great deal? The idea here is to find, as writer and theologian Frederick Buechner said, "the place where your deep gladness and the world's deep hunger meet," and in this case, it's not necessarily gladness in terms of happiness but in terms of what compels you, in essence, your soul's work.

The Power of Internships and Community Involvement

Years ago, after teaching a course titled Intimacy and Violence at Harvard, a student named Morgan asked me to direct her senior thesis on women's experiences of domestic violence in rural Montana. She exquisitely integrated an internship with qualitative in-depth interviews with survivors and managed to craft a senior thesis while making a significant contribution to a nonprofit organization not far from where she was raised. Projects like this give students the tools to seek knowledge and truth, rethink their place in history, imagine the future direction of the world, and dream about how they might engage in tikkun olam, a Hebrew expression for repairing the world. Ideally, students like this return to campus energized to pass along this torch they've lit, inspiring other students to become actively engaged in civic participation and leadership that stimulates responsible and ethical decision-making. I must share with you what Morgan went on to do since it's as far from domestic violence in rural Montana as is possible. She moved to Washington, DC, started a floral company, and then, with two other women, started a band. They've since released songs on Apple Music. It all makes sense. Morgan was always passionate about cultivating the conditions from which she and other living things could flourish. She chased gardens, growth, and beauty. She followed her heart. And it's working out.

As a junior in college, I began to think seriously about graduate school and realized that even though it wasn't required, it would be great practice to do a senior thesis. Because I was interested in homelessness, I decided I wanted to work in a shelter home for youth and interview them which I knew was rarely done with young people due to complications with permission. I found a volunteer position at a shelter home and spent my summer in Madison hanging out with the kids, taking walks and talking with them, splitting up fights, tutoring them, and shadowing the workers. I interviewed the kids, and all of them told me about the extent to which they had witnessed and experienced family violence. That paved the way for my master's thesis and dissertation, both of which related to violence and the sociology of emotions as well as work in domestic violence agencies as a counselor and clinical supervisor.

Research shows that students who've had at least one internship during college will fare better when seeking employment. Some students are able to find paid internships, but it's just as likely for these experiences to have little, or no, compensation. You may need to coach your parents to be sensitive to this dimension, understanding that the internship isn't fluff, but may just be the key to opening up doors to paid employment for the future and can be a springboard to meet people in fields that interest you, to shadow people, etc.

Sometimes internships are just the thing needed to create spark and purpose in a student. Take Nellie, for example, who was an average student in my introductory sociology course and later enrolled in several upper level electives with me and started to shine. I was curious what had shifted, and she attributed her motivation and improved performance to her internship. She said:

"What made me feel more passionate about my studies was mostly driven through the case manager I worked directly with. She'd ask me about what I was learning in each of my classes that week, and would always find a way to connect it to the work the organization does. I found this to be incredible because a lot of my courses, though I found them interesting, I didn't fully see how they connected to a profession, and she got me to see how they do. I had the opportunity to research things going on in our community… The root of it all was that I was able to gain a new perspective on the different kind of work I could do in my future which made me significantly more motivated to learn… I've started to learn how to have balance and healthier habits in my life which is benefiting my studies as well. I never realized how important self-care is until now. This was a big thing the case manager and I spent a lot of time discussing."

Study Abroad

The opportunity to study abroad is a quintessential part of the college experience for many students. For some, this is the first time traveling to another country. For others, it's a chance to see a new place beyond where they may have traveled with their families. Others see it as an experience to deepen and extend language learning they've done in the classroom and are excited at the prospect of finally engaging in daily life with locals and gaining more intimate knowledge of another culture. Study abroad is a chance to be immersed in another culture, its customs, rituals, food, and sights. For some, the adjustment to study abroad is as profound as the transition to freshman year of college.

Depending on where you're attending college, study abroad is either common, or you can't tell who's doing it and who isn't. There might be a sense of missing out that accompanies feeling left behind. Some students might choose to be away for a semester while others choose a year. Some pair this with being away in the summer so there's additional time for travel. Upon returning, it's not uncommon for those who study abroad to experience internal conflicts with reentry in terms of realizing they've changed, feeling critical or resentful of their home country, and wishing they could go back to living abroad.

Catherine, a senior at SUNY–Binghamton, was raised to believe that study abroad was just as much of a given as going to college. Her parents did it, found it life-changing, and wanted her to have this experience, too. She shared with me that she was surprised both by how awful it felt in the beginning and how much she wound up adoring it:

"The biggest thing to know about studying abroad is that it's going to be really, *really* hard for the first month, *and that is okay*! I am a pretty experienced traveler so I rolled my eyes at the idea of culture-shock, but it's a very real thing, and is even worse when you're away from everyone you've ever known. Paris didn't start feeling like home until mid-March, so it took me about two months to really settle in. I think there's an expectation that has been exacerbated with social media that studying abroad will be a movie set to the *Mamma Mia* soundtrack. That's not the case! I cried every single day for the first two weeks (resulting in a text from my father at one point that said that Paris seemed 'more like the city of tears than the city of lights'), and still ended up having an amazing experience. The best way to put it is that it feels like freshman year all over again—everything is new and scary and there's a constant feeling that you're the only one feeling sad, and that you're wasting precious time. I tried to do one French thing a day, which mostly ended up being buying baguettes, and that always made me feel better…"

Reflecting on how transformative this was for her, Catherine said:

"I really love the person that I became while I was in Paris—I became so much more independent and capable, and it taught me a lot about how resilient I am… I learned that I'm even more of a leader than I thought—I organized a lot of hangouts for everyone in my grammar class (all international students and Americans from other schools!) and it ended up being how I met my boyfriend… It made coming home hard, because I didn't feel like the same person and was worried that it would negatively impact my relationships, but it ended up showing me the friendships that can withstand distance and time apart, which is important to know since we're all graduating soon. In terms of the future, I feel much more able to do new and scary things despite being an anxious person who hates change. I've been applying to jobs I probably wouldn't have applied to beforehand because I feel confident in my abilities to adapt to unknown settings and bridge cultural gaps, which are both things I learned going abroad."

Still, there are students who have the chance to go abroad and choose not to. In fact, I was one of them. My father encouraged me to study abroad, emphasizing that he and my mother would find a way to work it out financially. Even though we had traveled to Europe as a family, he wanted me to have an opportunity to study in one of those countries or a new one of my choice. Since I did well in my French classes, he assumed I'd want to go to France to perfect my language ability. But after having a somewhat rocky freshman year and an incredible sophomore year, the last thing I wanted to do was leave at that point. In fact, my plan was to stay in Madison the summers after my junior and senior year. Students who identify with this way of thinking might benefit from trying to travel and study abroad during a summer in college, perhaps in the summer after the sophomore or junior year. In this case, they could meet up with college friends who are studying abroad so as to be there either immediately before the friend's study abroad program begins or right after. Summers away like that can be a good compromise and potentially more economical as well. My response to my father's generous offer was that France—or wherever—

would always be there but my opportunity to experience UW–Madison as a college student was more bound to that time in my life. I couldn't bear to leave it. In chatting with my friend Meg, I was surprised to learn she had made the same decision. Echoing my sentiments, she said she found her years at Oberlin to be a special oasis and knew she'd travel at other times in her life. In thinking about it now, perhaps it's that Meg and I saw going away to college as its own type of study abroad.

CHAPTER 20

WHEN SCHOOL'S NOT IN SESSION

Lesson 97: How to Have a Fun *and* Safe Spring Break

Just the words "spring break" conjure up images of the most raucous and hedonistic activities one could imagine. Students enter college already aware of spring break, longing for all it beckons, or at least all it represents—warmer weather, the promise of sex, drinking, flip flops, vacationing with friends, etc.

It generally marks a student's first possibility of a trip somewhere with friends and/or dating partners and without parents. Most students go home over Thanksgiving break and during the winter holidays, but come March, it can be a whole different story. Here, I address some things you might want to consider:

- Beware of spring break scams so you can exercise good judgment in questionable situations.
- Peer pressure for binge drinking is even stronger during spring break, so think of ways you can make it safer.
- Consider alternative spring breaks that involve rebuilding towns and cities, especially after natural disasters. Some colleges sponsor these trips. For students who aren't sure they want to commit to a whole semester or year of study abroad, this can be

a great, condensed opportunity to learn, grow, and contribute in a new place.

- Consider retreat style spring breaks that focus on self-care—making and eating nourishing food, doing more exercise, yoga, meditation, sleep, etc. These need not be costly spa activities at all and are practices that can be done with a few friends or a small group at home or an affordable rental property.

- Consider a break that has some degree of catching up on work, getting ahead on major projects, or jumpstarting better study habits, particularly if you're struggling. And build in rewards for these efforts—a day trip, movies, time with friends, etc.

- Have plans for regularly checking in to let people who care about you know you're safe. Before you go, consider sharing with your parents the contact information of your friends and their parents, in case of an emergency.

- If you're traveling with friends and can make a stop at home, it can be a nice way for your friends and family to know each other, perhaps over a homemade dinner or a meal out. This helps to build trust for everyone involved.

- Spring break might mark the first time you're traveling to visit a girlfriend or boyfriend, or the first time that person is coming to stay with your family, or the first time you're meeting that person to travel together, just the two of you or with friends. This can be hard for parents to swallow because it's another reminder of how grown-up you've become. If someone you're dating will be visiting you at your home, be sure to have frank conversations, both with your parents and with your boyfriend or girlfriend, about expectations and parameters at your home, particularly as related to sleeping arrangements, scheduling, meals, etc.

- Remember that it's normal to feel insecure about your body, and this is true for women and men. Young women in particular feel extreme pressure to wear new bikinis and skimpy sundresses that resemble whomever looks the hottest on Instagram. Instead, initiate conversations with your friends that emphasize good health and loving one's body.

- Hopefully spring break brings a welcome change of pace so you can return to campus more rejuvenated for the final push of the academic year. The remainder of March and April prove to be important as students seek out internships, study abroad programs, summer jobs, and finalizing their plan of study for the next academic year.
- When talking about spring break with your parents, consider the following:
    - » Help them understand that spring break can be a microcosm of what's happening on a near daily basis at school the rest of the year. Gently show them that if you can be trusted at school doing these things the other weeks of the school year, that you've got this and will be okay.
    - » If you don't have a credit card of your own, and if you're able and comfortable doing so, ask your parents for credit card privileges for emergencies during trips, and talk in advance about what constitutes a real emergency. And, if you don't have a credit card, it's a good idea to get one soon to begin to establish good credit.
    - » Encourage them to take a spring break of their own! Spring break isn't just for students. Parents are often stressed and sandwiched between their own careers, caregiving for kids away at college, kids still at home, and often their own aging parents. So, perhaps nudge them to do something nice for themselves.

Lesson 98: Navigating the Challenges of Returning Home for Breaks and for the Summer

My mom used to tell a funny story that when I was home during a break from college, she heard the dryer going at five a.m. when she got up to exercise before work and wondered why it was even on. Was the dryer mysteriously going on by itself? Would it start a fire? Then, she realized it was because I had likely been up late into the wee hours of the morning doing laundry. I was going to bed as my parents were waking up; I was eating breakfast when my parents were thinking about lunch, and I was headed out with friends when my parents were going to bed. At that time, that schedule felt perfectly normal to me. It mirrored how I was living my life at college. I was doing well in my classes, was involved on campus, and had dear friends, so these scheduling idiosyncrasies didn't seem problematic. That is, until I was back home with my parents. Apparently, yet unintentionally, I threw the house—and my relationship with my parents—into a topsy-turvy mess.

Now, I routinely listen to students as they share their ambivalence about returning home. They cannot wait to sleep in their own beds, hang out with their beloved family pets, have home-cooked meals, and see their old friends from home. Yet, simultaneously a good number of them tell me that they're anxious about interactions with parents, siblings, and friends because they worry about issues of criticism and acceptance given the ways they've changed since coming to college. They worry about restrictions imposed on their daily lives, and they express concern that their parents could withhold certain things like tuition or spending money if they make decisions that aren't in keeping with their parents' wishes.

Some students choose to attend college within a few hours of home, making it easy for students and for parents to just jump in the car for visits. It's a good idea to communicate expectations about that. Students likely won't want to be dropped in on, and at the same time parents might not want to be dropped in on either. Kids may feel that they should be able to walk through the door at any time they want because it's home, but maybe that's not actually the best idea. These are all things to respectfully discuss in advance so everyone is heard and understood.

There's often tension between wanting to enjoy creature comforts at home while retaining the newfound independence that has been gained at college. Consequently, students present a blend of the shadows of a more immature, self-centered-child self and the anticipation of a fully-developed-adult self, and this presents challenges when thrust back into the childhood home. The clear social and emotional growth point of college is for students to individuate from their families of origin. By extension, students will function better at home when parents respect their adult child's privacy and refrain from babying. At college, students are regularly making decisions on their own, some of which would thoroughly aggravate and upset their parents, but once back at home, students still need the practice of making their own decisions, living with the consequences of them, and advocating for themselves.

The typical combination of joyful anticipation and some trepidation is not only felt by students but many parents as well. Without a doubt, the act of leaving home shifts the family dynamics, and this can be deeply felt upon a first visit back. The gift of a successful college experience is that students can be exposed to worlds they never knew existed and then try some of these ideas and sensibilities on for size. You can remind your parents to think back to when you were little to remember how some core qualities, interests, and choices have remained intact throughout the years and how some things have changed. Encourage them to be curious as to who you're becoming and ask that they try to cut you some slack as you spin around and twirl out new ideas and identities. In the same way they were likely interested and entertained by your expressions as an infant, your new words and gestures as a toddler, or your ideas in fourth grade, they're well-served by bringing this same spirit of curiosity to interactions with you now as their adult child. The thing to remind them of is that some of these attitudes, choices, and behaviors stick and some don't, so it's not worth getting overly hung up on, attached to, and critical of every preference, style, choice, or shift.

Students often return home expecting and wanting everything to be enshrined, especially their bedrooms, while at the same time wanting to dash out of the house to meet friends. They're often shocked or distressed to learn their bedroom has been transformed into a home office, art studio, gym, or guest room. But remember that life must go on when you leave home just as life goes on for you at college.

One of the biggest challenges of visits home is communicating and negotiating about the basics of daily life and the scheduling and routines that go along with it. This is where it's good to sit down face-to-face and have an honest exchange about expectations related to things like: time with friends, curfews, sleeping in, work schedules, household chores, car sharing, meals, technology use, and family outings. You'll benefit from remembering how your behavior impacts others. Just as it's a good idea for parents to resist the urge to call and check in often when students are at college, it's considerate for students to check in at agreed upon intervals to let parents know if they'll be coming home for dinner, that they're safe, etc.

College students who return for visits home where they have much younger siblings often face unique challenges as do the parents. Adult children are used to a level of freely coming and going at college that simply would not apply to a ten- or twelve-year-old. It becomes much easier for parents to sympathize with the younger children or to expect older children to step in and shuttle younger children around or modify their social lives to accommodate their younger siblings. In reality, adult children require compassion as well for trying to juggle multiple demands of different sorts of life experiences. Parents, and especially mothers, who perhaps may have overly directed some of their time and intellectual and emotional energy into their child's lives may encounter the most difficulty getting used to the shifts in their adult child's new priorities and desire to spend less and less time with the family; it may feel like rejection of a sacred space that the mother had long nurtured. It's good to remember that when students leave for college, many parents, and especially mothers, find themselves rudderless and depressed.

It's natural for parents, relatives, and family friends to be interested and to want to ask you a barrage of questions about the college experience that may include how much you like the college you chose, your intended major, your grades, potential for study abroad, choices related to participating in Greek life, thoughts of staying on or dropping off of an athletic team, plans for breaks, internships, and jobs, and even questions about post-graduation. After a while, this can feel like an inquisition, so gently invite people to talk about other things as well.

Parents who are coupled often find they need to rearrange themselves after an adult child departs in order to negotiate newfound freedoms and blank spaces. As a result, students may return home surprised to find that their parents have developed new routines and interests alone and as a couple, perhaps seeming closer, happier, and more affectionate. Other students may return home to witness their parents' marriage unraveling. Statistics reveal that the rate of divorce has doubled for those over age fifty. This strikes me as a significant time marker since many parents of college students and college-bound students are close to that age. When kids venture off to college, it can be a "What now?" moment for parents, both in terms of what to do with themselves and the direction of their own careers and lives, and in terms of the direction of their intimate relationships. The questions that plague students interestingly manifest for parents in these tender moments of transition, ones like: "Who am I?" and "What should I do with my life?" For parents, these questions are often bound up with the quality and well-being of the marriage or relationship in which they find themselves. As students, you might consider seeking support and counseling for your own feelings about this.

Some students return home for breaks already aware and prepared to grasp the ways in which their family life has changed and is changing. Take for example, Sarah, whose life even before entering college was already turned upside down by what she called "true tragedy at home" with her sister's cancer diagnosis and brain injury. While she couldn't be sure exactly what she'd be walking into with each visit home, she was acutely aware that her family life had forever changed. She communicated to me a combination of relief, self-acceptance, and resolve that seems to have come both from growing so much while being away at college and from her new position as an insider and an outsider to family dynamics:

"My family dynamic has calmed down significantly. We're adjusting to this new version of life. I still see myself as the entertainer, always trying to make things happier or lighter. But my role at home continues to change every time I come home from college. This is because of two reasons...The first one is I have outgrown the versions of myself that survived and thrived in the house that I grew up in. I am a new version of myself. The second reason is my family dynamic is constantly shifting. Life at home has found a new rhythm that I am not a part of because I am four hours away."

What Sarah reveals here about shedding older versions of herself and embracing new ones echoes back to Kathryn Feltey in the first part of the book who set out for college decades ago aware that she was leaving her childhood behind, open to her new life and who she would become.

Once home, students are often itching to return to campus. This can leave parents feeling slapped in the face and rejected. But in reality, it's perfectly normal and pretty wonderful if you're eager to get back to campus. It's useful to remind your parents that they raised you to go off and become independent, and you're doing just that. Wanting to get back to college means you've chosen a place you like and can call home and are engaged in crafting a vibrant life for yourself. What more can anyone ask for?

Lesson 99: How to Best Plan Ahead for a Productive and Fun Summer Break

Will the summer involve an unpaid or paid internship, a part-time or full-time job, summer school, travel, staying at college, going home, or living somewhere else entirely? How might you engage in activities now that help you secure some plans for a dream summer?

Perhaps you'll want to consider writing a solid résumé, networking, making appointments for informational interviews, attending career fairs, etc. You might take advantage of what the Office of Career Services has to offer at your school and arrange to meet one of their counselors to discuss your hopes and dreams. It's not the job of parents to locate and maneuver all of this. Students who don't have the motivation to find the services themselves, or who oversleep the job fair, are never in high demand.

This is a great time to begin to utilize the alumni network; sharing an alma mater is a point of pride, and alumni will be glad you reached out to them. Students are generally well-served to have a paid job in the summer from which they can obtain some summer spending money and quite possibly money for returning to school in the fall.

If you enjoy the surrounding area in which your campus is situated, you might consider staying for a summer. This is especially true if you attend college in a vibrant college town, a fun city, or a place that is particularly spectacular during the summer months when you can take full advantage of the outdoors and savor things like hiking, kayaking, tubing, outdoor concerts, picnics, and farmers' markets. Most campuses, and the areas surrounding them, take on a different vibe in the summer that can be a terrific combination of relaxing and energizing.

CHAPTER 21

HEADING TO THE FINISH LINE

Lesson 100: How to Successfully Launch Yourself as a Senior

> "I'm not surprised that life after college is...a bit bleak. It's partly the times of today, but it's also the fact that college is the last 'safety bubble' of life... As a student, I was surprised how much growth and change I could notice in myself year by year, even sometimes semester to semester. College, for my adult development, was like a great big shot of 'grow up juice.' "
>
> —Chris, a former student

After having individuated from families of origin to adjust to living at college, students like you are once again leaving and individuating, this time from the community of the college. How might you strike out on your own buoyed by a greater, deeper sense of community and with the knowledge and creativity to be able to create community wherever you go? How might colleges and universities help to handle this transition with more grace and agility? I see many graduates quickly stumble and become adrift. This is simultaneously a private trouble and a public, systemic issue. When I talk with my own students and those enrolled elsewhere, what becomes clear is how lost so many of them feel approaching, and during, senior year.

What we see is a fetishization of the freshman experience and yet no equivalent infrastructure of support for seniors. While we have first-year experience classes that have taken hold across the country, we don't have an equivalent robust program for seniors, something like a Senior Launch program that I've envisioned. We clearly need something like this to bookend the college experience. Students often share with me how much guidance they need for "adulting." They're hungry for life lessons, life hacks, and overall inspiration for leading their best lives. Hell, I'm fifty-five, and I still crave all of that.

Seniors should consider taking advantage of career fairs and other sorts of workshops, talks, and events sponsored by the Office of Career Services on campus. There are often staff members there who can assist with crafting an effective résumé and cover letter. They might assist with how to best assemble a portfolio that is needed for your line of work.

Students benefit from talking with their peers about these things and swapping ideas of what works. Even if schools lack the support for this, seniors might benefit from starting their own senior launch groups as a means of support on professional and personal levels. A great example of this is Ben, who with one of his closest friends, started a podcast at their college in which they interviewed business owners, professors, and community leaders about creatively crafting a career and a life. Ben told me that numerous teammates and friends kept asking them how they stayed motivated, organized, and balanced in college, and while they acknowledged they had cultivated habits that served them well, they were aware of all the things they still wanted to know before leaving college that could strengthen their launch. Taking the initiative to collaborate on this podcast and to continue it after graduation positioned them well as they straddled the two worlds of being college seniors and new graduates starting jobs.

As a senior, I sought permission to take a graduate class on family violence. Doing so shifted the trajectory of my life in powerful ways. It was in that class that I became exposed to the most groundbreaking work on abusive men and got introduced to the first abuser intervention program in the country where I later was employed for many years while in graduate school in Boston and where I currently serve on their Board of Directors. Isn't it incredible that this all started in a class during my senior year?! It was that class that helped me see that my interest in homeless women and children was indeed an interest in violence against women since so many women who are homeless are trying to escape violent relationships and are vulnerable to violence on the street. I was aware that the experience of enduring violence left one metaphorically homeless. It was in that class that I began to develop the language and understanding of abusive dynamics that later helped me to untangle that knotty narrative in my life, having grown up in an abusive home. In fact, I'm confident that the roots of my first book, *Welcome to Wherever We Are: A Memoir of Family, Caregiving and Redemption*, were planted in that class. What's more is that professor, Mary Gilfus, left UW–Madison for a job at Simmons College in Boston where I was already living, and invited me to be part of a research group related to gender and violence. The group met often to host speakers and discuss research, and a small group of us wound up co-authoring an article about research on violence against women. It was significant to me in graduate school to be invited to co-author a peer reviewed publication that appeared in one of the foremost journals on violence and that continues to be widely cited.

Senior year is fraught with complicated emotions. Some students feel nostalgic, finally adjusted, settled, and wanting to remain cocooned on campus forever while others are itching to get out, feeling they've outgrown the place. And many students are somewhere in between, knowing they'll miss their friends and certain aspects of the spontaneity of social life that college affords while excited, uncertain, and nervous about all that lies ahead.

Seniors benefit from trying to take it all in, soaking up the variety of things that are offered on campus and in the larger community and meandering in places they intended to go and forgot about. Students can find comfort in the fact that they can always return to campus and the surrounding area at a later point, either alone or to reunite with friends. Students benefit from trying to remember to balance out the level of seriousness and concern for the future with reveling in the present moment and some of the freedom that college provides. These are huge lessons to take into one's life beyond college as most of us experience the tug of future worries while wanting to savor the present moment. Balancing work and play are pivotal, and college is an ideal place to hone this.

Speaking of life lessons, remember how I've said a number of times that failure is okay? Students benefit from trying things they've longed to do, even if that means sucking at it. Because who cares and who's watching? Perhaps you've wanted to learn to dance, sail, play tennis or golf, or you wanted to try painting, rock climbing, or learning Mandarin. The thirst for lifelong learning is the best thing to take with you on your journey beyond college. Practically speaking, it will set you apart from others on the job market, it will position you for greater success for the duration of your professional life, and it's sure to make you a more interesting person, friend, partner, parent, or whatever you choose to be one day.

By now, you're seeing how education must go beyond the traditionally conceptualized three R's of "reading, 'riting and 'rithmetic" in order to be relevant and responsible. I think of it as seven essential C's you always want to be cultivating: curiosity, creativity, connections, contemplation, critical and connected thinking, compassion, and communication. In her landmark book, *The Artist's Way,* Julia Cameron identifies three practices to cultivate these qualities: daily walks, writing three pages of handwritten stream of consciousness every morning, and taking a creative excursion as regularly as possible. These are motivational tools you can easily implement in your senior year and after graduation.

Another life lesson accentuated in senior year is the awareness that you'll never live exactly this way again. The reality is that given life's impermanence, things are always changing and we're likely to feel that way many times in our lives, but there's something so unique about the setup of college that the anticipation of leaving it and the transition out is almost like no other. A favorite former student, Chris, told me, "I made sure to make the most of every minute because even back then, I knew one day I'd wish I could go back." Chris's remark reminds me of something powerful that's inscribed on the campus of Miami University: "To think that in such a place, I led such a life." If you're lucky enough to have a fulfilling college experience, it's almost impossible not to feel this sense of reverence. I, too, marvel at the sense of place I got to experience and the life I got to make.

One of my best college friends, Leslie, has often remarked over these intervening decades how truly amazing it was to be able to walk downstairs in our apartment building to visit me; thirty-three years have passed since we lived in such close proximity to each other, and though we love each other dearly we can probably count using less than ten fingers the amount of times we've seen each other since graduation. There's grief in acknowledging that reality. But we've lived far from each other, we each married, and life happened as it does. Nevertheless, a dear college friend ends up being in a class by themselves.

As seniors, it's good to reflect on the vast array of people who helped you get to this momentous time in your life. The circle of people might include grandparents, parents, siblings, teachers, and friends. Try to express this gratitude verbally and on paper to those that made a difference.

This is a great time to craft short and long-term goals. Commit them to paper. Reflect on them every few months so you can tweak your habits to support your goals. When you make your lists of goals and to-do lists, be sure to make a done list of what you've accomplished. Doing so reminds us to take stock of the big picture.

Speaking of pictures, now's a good time to clean up your social media profile. Be honest—if you could access all you've posted or been tagged in, would you hire you or admit you to a selective program? Decide what serves you and clear out the rest.

One thing is for sure: new growth happens from change.

Lesson 101: Marching Toward the Graduation Stage

"Now this is not the end. It is not even the beginning of the end. But it is, perhaps, the end of the beginning."

—Winston Churchill

We're steeped in rituals and celebrations surrounding college graduation. There's the profound exhale and joyful relief we experience among graduates and their families—the exhilarating sense of accomplishment, the anticipatory promise and hope for the future, and an almost audible chorus singing in the background the title of that Dr. Seuss book, *Oh, the Places You'll Go.*

The truth is, so many graduates don't have a clue. They have no idea of the places they'll go. And they're the first to admit it.

As a culture fixated on doing over being, work over leisure, future over presence, and predictable control over uncertainty, this time after college that appears at best ambiguously structured is puzzling and disappointing to many parents and grandparents. They may experience a young person's reluctance to embark full throttle on gaining direction and momentum as worrisome, maddening, and embarrassing. The reality is most students go to college directly from high school with no time to truly pause, reflect, and explore what they most need and want from the future and to determine if college is even the necessary and immediate next step or what they might want from it. Moreover, mental health challenges and trauma histories that plague some students can be more paralyzing upon graduation when there's the anticipation of less infrastructure for support. Most students don't want to return home to live, nor should they, yet financial realities can make living independently almost impossible, forcing young people to choose living arrangements, schedules, and jobs that can be compromising.

If young people are going to be successful, they need opportunities to develop a thick skin. Now is the time to try any job or any passion and see where it leads. Sometimes this involves the willingness to turn your backs on societal and familial expectations. If there's ever a time to be curious, to explore, take risks, travel, and experiment, it's right after college. Just as an undecided major allows students the chance to test out the waters, not knowing exactly what one will do after graduation can have those same advantages. The most prestigious internships and jobs right after college may seem terrific yet it might not be the right time. And that's okay. Young people shouldn't be pressured to say yes to every opportunity just because it presents itself. Maybe "no" or "not right now" are important answers to cultivate. Saying no helps us say yes to other things.

Lesson 102: What to Do When You Need Recommendation Letters

An important life skill is learning how to effectively seek out references. It might seem obvious, but it's not. It's good to have a few professors who know your work, both your performance and your work ethic, and ideally who know you in and out of the classroom and can speak about you in as multidimensional way as possible. You may need recommendations for things like scholarships, internships, residential life positions, transferring schools, jobs, and graduate school. Here are tips to guide you through the process:

- It's important to talk candidly with prospective references about the extent to which they feel they can properly support your candidacy.

- It's best to ask professors who taught classes in which you earned a B or better.

- If you're applying to transfer or eventually need recommendations for graduate school, have your résumé and personal statement ready to send to people writing in support of your application so they have the information necessary to craft the best letter.

- Let them know exactly what you're seeking to accomplish, where you're applying, and the names of the programs, and be sure to let them know what to expect and when.

- Students looking for a job sometimes mistakenly think they need reference letters when in fact, they typically need to provide contact information of people that prospective employers can call or email.

- Students distinguish themselves when they give people ample notice about needing recommendations, preferably two to four weeks. There's nothing worse than receiving an out of the blue electronic request for recommendations or a phone call from an employer before the student has even reached out.

- When submitting your application, always waive your right to see the letters. This is because most people want to be able to freely express themselves. Some professors will send you a copy of what they've written so you have it for your records and because they believe students should get to read what has been said about them.
- Send a handwritten thank-you.
- A professor may decline your request because of constraints with their own schedule or a concern they won't be able to recommend you as strongly as possible. Regardless, if they took the time to respond, send them a brief email thanking them for getting back to you. Any lack of follow-through on your part reinforces reasons for not recommending, and if you wind up having this professor again you'll be glad you never dropped the ball as they may keep you in mind for other opportunities.
- As soon as you've heard a decision one way or the other, send an update to the people who supported you. If you got what they recommended you for, it's thrilling to share in your joy.

Lesson 103: Get Comfortable with Interviewing

When thinking about launching yourself into the world beyond college, interviewing is key. While it feels like a high-stakes, nerve-racking process, it's helpful to reframe it to see how it's great practice and often filled with valuable lessons. The way employers handle the search process reveals what it would be like to work with them; similarly, the way candidates behave speaks volumes about what they'd be like to work with and who they are as human beings.

You'll learn a lot about yourself from being interviewed. Sometimes your response to a question helps you think about something in a new way, and you'll likely discover after being interviewed at different places that you're developing a better sense of the range of questions that might be asked of you and how to best respond. Through an interview you might realize you're less interested in the position or that line of work than you thought.

There will always be employers who ask ridiculous questions such as if you could be a small appliance, what would you be, or if you could come back to life as an animal what would you be. You'll find yourself second-guessing if you should have said a blender instead of a coffee machine, or worry it may have been a bit over the top to say a giraffe. Yes, indeed I, and most people I know, have been asked these dumb questions that made us question why we applied, but at the same time they were good practice for coming up with intriguing responses on the spot.

Interviews facilitate networking and bridge-building. What I mean by that is that even if a place turns you down or you decline an offer, if you're confident you developed a good rapport with those with whom you met, it behooves you to stay in touch. This person may eventually become a colleague in the field or land in another position where you'll want the connection. You'll likely find the world gets smaller and smaller the older we get, and nurturing relationships is key.

Here's a good story to illustrate this. Though I landed my current job in 2012, I had previously interviewed at my university in 2010, was offered the position, and turned it down. It was an agonizing decision since the academic job market is overwhelmingly competitive, and I worried I was giving up my shot at a tenure-track position. But I intuited it would be a bad idea to move across the country with my now ex-husband when what I most needed to do was initiate a divorce and move somewhere alone to start fresh. After that first trip to South Carolina in 2010, I found I enjoyed the people I met, and I stayed in touch with a few of them, one of whom is Pat, the former executive administrative assistant who became a dear sister-friend. In fact, she's the one who called me in Boston to let me know about the job opening in 2012 and encouraged me to reapply. I was worried they wouldn't look favorably on me again after I had turned down their first offer. There are job candidates who ignore or are unkind toward administrative assistants and other helpers along the way, and this experience goes to show how many are influential at their workplaces. While Pat wasn't involved in formally interviewing me, she had multiple opportunities to see me in action and communicate her impressions to decision makers, and this helped immensely.

Staying in touch with Pat for the two years before I joined the university was the result of an unusual conversation that happened during my first trip, and it's one worth sharing here. She and I bonded over something tragic, and something most people would have preferred to run from. When Pat took me to the Savannah airport so I could catch my flight back to Boston, I exited the car, grabbed my suitcase out of her trunk, and spotted a bumper sticker on her rear window that said "In memory of Squints," a name that seemed rare and endearing, so I asked who it was. It turned out to be her son, Jason, who died by suicide. Sadly, I knew too much about suicide going back all the way to the first grade when a friend's mother took her own life, and over the years, I befriended numerous people who lost someone close to them through suicide. Rather than feel like I put my foot in my mouth when asking about the bumper sticker and trying everything to quickly and awkwardly escape the conversation, I trusted that she saw my question as an open invitation to talk. It turns out we continued talking under the departure sign for about forty-five minutes until I risked missing my flight. This experience jumpstarted our friendship and created the foundation that made it possible for Pat to contact me the minute a new position opened up.

Another thing to remember is that the way people leave their jobs is telling. Exiting respectfully is huge, and that's true of any relationship you're in, professionally and personally. It's great to stay connected with people from places where you worked since they may land new jobs in the future and think of you for openings years down the road. They might be strong references when you're applying for other things. Some places may invite you back if new opportunities emerge down the road for which you'd be well-suited.

The thing I've learned about interviewing is to be open to the surprises and connections they bring. Years ago, I was interviewed at a public university in Massachusetts and was asked about teaching statistics, something I had less than zero interest in doing. I was honest and said I could pretty much teach anything, but that if students were to get the best of me, it wouldn't be through statistics. Unsurprisingly, it turns out they wound up hiring someone else. It was a job that in retrospect I'm glad I didn't get, but at the time it seemed promising because it was only about thirty minutes from where I lived with my ex-husband. Some years later I was at a sociology conference and ran into the man who directed that job search, and he said, "Hey Deb, you need to finally know something…you were our first choice and I wish we hired you." Laughing, I said "Well then, why didn't you?!" He said, "You should've lied and said you could teach stats," and I replied, "But what kind of colleague would that make me if I was lying to you before we even started working together?" We've remained friends, and I invited him to South Carolina to give a keynote lecture and musical performance at a conference I helped organize. The overriding lesson here is to keep the channels open for communication, connection, surprise, and serendipity.

I want to highlight a few practical considerations related to interviewing. You might find you don't have appropriate clothing to wear to an interview. If you're unable to borrow from someone, remember that the Office of Career Services on campus may be a resource for you. Many will have closets of donated suits and dress clothes for men and women. If you need this, there's nothing to be ashamed of, and you're not alone. Many people are unable to afford these expensive items, and there are often generous folks in the community who want to support students in fulfilling their dreams.

Be sure to research the place you've applied to and find out the backgrounds and expertise of the people with whom you'll be meeting. Go to your appointment with a bag containing a paper notebook, copies of your résumé, writing utensils, and a thermos of water. If you've done your homework in finding out information about the company or organization, then you have a stronger basis from which to ask compelling questions.

Always remember to send an email thanking the interviewers, and include detailed examples of what was memorable about the conversation.

CONCLUSION

FOLLOW YOUR PASSION, FOLLOW YOUR BLISS

"If you follow your bliss, you put yourself on a kind of track that has been there all the while, waiting for you, and the life that you ought to be living is the one you are living. Wherever you are—if you are following your bliss, you are enjoying that refreshment, that life within you, all the time."

—Joseph Campbell

I want this time in your life to be an opportunity to think about how you might become healthier, happier and more successful people in the face of global uncertainty, crisis, fear, and change. I hope you'll think about how and where you can be of the most service and how you can channel your energy to effect change—change that can have ripple effects.

Going forward, I encourage you to think about what you want to hold on to, what you could let go of, and how you want to be remembered, and I hope you'll make choices that align with those desires. I urge you to stay open to all the ways that the fullness of the college experience can offer you an alternative approach for how to craft a life worth living.

Gina, the mother of a college junior, shared with me what she sees as the top priorities for college students: "…human connectivity, collaboration, creativity, self-confidence, resilience, optimism, and self-care... While hard work is important, we're often taught to forgo our happiness in order to achieve success in the future. But happiness is allowable, and, in fact, happiness is often a vehicle to success."

Like Gina, I want all of this for you as well. Gina's right about happiness. It's not an extra, rather, it's central. I'm reminded of a quote I try to live by: "Let us linger here awhile in the foolishness of things." I first spotted it on a poster when I was a student at UW–Madison. Years later when visiting, I bought the poster, framed it, and hung it in my home office. It's a constant reminder of the aliveness of the present moment and what's available to us when we commit to linger, reflect, observe, and play.

Remember how in the beginning of this book, I talked with you about college being a kind of hope structure? My wish for you is that throughout college and far beyond you'll continue to dream about how you can chart a course for and about hope, even and especially in the moments it feels like there is none. And as you do this, remember to look up, look out, and before you do either, always, always, look and reach inward.

AFTERWORD

When I set out to write this book, I had no idea how prominently my own mother, recently deceased, would figure into it. For years I had consciously and unconsciously soaked up lessons from her about teaching and learning since she had taught junior high and high school for twenty years and directed a youth mentorship program, all the while holding unconventional ideas about education.

Just as students need and want their parents in college as a sort of North Star, they need and want to be free of some of that influence to be able to strike out on their own. As it turns out, I've experienced this in the course of writing. It's hard to describe how much I wish that my mother was alive to talk about all this, to challenge me to think of something in a new way, and to laugh at the places where I came to realize that she was right. As I continue to strike out on my own, I'm tethered to her still.

No wonder I spent so many mornings before I'd write staring at the art she created, sifting through the thousands of paintings she made, caressing the paper, marveling at how she loyally showed up to make art every day, regardless of the kind of day she was having, and was willing to make mistakes and stay open to the joys and surprises that art-making can bring.

I've spent my career meditating on what education is about, trying to approach it as artfully as possible. I see now how much education and artfulness are braided together in my life history and in how I see the world. All of this serves to highlight for me the ways that teaching itself is art, demanding unbridled imagination, wild abandon, constant experimentation, and great risk. Of course, the same can be said about the entirety of the college experience.

This gift I was given, to be able to see college this way, I give to you as it contains everything you need to know to succeed in and out of the classroom: commit to creating a college experience that is as bold, courageous, and innovative as possible, where you stay open, observant, and curious, and that leads you to crafting a life after college that is artful and uniquely yours!

ACKNOWLEDGMENTS

There are countless people to thank who helped make this book a reality. I'm especially grateful to two important mentors, Catherine (Kay) Valentine and Gordon (Gordie) Fellman. They each showed up for me exactly when I needed it most in graduate school and supported me in crafting this career. My love for each of them transcends their deaths.

I'm grateful to Mary Gilfus, one of my favorite professors and human beings in the world. Kathleen Kautzer, Professor Emerita at Regis College, was such an incredible role model to me as I started in my first tenure-track position, advocated for me in every way imaginable, and cheered me on with my writing. Gordon Haist, former Executive Vice Chancellor of Academic Affairs at the University of South Carolina Beaufort, embodied everything one would hope for in an academic leader and showed me at every turn how much he trusted, valued, and believed in me. Higher education across the country would surely benefit if he could be cloned.

I thank my more distant mentors, Parker Palmer and the late bell hooks, for each of their groundbreaking contributions to teaching and learning. Their work underscores the importance of being mindful of the whole person when we teach—both the whole of the student and the whole of the teacher, and they share the idea that good teaching is about the capacity for connectedness, over and above any sort of teaching methods.

Thanks to Abby Seixas for helping me access the deep river in almost everything and for identifying essential practices for anchoring into ourselves that shape my teaching and writing.

I'm grateful to George Greenfield, my agent for my first book who has remained a friend and with whom I shared important conversations when I was in the thinking stages of this book. When I told him what I was observing among college students and parents, his response was spot on: "They're going to college together and apart." This has remained a pivotal framing in my thinking.

This book might not exist if it weren't for Gary Drevitch at *Psychology Today* and Sarah Bray, a former editor at *Inside Higher Ed* for whom I've had the pleasure of writing since 2016 and 2017 respectively. They each gave me a platform from which to test out my ideas for a much larger audience, and I'm beyond lucky for the connections that emerged. A few years ago, after Sarah decided to run one of my articles, literary agent Isabelle Bleecker contacted me after reading it and offered me representation. It remains one of the best emails I've ever received, and working with her, one of the best choices of my career. I'm most appreciative of her immediacy, approachability, practicality, wit, warmth, and reassurance. I thank her work partner, Jennifer Thompson, who has lent support and good cheer. I'm especially thrilled that Isabelle pitched this book to Mango Publishing as it has proven to be a perfect home for it.

I am grateful for my editors, Hugo Villabona and Naomi Shammash. They've been like sprinters nimbly passing the baton in a relay race while making it all feel manageable and seamless rather than strenuous and stressful. Thank you for immediately getting what I was trying to do, and for all the kind support at every turn. And, I deeply appreciate Elina Diaz's artistry with the great cover design. I also wish to thank Chris McKenney, Nate Parker, Brenda Knight, and Laura Victor. I am one lucky author.

With this book, I honor my relationships with so many treasured former students turned friends, some of whom show up on these pages. Those whose names don't show up here are still loved and made an indelible imprint on how I came to think about these issues. I'm grateful to everyone I interviewed for this book including students and parents. Special thanks to Ben Cowan, my nephew by sister-friendship, and Sara Metz, my niece by marriage, for sharing in my excitement and being such terrific people to bounce ideas off of for this book.

Enormous thanks to Jayne Violette and Kimberly Cavanagh for being dream colleagues and friends I fell in love with instantly, and for always giving me a safe and fun(ny) place to land.

Writers need a posse for taking care of their body and spirit, and I'm grateful to have the best in my corner. Special thanks to Jenn Stevenson for helping me feel strong again, Habiba Bennett for providing a sanctuary to savor the deepest relaxation, and Elaine Jeffers for keeping my head on straight, quite literally, and for connecting me to Kathryn Feltey whose wisdom informs this writing.

Thanks to my own college besties: Laura Feig, Tom Fishlove, Julie Fohrman, Leslie Perlmutter, Marian Raab, and Bari Weisman. I love you all.

Other dearest friends have been especially motivating and helpful to me in getting to the finish line. They are: Halle Saperstein, book cheerleader extraordinaire; Livia Condon, for the intensely sparkling conversations that could go on all day and night on everything related to living a creative life; Jenn Palmer, for becoming one of my best friends even when that's harder to find the older we get, for changing my mind about online classes, for signing up for my class in the first place, and for being one of the funniest dinner dates; Kate Malarney, who in the darkest moments knows how to find light and spread it fiercely and whose parenting inspires me; Michael Ryan, for valuing my writing in a way that's without parallel, for all the love, and especially the shadow love; Janine Schipper, for giving me Janine in January, for the wisest perspective on all our parallels, and for being the sort of friend everyone should be lucky enough to have; and Erica Cowan, better known as #myfwendewicamiwah, for always asking about the book, carrying my whole history, channeling what would be my parents' excitement if they were alive, and being beyond exuberant about my writing.

My deepest gratitude, overwhelming sense of awe, and forever love go to Michael Robertson. He's my favorite person on planet earth, my muse, and my first and favorite reader who has the unique capacity to energize and calm me always. With him, anything seems possible and worth aiming for, worth hoping for, and certainly worth trying. It turns out these are essential elements of a writing life.

ABOUT THE AUTHOR

Deborah J. Cohan, PhD, is an award-winning public sociologist, sought-after speaker and trainer, and author of the critically acclaimed memoir, *Welcome to Wherever We Are: A Memoir of Family, Caregiving, and Redemption* (Rutgers University Press, 2020). Cohan is a professor of sociology at the University of South Carolina Beaufort, a regular contributor to *Psychology Today*, and a frequent contributor to *Inside Higher Ed*. Her work has appeared in *The New York Times* Modern Love column, *Teen Vogue*, *Newsweek*, *Ms. Magazine*, and others. Regularly featured as an expert for media on a range of issues, Cohan has been cited in outlets such as CNN, BuzzFeed, MSN, *TIME*, *US News & World Report*, *Elite Daily*, *The Washington Post*, *Vox*, *Slate*, *Salon*, *Vice News*, *Huffington Post*, *The Chronicle of Higher Education*, and numerous others. For more information about her, please visit deborahjcohan.com.

Mango Publishing, established in 2014, publishes an eclectic list of books by diverse authors—both new and established voices—on topics ranging from business, personal growth, women's empowerment, LGBTQ studies, health, and spirituality to history, popular culture, time management, decluttering, lifestyle, mental wellness, aging, and sustainable living. We were named 2019 *and* 2020's #1 fastest growing independent publisher by *Publishers Weekly.* Our success is driven by our main goal, which is to publish high-quality books that will entertain readers as well as make a positive difference in their lives.

Our readers are our most important resource; we value your input, suggestions, and ideas. We'd love to hear from you—after all, we are publishing books for you!

Please stay in touch with us and follow us at:

Facebook: Mango Publishing
Twitter: @MangoPublishing
Instagram: @MangoPublishing
LinkedIn: Mango Publishing
Pinterest: Mango Publishing
Newsletter: mangopublishinggroup.com/newsletter

Join us on Mango's journey to reinvent publishing, one book at a time.

www.ingramcontent.com/pod-product-compliance
Lightning Source LLC
Jackson TN
JSHW031347080625
85581JS00001B/1

* 9 7 8 1 6 8 4 8 1 8 5 2 5 *